OPERATION GREYLORD

The True Story of an Untrained Undercover Agent
and America's Biggest Corruption Bust

OPERATION GREYLORD

The True Story of an Untrained Undercover Agent and America's Biggest Corruption Bust

Terrence Hake with Wayne Klatt

AMERICAN BAR ASSOCIATION
Defending Liberty
Pursuing Justice

Cover design by Elmarie Jara/Ankerwycke.

In 1215, the Magna Carta was sealed underneath the ancient Ankerwycke Yew tree, starting the process that led to rule by constitutional law—in effect, giving rights and the law to the people. Today, the ABA's Ankerwycke line of books continues to bring the law to the people. With legal fiction, true crime books, popular legal histories, public policy handbooks, and prescriptive guides to current legal and business issues, Ankerwycke is a contemporary and innovative line of books for everyone from a trusted and vested authority.

Printed in the United States of America.

18 17 16 15 5 4 3 2 1

ISBN: 978-1-62722-919-7
e-ISBN: 978-1-62722-920-3

Library of Congress Cataloging-in-Publication Data

Hake, Terrence.
  Operation Greylord: the true story of an untrained undercover agent and America's biggest corruption bust/Terrence Hake with Wayne Klatt.
     pages cm
  Includes bibliographical references and index.
  ISBN 978-1-62722-919-7 (alk. paper)
  1. Hake, Terrence. 2. Lawyers—Illinois—Chicago—Biography. 3. Judicial corruption—Illinois—Cook County. 4. Corruption investigation—Illinois—Cook County. 5. Undercover operations—Illinois—Cook County. I. Klatt, Wayne, author. II. Title.
  KF373.H229A3 2015
  364.1'3230977311—dc23

                                                                2015016224

Discounts are available for books ordered in bulk. Special consideration is given to state bars, CLE programs, and other bar-related organizations. Inquire at Book Publishing, ABA Publishing, American Bar Association, 321 N. Clark Street, Chicago, Illinois 60654-7598.

www.ShopABA.org

Dedicated to

Mort Friedman

a lantern in the dark

Contents

Cast of Characters

These are the major people involved in Operation Greylord.

The Investigators

MICHAEL FICARO: an assistant state's attorney who broke in Terry Hake and gave Operation Greylord a push at the earliest stage

TERRY HAKE: an assistant state's attorney who agreed to gather evidence in the felony courts and then as a fixer in the municipal courts

LAMAR JORDAN: one of Terry Hake's contact agents

SCOTT LASSAR: an Assistant U.S. Attorney who helped guide Terry Hake

BILL MEGARY: an FBI contact agent whose work ensured the success of Greylord

DAN REIDY: an Assistant U.S. Attorney and the planner for Operation Greylord

DAVID VICTOR RIES: an FBI agent who set up a law office and began gathering evidence in the municipal courts

CHARLES SKLARSKY: an Assistant U.S. Attorney, who contacted Terry Hake about going undercover in operation Greylord.

The Corrupt

*BARRY CARPENTER: a two-bit fixer married to Terry Hake's friend Alice, a fellow assistant state's attorney

*FRANK CARDONI: looking like a magazine ad, this defense attorney joined the BMW set by specializing in cases before Judge John Reynolds at a North Side police station

*MARK CIAVELLI: Terry Hake's best friend in the courts, who left the State's Attorney's Office to become a fixer with his law partner, Frank Cardoni

---

*indicates the name is a pseudonym

HAROLD CONN: used his role as a deputy court clerk to pass bribes on to judges, sometimes in public

JAMES COSTELLO: "Big Bird," a hallway hustler in need of a friend who taught Terry Hake how the courts really worked

JUDGE JOHN DEVINE: snidely called "Dollars Devine" for his open greed in Auto Theft Court

JUDGE MARTIN HOGAN: another man you bribed if you were caught stealing an auto

MEL KANTER: "Candyman," one of the Traffic Court fixers known as "miracle workers"

JUDGE ALAN LANE: so corrupt he hinted at it on his vanity license plates

JAMES LEFEVOUR: "Jingles" and "Dogbreath," a policeman serving as a bagman in the municipal courts under his cousin, Judge Richard LeFevour, whom he resented

JUDGE RICHARD LEFEVOUR: in public he reorganized the municipal courts to end corruption, but secretly he packed the courts under him with equally grasping judges for a share in their bribes

JUDGE THOMAS MALONEY: his pretense of being a law-and-order jurist collapsed when he became the first American judge convicted of taking bribes in murder cases

JUDGE P.J. MCCORMICK: suggested Terry Hake lie about a case in his courtroom

JUDGE JOHN MURPHY: his greed in Traffic Court made him one of the first targets of Operation Greylord

JUDGE WAYNE OLSON: while presiding in Narcotics Court, he took bribes from fixers waiting in line

JUDGE MAURICE POMPEY: a jurist so cautious that Greylord could not touch him

JUDGE JOHN REYNOLDS: his side business was freeing defendants at a North Side court

LUCIUS ROBINSON: this bagman for Judge Pompey seemed like an ordinary court clerk, but could outsmart some of the fixers

JUDGE ALLEN ROSIN: hid his corruption from his family, but one day snapped, shouting in court, "I am God!"

BRUCE ROTH: a fixer who tried to get his law license back after being convicted of bribery

PETER KESSLER: this immigrant lawyer was a big money hallway hustler until he found his conscience

BOB SILVERMAN: "Silvery Bob," a dapper defense attorney who spread corruption wherever he worked

JOE and JAMES TRUNZO: identical-twin policemen and bagmen in the traffic courts

JUDGE FRANK WILSON: took a bribe to free mob hit man Harry Aleman, making him give up his career and live in disgrace

CY YONAN: a fixer specializing in having judges throw cases out

Introduction

"The judge is condemned when the guilty are acquitted"
—Scottish proverb

Today, crime victims and their families are fairly assured of seeing justice carried out, but it wasn't always that way in Chicago. The system was so crippled by corruption when I became a young prosecutor that no one knew how to fight it. But then the U.S. Justice Department chose the city for an experiment in reaching the roots of judicial bribery. Although there would be a personal cost for me, I was privileged to have been inside Operation Greylord from the beginning.

It used to be thought that lawyers corrupted judges, but we found that judges were pressuring defense attorneys for bribes and even setting their own rates. By freeing criminals, the judges were in effect taking part in their rapes, robberies, and murders. During our undercover investigation, we learned that perhaps half the judges in the nation's largest circuit court system could be bought or made to comply. They were merely scarecrows draped in black robes. Those who refused to sell their ideals had their careers sidelined by being assigned to the lesser courts.

Any case could be rigged, from a traffic ticket to a mob hit. There even was a rumor that some innocent people were being convicted just to make crooked jurists appear tough on crime.

City hall and police headquarters were interlocked with the courts by corruption, with each protecting the other. It had always been this way, good people said with a shrug; but, as we learned, it hadn't.

For me the most shocking perversion of justice was the freeing of notorious mob killer Harry Aleman. On the night of September 27, 1972, truck dispatcher William Logan was leaving home for work when Aleman called out from the shadows, "Hey, Billy!" As Logan turned around he was cut down by three shotgun blasts.

A neighbor walking his dog saw the short, slender gunman heading for a car, and a woman talking on the phone glimpsed the man's face through a window. She shuddered because he looked so much like Aleman, whom she remembered from her old neighborhood.

Law schools never prepare students for reality, and many honest prosecutors were quitting rather than either becoming tainted by the system or losing at every turn. I was just starting out in the State's Attorney's Office—known in some states as the district attorney's office—when experienced prosecutors practically danced in delight over Aleman's indictment, the first airtight case against a hit man in "Murder City's" bloody history. We thought it was the start of a new era.

All of us were stunned when the judge ignored testimony and set Aleman free to kill again, and again, as the syndicate's bogeyman. Just the mention of his name made people keep quiet or pay their debts.

"Outfit" leaders grew so arrogant that they shrugged off fairly new federal anti-racketeering laws as if nothing could touch them. And so the Justice Department decided to make Chicago a test case for an experiment: a coordinated counteroffensive using wiretaps and moles in several capacities.

No single person was involved in every aspect of what became the one of longest and most successful undercover operations in FBI history. I was involved in the criminal courts aspect. It began in 1980, when I was a twenty-eight-year-old prosecutor, just three years out of law school. I complained to my mentor in the State's Attorney's Office about the case fixing in the murder, rape, and child molestation court in Chicago.

I was ready to quit in disgust because these were the most serious cases in our criminal justice system. My mentor decided to forward my complaint to the State's Attorney and his Special Prosecutions Unit, coincidentally as the federal government was planning its experimental investigation. When the Justice Department decided to take the State's Attorney into its plans, my name came up as a person the FBI might want to talk with. No one knew at the time how massive Operation Greylord would become, leading to an overhaul of the entire system, as well as three suicides and more than 103 individuals being charged, seventy by indictment.

I spent three years passing myself off first as a crooked prosecutor and then as a fixer, a defense lawyer with connections to certain judges. But when I served as a defense attorney, all my "clients" were undercover FBI agents who had faked minor crimes so that they might appear before targeted judges.

I think only someone as hopelessly naive and optimistic as I had been would have volunteered to put himself in such danger and, in effect, give up his law career. I found myself a sheep wandering in a wilderness of wolves.

This is the first inside account of the takedown that involved several unprecedented steps, beginning with bugging a judge's chambers to pick up conversations about bribes. Then for the first time in America, a judge was convicted of taking bribes in murder cases.

And finally, Aleman was tried a second time for the same killing. In the furthest-reaching decision arising from Greylord, the Illinois Supreme Court ruled that double jeopardy protection does not apply when the outcome of the first trial is predetermined, and the U.S. Supreme Court did not take the appeal. It took twenty years, but justice finally won out, Aleman was sent to prison, and the mob was no longer invincible.

You are about to see what it was like to move among sleazy and dapper fixers in courts, restaurants, and even the race track, and to talk in bribery code to judges and bagmen. The burden of playing this game without rules came close to wearing me down. When I testified in one of the trials, a top defense lawyer tried to break me on the stand by attacking my most vulnerable point: my guilt over making friends among the shysters so that I might betray them. That is the agonizing necessity for anyone working undercover. I recovered on the stand, and federal judges banned any mention of Greylord to avoid giving prosecutors an edge in the corruption trials.

I was honored to be part of the investigation, even though my life has never been the same. Our investigation was conducted simultaneously with the Justice Department's assault on the Chicago mob hierarchy, based on information from a gambler who had been shot and left for dead. The evidence showed how the crime syndicate paid off Chicago politicians with money skimmed from Las Vegas casinos, using Kansas City mobsters as middle men.

I was not part of the crime syndicate probe, but watched with pleasure as the two crackdowns—occasionally involving the same people—exposed and crushed the old-line mob. The two-pronged assault on what had seemed an impregnable fortress helped establish a framework for investigating corruption anywhere in America. But as long as there is a feeling that lawyers should never gather evidence against their colleagues, there will be a need for investigations like Operation Greylord.

All conversations in this book are drawn from my memory, testimony, secret tape recordings, court transcripts, and FBI reports. Events involving crooked lawyers and judges have been reconstructed from thousands of pages of transcripts from the major trials. Persons represented by fictitious names are marked with an asterisk (*) at first reference.

PART 1

ENTRY LEVEL

1

A GAME WITHOUT RULES

June 1980

There had to be a way of infiltrating the systemized corruption in Chicago courts, of sneaking through the wall that had protected shysters and judges for more than half a century.

In the early 1970s, three people in the New York City District Attorney's Office were convicted of taking fifteen thousand dollars to quash a weapons charge against an undercover agent posing as a street criminal. But the evidence had been gathered by having agents commit perjury before a grand jury and judges. A shocked appeals court sided with the defense and held that the investigators had allowed their contempt for bribers "to spill over into disdain for all participants in the system."

The Justice Department realized that any future investigation of corruption in the United States would have to work within the integrity of the system as a whole, and that meant never tape recording in courtrooms and grand jury chambers. It absolutely needed a mole, like me. But initially I had gotten nowhere despite weeks of trial and error.

The Justice Department had shown me a list of people almost certainly on the take, and Narcotics Court Judge Wayne Olson was one of the most notorious for taking bribes in drug arrests. Although murder is worse than drug peddling, most killers don't have the connections and money that cocaine dealers have. Bug-eyed Olson had been canny enough to protect himself from investigations for years, yet I had to get evidence against him if I was to reach any more important judges.

Knowing Olson's volatility—in a fit of temper he had once accidentally killed a man—the chief judge of the criminal courts kept him in the lowly job of deciding whether evidence in hundreds of drug arrests was

strong enough for trial. This allowed Olson to arrange regular payoffs from defense attorneys, who sometimes even stood in line to pay their respects. They were bound to relay any suspicions to Olson. How could I fool them all? All I had been told was, "Don't worry, Terry, you'll find a way."

I could tell early on that some judges were in with the fixers from the way they continually ruled for the defense, and I was sure everyone at the marketplace of justice was laughing at my naïveté behind my back.

During this hazing period, I was doing my best to look as if I had already come around. My contact agent had offered a few suggestions—mainly that I grow a mustache and wear flashy clothes. I thought my mustache only made me look like someone trying to look tough, and I stuck to my conservative suits. If I was going to change my public life, I would need to keep enough of the real me to remember who I was.

One way I came up with for making myself look less like a choirboy was being seen shaking hands with defense lawyers. I also pretended to look the other way as attorneys paid off court clerks for favors, and from time to time I went to bars and restaurants with Olson. But so far no one had made me an offer.

In fashionable society long ago, you were not accepted until someone introduced you to the proper circles, and so it might be in the underworld of courthouse payoffs, I thought. What I could use was an established fixer who would go up to Olson and say something like, "This guy is all right."

I wondered who among the dozens of lawyers working in the gray aging courthouse might take me under his wing. I considered each of the attorneys standing beside their clients or riding with me in the elevator. The one I needed would have to be a small-timer who was both dishonest and yet trusting.

The person who kept coming to mind was loud-mouthed James Costello. He was held in such low regard that no one ever took him seriously, and yet I probably never made a better choice in my career. Jim stood six foot three, and his unwieldy hair looked like a fright wig. Derisively called "Big Bird" after the Sesame Street character, Costello could be friendly and abrasive at the same time. He never tried to hide the vestiges of the tough South Side neighborhood where he grew up. Although Jim wore dark glasses to seem professional, he spoke like a street punk and kept pushing himself where he wasn't wanted.

About all I knew at the time was that if Jim happened to be scraping for clients, he would slip twenty dollars to a court clerk for the names of people who were due in court but did not have a lawyer. Even clerks assigned to decent judges would sell the lists. With a photocopy under his arm, Costello would inch his way through the crowded first floor hallway by Narcotics Court and boom out the names.

Suspects posted ten percent of their bonds to be freed until their preliminary hearing, and the amount was refunded when their case ended. But hallway hustlers like Costello charged that ten percent for what amounted to a few minutes of routine work.

Most of the defendants waiting outside the court were African-American, and Costello thought he had a natural rapport with them. He would adopt a white man's imitation of black speech, glad-hand a few, and say things like "Hey, my man, how yuh doin'?" Sometimes he would address men he had never seen with a black handshake and ignore their look of scorn or bewilderment. Jim thought he was cool. Others thought he looked ridiculous.

Jim would practically press himself against a potential client and rapidly say, "You got a lawyer? You got one now. I'll handle your case and you pay me your bond, and that'll be my fee. Is it a deal? Don't worry, you'll beat this thing, I know the judge. Just don't say anything, leave it to me." All his hustling was done inches from a wall sign stating: SOLICITATION OF BUSINESS RELATING TO BAIL BONDS OR TO EMPLOYMENT AS COUNSEL IN THE COURTHOUSES IS PROHIBITED.

Unlike some fixers, there was no disillusion behind Costello's corruption. He had wanted a place at the feeding trough from the beginning. Rather than being ashamed about prostituting his law training, Jim mistook his success in getting clients off for legal skill.

One look at Costello working the hall suggested that all he cared about was a fast buck, but there had to be more to it than that. Without realizing it, I had already taught myself the first lesson in undercover work: sizing people up and sensing what they really wanted out of life, and using that against them. What he really wanted—and never in his life would obtain—was respect. Fellow attorneys knew Jim as a loser, but I saw him as someone badly in need of a buddy.

Jim had built a practice, such as it was, largely by reaching people before they learned that the Chicago Bar Association customarily assigned a lawyer for defendants who could not afford an attorney of their choice but could post nominal bond, disqualifying them for a public defender. From time to time a defendant slipped by these hallway hustlers and appeared in court on his own. It fell upon the judge to assign the bar association lawyer to any unrepresented defendant. When the bar association-designated lawyer wasn't around, Judge Olson would send the accused to Costello or one of the other attorneys paying him off.

Bonds for drug charges typically started at one hundred dollars. Costello would pick up half a dozen clients a day. The bond checks would be mailed to him by the clerk's office. After deducting the legal ten percent for court costs and then the bailiff's illegal cut, he could take in more than five hundred dollars a day. But his net profit depended on how much went to the judge. All this kept Costello scrambling for a quick turnover, even if it meant pleading clients guilty when elements in their case could have brought an acquittal. In fact, a successful hustler could earn more than one hundred thousand dollars a year with just "bullshit cases."

This was pretty much about all I had been able to turn up on my own, and I was disheartened to feel that so far I was letting down all the people counting on me.

April 1980

Two months earlier, I had been called at work in a police station and asked to report to the FBI offices downtown. As I walked in, wall photos of all past Chicago office special agents in charge seemed to look down at me, and I wondered how I could measure up in the eyes of the three Justice Department officials scrutinizing me at the long oval table.

Assistant U.S. Attorney Charles Sklarsky had a friendly yet nononsense way about him. But doing most of the talking was another assistant U.S. Attorney, Dan Reidy, who I would learn later was the architect of Operation Greylord. He had an interesting face, with his dark brown hair and reddish mustache. Studying me but hardly saying a word was tall and thin Assistant U.S. Attorney Scott Lassar. All three would be important to me over the next three years.

My responses to their formal questions were so dry and brief that I could tell they wanted someone with more experience—and preferably someone who looked unscrupulous, rather than a young man of medium height with reddish-blond hair, unlined features, and a soft voice. Other lawyers had told me I looked like a choirboy.

Reidy asked if I had ever been offered a bribe. No, I said. What would I do if I were offered one? I would report it to the head of my division, I answered. Did I know anyone who took bribes? No. How did I know about the bribery? It was just common talk, I replied. Scuttlebutt.

As my scrutinizers asked about my personal goals, their eyebrows lifted when I let out that I had in law school applied for a special agent position at the FBI. From then on, the interview became more relaxed. "You will have to wear a wire" if I passed a second interview, Reidy said in his steady voice. That sounded exciting, but it hardly seemed like *me*.

Eventually he got around to outlining what we were all in this room for, and my heart started beating faster. "We want you to take bribes to drop cases. You must agree to testify in court after the arrests are made, and that will mean public disclosure of your role."

"But what about my safety?" I asked, suddenly feeling a little weak-kneed. "I mean, after my initial complaint and the State's Attorney's Office wanted to do something like this, a few people tell the State's Attorney's Special Prosecutions Unit was talking to me." I remembered how a fellow assistant state's attorney—who later became a judge—saw me starting to open the door of the special prosecutions office and told me I would not want to rat on my colleagues.

"And just how secret is all this going to be?" I asked the officials.

"That's nothing you have to worry about, Mr. Hake," Reidy assured me. "We won't allow any information about the investigation to come out until we are absolutely ready. We will even give you a code name for all the FBI files to guard against internal leaks."

"Suppose they find out anyway?" I wasn't thinking about myself so much as my family and my new girlfriend, Cathy. I had every reason to believe our relationship was going to last.

"We will do the best we can to protect you," Reidy said. "It's an understandable concern, but crooks generally don't mess with federal witnesses. Besides, attorneys and judges are not the sort to go around killing people."

Maybe not, I thought. But some of those lawyers had crime syndicate ties from their clients or took out mob loans, and rumor had it that a few of them were heavily into cocaine. I could imagine a fixer mentioning he would like to see me dead, and one of his friends doing him a favor.

"The best way to ensure your safety is to keep your mouth shut and not tell anybody, not even your family or your girlfriend." It seemed that Reidy was reading my mind. "We're going after some pretty smart guys. Just a worried remark from somebody might make them suspicious."

Indeed, the possible danger seemed remote at the time. But another concern was troubling me. "When someone from the State's Attorney's Office talked to me about going undercover, he said I wouldn't be able to practice law for about five years."

"Well, he was wrong," Reidy said. "You probably won't *ever* be able to practice law in Cook County again. There is no way of getting rid of everyone who is crooked, and the ones still left would fight you all the way."

"So I won't be a trial lawyer anymore," I said, as if to hear myself say it. Here I was, in my twenties and yet seeing all my dreams of prosecuting major cases evaporate.

"Not in Cook County," Reidy stressed. "Do you think you can live with that?"

This was the make-or-break moment, but I couldn't back out now. I wasn't raised that way. All I could think about was my mentor, Mike Ficaro, the corpulent assistant state's attorney who swore me in as a lawyer in a rubble-strewn vacant lot on a cold, windy, rainy Halloween evening three years before.

"How much does Ficaro know about this?" I asked.

"Nothing," Sklarsky broke in, "and don't tell him. You're only going to be effective as long as you can keep quiet about this."

That was it. They were asking me to pose for as long as needed as someone I would have scorned, and now all we were doing was sitting around a table as if chit-chatting. We shook hands, and the three officials told me to take as long as I needed to think it over. As I got up to leave, Reidy had an afterthought. "Terry," he said, "did you tell anyone about the undercover project the State's Attorney asked you to participate in?"

"Just my mother," I replied, too ashamed to admit that I had also mentioned it to my closest friend in the prosecutor's office. If these important men knew I had confided in someone within the court system, they might call the whole thing off. But wouldn't there be serious consequences if they ever learned I had held something back?

"And I told *Mark Ciavelli," I hastily added. "He's a friend of mine in the State's Attorney's Office."

Mark and I had gone to movies and restaurants together to ease the tension of our work in the felony review section, where we worked in police stations to inform detectives whether their arrests were strong enough for felony charges. As we sat in Mark's car, I let him know that someone high up in the State's Attorney's Office wanted me for an internal investigation.

Mark threw me a startled glance, but I hastily added that I had backed out. "You did the right thing, Terry. Nobody likes a squealer. Anybody who goes around spying on other lawyers can just throw their career out the window. The other guys would cut you out of everything, you wouldn't get any cooperation."

Now, with these three important men from the Justice Department studying me, I was being given a second chance to do what was right.

"What kind of man is he?" Reidy asked of Mark, apparently mulling over something.

"He's honest, I know that. Mark used to be a cop in the suburbs. His father was a cop, too, and his brother's a lawyer. He's got a good family."

"Well, we can talk about it later. Don't mention to Mark what you're doing. Since you live with your parents, I suppose you'll have to tell them—if you want to go ahead with this thing."

If? I had to restrain myself from blurting out "Yes!"

Then Chuck Sklarsky had a parting thought. "There are always surprises whenever anyone goes undercover, Terry. You soon find out you don't know people as well as you think. It is even possible that some of my own friends from the State's Attorney's Office and the defense community are involved."

Well, Chuck, maybe your friends, but not mine, I thought, feeling great as I walked out of the office. It seemed strange that not long ago I had considered abandoning my legal career in disgust at the corruption all around me. Now I didn't want any other job in the world.

I returned to work in the police station but my mind was no longer on the job. Going home that evening, I decided to keep the plan from my father as long as possible. John Hake was a good traveling salesman but a terrible secret-keeper. I could just hear him asking in a crowded restaurant, "Did you hear about my son, the FBI mole?"

My mother, Sarah Kearns Hake, was another matter. She had always been the moral core of our family and had reprimanded me when I stole an ear of corn from a farmer's field just because other kids were doing it. How proud of me she would be, I thought.

When I hurried inside my parents' suburban home and told my mom, I expected her to be as excited as I was. Instead, a cloud came over her broad Irish face. She seemed to look not at but into me and asked, "Are you sure this is what you really want to do?"

"It has been, all my life." Ever since I watched *The FBI* television show.

"It sounds dangerous to me."

"Believe me, Mom, it'll be all right. I'll be working with the FBI."

With that expression of misgiving we Hake boys knew so well, she sighed and said, "All right, then you might as well do it."

Over the next few days, as I thought things over, Reidy and Sklarsky looked up my old application for a job as a special agent, as I could tell from the confidence in their faces at our next meeting. The oval table, the iron-gray rug, the wall of photos—everything was the same, except the mood was more laidback.

But I was stunned when they outlined the scope of their project. "We want you to go after attorney Bob Silverman," Sklarsky said. Until now I thought they had only wanted me to get evidence on a few minor fixers. "Silvery Bob" Silverman was one of the most visible, well-liked, and successful defense attorneys in the city. He represented several mob figures even though his brother was a judge admired for his integrity.

"We're not only after the fixers," Sklarsky went on, dropping another bomb. "We want the judges. There's never been a judge in Cook County who's been convicted while still on the bench, and we want to show that nobody is immune. Some of them you know, like P.J. McCormick*. Others you'll have to find ways to get close to, like Wayne Olson, Jack Reynolds, and John Murphy."

I couldn't even grasp it all, let alone fully believe they expected me to help them do all this. Because I'd spent most of my time working at police stations, I had just a few weeks of felony trial experience. What did I know about subterfuge and rigging cases, let alone laying traps?

But, then, where could I have learned it? No one had ever tried anything like this before.

"We understand it might take a few weeks before you can start getting payoffs," Sklarsky added, "so don't get discouraged if nothing happens for a while. Hopefully, you won't be working all by yourself, but for right now you'll be alone. Do you know anyone who might come over, like your friend Mark Ciavelli?"

"I could ask. I know he'd be good."

"You'll know when the time is right, but clear it with us first. Now, do you have any questions?"

"Yeah" came out of my dry throat. Though I felt a little ashamed for thinking of myself at a time like this, I asked, "Suppose everything turns out all right and you get what you want. What happens to me then?"

"For obvious reasons, we can't make any promises," Reidy said in carefully measured words, "but the federal government is a pretty big place. You won't be forgotten."

"Okay, then. How do I start?"

"We want to put you in Olson's court," Sklarsky said. "If you get something on him, then maybe you can move up to other judges."

"How many are there?" I asked about the suspected jurists.

"That's one of the things we're hoping you'll be able to tell us."

That gave me something more to take home.

During the anxious weekend before I could be transferred to court work, I wondered how many other attorneys had been approached about going undercover. When Reidy finally got around to the subject some time later, he told me, "You were chosen from a list of one." From this I inferred that no one else had complained about the corruption.

So there I was, pretty much as I had been on the first day of my undercover work, but deciding that Jim "Big Bird" Costello was my best bet for an entrance into another world. Like my father I'm naturally friendly, but until now I had always kept my distance with hallway hustlers, as if they went around with a little bell saying "unclean . . . unclean." But now every morning I said hello to Jim and patted his arm and asked how things were going.

The essence of courthouse hustling was dressing well and talking knowingly so that a defendant from a high-crime neighborhood might believe he would be in good hands. That was about Jim's only qualification. He had been in private practice for just a year, but he already seemed part of the dull-gray architecture. At least Costello kept an office, unlike those who worked out of their cars, keeping a clutter of case files on their back seats and picking up messages from an answering service.

In our exchange of small talk that first week of our friendship, I learned a few things about him. Like me, he had studied at Loyola University in Chicago and spent some time as an assistant state's attorney. But whereas I grew up in a nice suburb, Costello came from a tough South Side area, and after an army stint he was a policeman for a dozen years. That was when he learned how things were done in one of America's most corrupt cities. The City That Works. And he began taking bribes.

A little more confident now, I felt that I could play my role better if I stopped trying to look like someone I'm not, so I shaved off my mustache and acted more naturally. In my first overt move, I asked Costello if he wanted to have lunch down the street at Jeans Restaurant. "Yeah," he said.

We crossed the railroad tracks running past the courthouse and walked half a block down California Avenue to the corner restaurant and bar. Prosecutors had their witnesses eat there because it was close, and Jeans would bill the State's Attorney's Office. Since court workers dropped by to talk shop, the jukebox was just a silent ornament.

"You're a jerk to stay in the State's Attorney's Office," Costello said after the waitress took our order. "I was in it three years, and I just had to get out. Know what I finally did? I called in sick thirty days in a row while I was setting up my own practice. You know Mike Ficaro? He sent an investigator to follow me around and found out I was just sick of work, so he fired me."

As always, Costello was only saying whatever came into his head, and I found myself enjoying his company even though I was looking for a way to trap him. He jerked his head toward a few prosecutors sitting around the place. "Look at those dorks. They're making, what, twenty-five, thirty thousand a year and think they're tough shit. Let me tell you about the courts. There are certain ways of making things easier for everybody. Cops, you ASAs [assistant state's attorneys], the judge—everybody. Why clog up the calendar, know what I mean? If you go by the rules, you won't get nothing done."

Simple as that, a few words over a beer and sandwich. Costello was not suggesting that he ever did anything illegal. He was only letting me know that he hung around fixers and that I could, too, if I stuck with him. Then we went back to our work on opposite sides of the system, only now I was delighted at having found a chink in the wall. At last I could imagine myself walking down the corridors as defense attorneys ran after me with money in their fists. Only it didn't happen that way.

2
THE CLOSED WORLD

A Lawyer's Education

In a way, I was out of place as an assistant prosecutor because of my assumption that law school had taught us everything we needed to know. No one told us how an arresting officer might lie in front of a judge to make a good collar seem weak, or shown us the many ways attorneys could manipulate the system. I had to figure these things out for myself, and not with any sudden realization.

My first duties had been to present cases in the misdemeanor courts, where Judge P.J. McCormick taught me Chicago style justice. P.J. McCormick was called "P.J." by his buddies in the mob-run Rush Street nightclubs. He was a rather good-looking man in his forties who had the bull neck and forceful manners of a football coach. But he had pulled the rug out from under me in the case of two men from an apartment-finding business that cheated immigrants.

These employees had savagely beaten an Ecuadorian who demanded his money back because they had done nothing for him. Their attorney kept calling for continuances to discourage him from coming back. When the case fell to me, it had been dragging on for more than a year and P.J. apparently thought something had to be done before the victim filed a complaint against him.

McCormick found a devious way to make it appear that justice was being served. But the upside-down logic he used takes a little explanation. The worse offender had a record, so P.J. found him innocent to keep him out of jail. Then, since the less culpable man had not been in trouble before, the judge found him guilty and then called for a thirty-day pre-sentence investigation, something unheard of for just a misdemeanor. When the final hearing came around, McCormick placed him on court supervision. This meant that if the man stayed out of trouble, a "not guilty" would be entered on his record. So in the eyes of the law, the beating never occurred.

McCormick's probably taking a bribe did not exactly shock me. A few years before he had been accused of waving a gun at a man and threatening to blow his head off over just a parking space. Although McCormick conceded he owned a gun, he insisted that his weapon had been a big black cigar, and charges were dropped.

This led the newly formed Illinois Courts Commission to conduct a hearing on whether any action should be taken against him for putting the judiciary in a bad light. The commission had been founded with the best intentions, but its members did not want to cast a shadow on the system. So after a review of evidence in the thirty-two-caliber cigar case, P.J. McCormick was merely suspended for four months.

When hit man Harry Aleman was acquitted in the William Logan shooting, I assumed Judge Frank Wilson's verdict had been based on a peculiar assessment of the evidence. But once I was assigned to trial courts, I began seeing all too many apparently wrongheaded decisions being handed down, as if certain judges were operating on an entirely different set of laws from the ones we had been taught. Yet I never took that extra step of realizing that many of the judges were actually worse than the criminals before them. I needed to hold on to my illusion rather than gradually accepting things as they were.

My innocence ended when an Egyptian grocer was tried for raping a shy and pretty black employee. The man had viciously bitten the teenager on the neck and chased her around the store with a gun, threatening to kill her if she told the police. He was even overbearing in court. I put the girl on the stand and had her go over the attack. The defense attorney dispensed with the usual cross-examination and the judge dismissed the charges, freeing the defendant to do the same thing with some other girl.

I could tell the girl's parents thought that perhaps there was something in the law they did not understand. I led them to a hallway and told them that since there were no witnesses, the judge must have felt the case wasn't strong enough. Why add to their pain by explaining that I thought he had been paid off? Then the sheriff's deputy assigned to the courtroom, an African-American woman, drew me aside and berated me. "How could you have lost this case! Look at what you did to that poor girl and her family."

Disgusted at my helplessness, I drove that evening to my parents' red colonial-style home in suburban Palatine, where I had been staying until I could get an apartment. I ate without tasting the food and tried to get to sleep, but I kept hearing the sheriff's deputy saying "How could you have lost this case?" so often that her voice seemed like my own.

Turning points are strange. You don't know what is happening to you right away—a notion just grips you and won't let go. And then, somehow, you're not the same any more. By the next afternoon, I was fed up with the legal profession and made my complaint to Mike Ficaro in November or December 1979. Now, just a few months later, I could see that Dan Reidy and Chuck Sklarsky had come up with the best chance the state and federal governments ever had for throwing fixers and grasping judges into prison. But without an insider at the criminal courts the plan would die. And so I agreed to join, with all the enthusiasm of someone unaware of what was in store for him.

I had been told not to confide in anyone outside my immediate family about my new role, but I couldn't keep my excitement from my girlfriend, Cathy Crowley. A few days after agreeing to work undercover, I felt comfortable enough with Cathy to take her to a wedding reception for a high school friend, even though I had known her for less than two months.

Cathy was a little taller than some girls I'd dated, slender and pretty with reddish-brown hair. We had met through my friend Mark Ciavelli, who sometimes worked with me in the police stations. Since I still lived in the suburbs, I was not part of the singles scene, so Mark had taken me to a St. Patrick's Day party on the North Side. There I noticed Cathy in a green plaid dress and asked if she would dance with me.

You can be with some people for years and never really know them. But with others you quickly find yourself talking to them as if they'd always been a part of your life. That was how I felt with Cathy. She was bright and fun to be with, and I found myself going from subject to subject as we kept up with the music. That was how I learned she was in her first year at Loyola law school, from where I had graduated in 1977.

Seeing that I was already acting as if I wanted to be with Cathy forever, Mark waited until she was out of earshot and then suggested that I offer her a ride home. Among the things we three laughed over were the latest antics of Judge P.J. McCormick. He had been stopped for driving too slowly on a highway. He alledgedly was so drunk that he tried to escape by taking the state trooper's car.

June 1980

At a red light on the way back from the wedding reception, I turned down the radio in my eight-year-old Plymouth Fury and said, "I'm transferring to Narcotics Court on Monday."

"But I thought you liked felony review," Cathy said.

What would Dan Reidy and Chuck Sklarsky think if they knew I was about to divulge my decision to the daughter of a judge, who was studying to be a trial lawyer and whose family moved in legal circles? I just couldn't help myself.

"Well, I'm going to be working undercover for the FBI." There, it was out and I didn't care.

"Yeah, right," Cathy said. She turned up the radio and took another look at me. "You're pulling my leg, aren't you?"

I had thought I would become something of a hero in her eyes, but now I felt a little silly. "It's the truth," I assured her. "We had a couple of meetings downtown, and they told me the names of maybe half a dozen lawyers and judges they're looking at. Can you believe it, taking down *judges*?" My exuberance must have made me sound juvenile.

"My father was absolutely honest," Cathy assured me.

"Everybody knows that." Judge Wilbert Crowley had died with a spotless record about four years before.

There were a lot of things I hadn't told her about the investigation yet, and no wonder she couldn't understand why I was doing this. "You can't imagine how bad it is," I said, "you have to be in the courts all the time to see it. It's got to be stopped."

"And *you*'re going to do it? You're just starting out."

"It's practically as if I'm an FBI agent." That was my way of looking at it, even though at this stage no one else would have. "They've had me transferred to Olson's court. You don't mind that I'm going over? I mean, people will start thinking I'm a crook."

"No." Cathy tossed this off with a lilt. "I think it's neat."

"You can't tell anyone, all right?"

"Don't worry," she said. "Who would believe me?"

That Monday I walked up the concrete steps of the Criminal Courts Building with the start of a mustache, prepared to act like I was on the take at the first chance.

And so ended the period of my life when I could say and do pretty much anything I wanted to. From now on any spontaneity had to be held in check until it was safe to be myself, and even then I felt uneasy about it. Since I now had to work the corridors and the cafeteria as well as attend to my official duties, the Criminal Courts Building was becoming my real home.

The busy courthouse, described by the *Chicago Tribune* as a "columned, neoclassical hulk," sits off a short boulevard in a residential neighborhood at 26th Street and California Avenue, at nearly the geographic center of the city and a half-hour drive from downtown. As a reporter said when the place opened in 1929, it "is five miles this side of Keokuk, Iowa."

Maybe its remoteness had something to do with the way bribery took root. Without the distractions of large law offices, trendy shops, theaters, or major restaurants, the judges and lawyers formed an odd little society of their own, even shooting dice together in the back of Jeans Restaurant once a week. Some of those cozy relationships tightened a bit when a towering office annex was built next to the courthouse for judicial and state's attorney personnel, but many judges still counted defense attorneys among their friends. This closed society, in which trial judges often favored their lawyer friends, was something most new prosecutors felt alien toward.

Part of my undercover role was to avoid looking uneasy as I summarized the arrests of drug dealers at preliminary hearings before Wayne Olson, one of the loudest judges in the system. He was a large man who at forty-nine easily seemed ten years older. On the bench he had a tired but kindly expression, with such bags under his eyes that in public appearances he kept his lids raised, giving him a startled look. His permanent assignment, Branch 57, was one of the two Narcotics Courts in the building. The other judge was honest. The decisions coming simultaneously out of those two courts at each end of a short hallway were like noon and midnight.

Olson's courtroom must have been built in anticipation of some Trial of the Century, since the preliminary hearings occupied less than a third of the space. His bench was kept diagonally in a corner to catch the natural light from the tall, narrow windows. The two waist-high lecterns for the attorneys and witnesses were set at conflicting angles, so the total arrangement created a small maze. As a result, the empty jury box did not directly face the witness stand, and neither did the two rows of spectator benches. This made huge Room 100 look tipped toward one corner, with everything at an angle from something else.

Every few minutes someone was called before the judge, and another man or woman was led away. The hearings were just a drone barely audible in the front bench. There was no gaveling, no voices raised. Assistant prosecutors were continually referring to their case files from a stack on a gray metal cart, and assembly-line defendants were not even faces after a judge's first few months.

You could tell when Olson was feeling good because he eased the monotony of an overloaded court call with a stream of banter. When well-known defense attorney Sam Adam arrived in a red and white checked sport coat instead of his usual suit, Judge Olson said, "You know, Mr. Adam, there's an Italian restaurant somewhere in this city that's missing a tablecloth."

Another time a confessed burglar appeared before the saggy, baggy white-haired judge. Before sending the thief to the Vandalia prison farm, he asked the defendant if he had anything to say.

"It's my birthday, Your Honor," the burglar answered, hoping for a lighter sentence.

Olson stood up, clasped his hands behind his back, and sang, "Happy birthday to you, happy birthday to you. One year in Vandalia, happy birthday to you!" He then sat down and told the bailiff, "Get him out of here."

I arrived early on my first day at Olson's court so I could strike up a conversation with his clerk and occasional driver, *Charlie Squeteri. Even before the bailiff could say "All rise, the court is now in session," I saw an attorney approach Squeteri with money in hand to have his client called first. That would slash the lawyer's wait time so he could handle an additional client and make more money. Noticing my gawking, the attorney slid the cash back into his pocket. I obviously would have to stop showing such scruples if I was to be taken for corrupt.

Nothing happened for three days, but on Thursday of that first week a black policeman serving in an elite suburban undercover narcotics unit testified against a white dealer who had sold him narcotics. At our recommendation, the judge conducted the hearing in his chambers to keep the officer from being seen by drug pushers waiting for their cases.

Testimony established that the defendant had approached the officer and asked if he wanted some heroin, so there was no entrapment. Olson occasionally fingered his lip and then ruled that the officer had violated the rules against entrapment and therefore there was no probable cause for an arrest. Even though the Justice Department was sure Olson was crooked, the decision upset me. Undercover drug cases are the most dangerous of all police assignments, yet he might as well have slapped this officer in the face.

But Olson on the bench was nothing like Olson at leisure. I was one of three assistant state's attorneys (ASAs) assigned to a long, narrow office built into the side of his courtroom. The office—more like a hut— was not much more than an elongated closet, but dirtier. On the day after the entrapment ruling Olson took us to an Italian restaurant, and in his gritty baritone told us one delightful story after another. To him there was no such thing as justice; everything was just absurdity on both sides. I found myself almost forgiving him for ruling against the evidence. I'm sure that's what he had in mind by inviting me. Not that he paid the bill.

The undercover policeman's case was the first evidently rigged verdict I'd seen since my transfer from felony review, but my contact FBI agent, Lamar Jordan, told me we had no way of proving it. Even so, he asked me to copy the police report as the initial solid evidence against the judge.

Sometime later a fellow prosecutor, Brian Scanlon, told me that one day "Silvery Bob" Silverman and another defense attorney went up to him at different times while Olson was away and offered to split their fees with him if he would drop their cases.

"Did you do it?" I asked.

"Hell no," Scanlon said, "but it's funny. Those guys wouldn't have done that if Olson was in to take care of them. When another judge fills in for Olson, the shysters come out of the woodwork."

I had been trying to avoid my mentor, Mike Ficaro, even though he was so easy to get along with that his employees pulled pranks on him. I've heard they put fish in his water cooler and hid the chalkboard he used to keep score for convictions and acquittals. But that was before drug proliferation skyrocketed crime in the late 1970s and everyone was overworked.

As head of the criminal division of the State's Attorney's Office, Ficaro had a hand in most transfers within the State's Attorney's Office. Since he kept his eye on everyone working under him, I was afraid he might wonder why I had been taken from felony review without somebody clearing it with him. Catching up with me in a hallway that Friday afternoon, he asked, "So, Terry, what are you doing in Narcotics Court these days?"

The remark seemed offhanded, but Mike's girth was blocking my path and he gave me the same penetrating look that struck terror in defendants on the stand.

"I just decided it was time to move up," I said.

"Don't lie to me, you said you never wanted to go back to trial work." He kept standing in my way and waiting for an answer.

I had been specifically ordered not to mention my new role to Ficaro, but I was sure Reidy and Sklarsky didn't realize that Mike could see through me. I looked around to make sure no one could hear us and whispered, "You won't tell anybody?"

He shook his head, and as we walked a few feet down the corridor I told him what I was trying to do. Mike listened with his hands behind his back. When I finished, he asked if he could help.

"No, I don't think so."

"All right, Terry. But remember, my office will be open any time you need it."

Knowing that Ficaro was supporting me boosted my confidence. I would soon learn that he was helping me behind the scenes even though as part of the county system he would play no role in the federal investigation. In early June, just as I was becoming friendly with most of the court personnel, every court clerk and Narcotics Court bailiff was transferred to other assignments.

Although no money had been given to me, every day I expected to be found out. I was like someone who plugs in a lamp the moment a city has a blackout and thinks it is his fault. It turned out that Ficaro knew that the arrival of all these new clerks and bailiffs might induce fixers to take their money to me as Costello's friend rather than risk testing them.

I didn't appreciate Mike's interference at the time, since bribery was so persuasive anything could set off rumors of an investigation. But I learned that greed was so addictive that not even this could stop the bribery, and that Mike's transfer orders had given the stalled investigation just the push it needed.

Olson certainly didn't change his ways. An assistant prosecutor can expect to win at least three-quarters of preliminary hearings before an honest judge. But with Wayne Olson I lost eighteen of my first twenty. It took me several weeks to catch on that he was wordlessly urging me to start taking money from his lawyer friends if I wanted to get anywhere in my career.

But apart from developing an acquaintance with Costello and going to Jeans so that I might be accepted as one of the boys, there still was no change in my relationship with anyone in the building. But then as Costello and I were having lunch one hot July day, he ruminated about his time as a Chicago policeman.

"That's when I started taking dough," he said, as I tried not to seem especially interested. He added that he and his partner would share ten or twenty dollars from motorists who ran a red light. "At first you say it's not right, and what happens if you get caught, but people don't care. The money wasn't all that much, but it was something. It makes being a cop okay, after all you got to put up with." The money helped him attend John Marshall Law School at night. "I even took money from Silverman once."

Oh my God! He had just named the main lawyer I had been recruited for, Bob Silverman, the man suspected of single-handedly corrupting dozens of police officers, lawyers, and judges. Now at last I had something to report, and for the first time I wished I had been wearing a wire.

"That man is a gentleman, I tell you," Costello said in admiration. "Ever see Bob in action? Terry, that guy's got class."

Was Costello dropping hints that he would help me share the action? My hopes slowly deflated as I learned that he had mentioned Silverman only in passing. But it was clear now that all I had to do was make him comfortable and let his avuncular impulse take over.

"Everyone is dirty in Traffic Court, and I mean everyone," he said over cocktails on another afternoon. "I can fix drunk driving cases there, but I got to go through somebody." Since we both worked in criminal courts, there was no reason for Costello to tell me about Traffic Court in another part of the city—unless he was testing my reaction. I didn't ask for names, and hoped I seemed like an apt pupil.

As Jim explained the system, the cost of a DUI fix in the other building was usually three hundred dollars. Of that, the judge received two hundred. The rest went to the bagman for conveying the money and possibly to the arresting officer. With the seduction of corruption, a grateful client was bound to pass the attorney's name on to friends. No one was bothered about letting motorists go free to drive drunk again. When a court system is too big, defendants aren't real. Only money is real.

Summer 1980

Over that summer Costello kept lacing his funny anecdotes with hints of dishonesty. He studied my expression as I laughed with him despite my disgust. Slowly the process of behaving as if I had sticky fingers was washing away my natural emotions. But I still set myself back with sharp fixer Bruce Roth. He was one of those people who had left the prosecutor's office because of all the money beckoning on the other side, and the FBI had told me to keep my eye on him. He lived in the Gold Coast neighborhood near the lake and hung out with flashy cocaine dealers.

After Olson granted a motion to suppress evidence against one of his clients, Roth opened a briefcase smelling of new leather and I could see copies of arrest reports among his papers. The only way he could have obtained those reports, with the names and addresses of witnesses, was by subpoenaing them from me or bribing a police officer.

"Where did you get those reports?" I blurted out.

"I subpoenaed them," he said, with a look that told me: You know damn well how I got them.

"That's—" Even though I stopped short of adding "a lie," it was too late. He knew what was on my mind. *What are you doing*, I asked myself, *you're supposed to get friendly with this guy.* So I changed my tone and said through a smile, "Hey, forget about it, Bruce, all right?"

He snapped his briefcase shut and left. Maybe Costello thought I might be ready to join the 26th and California bribery club, but I was sure Roth regarded me as just another head-in-the-clouds ASA.

Indeed, the fixers never trusted any of us. We assistant state's attorneys were mere obstacles to work around, and in Olson's court there was hardly any point in having us there. The process of law had become just a show for the witnesses. Time and again cases were thrown out because the arresting officer had been given twenty to fifty dollars to change his story. That's cheap for perjury, but some of those officers were appearing a couple of times a week, week after week. Since "nickel bag" cases never made the news, no one kept track of how often police testimony contradicted their reports. Sometimes they wouldn't tell a blatant lie—they would fudge halfway and Olson would fudge on the other half.

There were some excellent defense attorneys working in the courts, and newcomers couldn't tell the skillful ones from those who bought judges. Bob Silverman, for example, was able to strut with assurance because he supposedly would not touch a case unless he knew he could put the fix in.

On a Friday that July, a veteran ASA called to say a friend of his was going to serve as the bar association attorney in the building. "Terry," the veteran said, "make sure his clients don't sit waiting all morning for their cases to be called, and give him a break or two." In other words, I was to bend over backwards to dismiss the charges or offer probation. Well, why not? I had to start doing small favors before fixers would trust me.

"I'll see what I can do," I said casually.

The brand new defense attorney, let's call him Sammy, was tall, tanned, and wore a tailored suit, but he knew no more about court procedures than a high school student. After Olson handled his final case, I returned to the small office for the three assistant prosecutors assigned to his courtroom. While one of us appeared on a matter, the others would get some of their own cases ready. Our desks were just places to throw reference books on, and we seldom sat at them. Since our window was virtually opaque with dirt, we used it only for ventilation and as a platform for the telephone.

Defense attorneys would drop by looking for an ASA or to sit on the sill and use our phone for free. Only authorized court personnel were allowed inside, but letting them in was our way of staying friendly with the enemy, since many ASAs later crossed over. Police officers would come in before testifying to explain the arrest to us, and court officers hung around to discuss everything but work. So many people popped in that if you kept anything in a drawer it might not be there the next day. Yet we managed to handle up to a hundred and fifty cases a day.

I was stacking files when Costello stepped into the long, narrow room and mooched a call so he could check on his phone messages, and before long Sammy poked his head through the doorway to ask one of his dumb questions.

"Say, Terry," he said, "do I need to file a demand-for-trial on the cases you dismissed for me?"

"Yes," I answered, a little tired, "it's a matter of routine to keep my side from reinstating the case later."

Overhearing us, Costello put the phone to his chest and asked with an edge, "What's up, Terry?"

Sammy had annoyed me so much that I muttered, "I'll talk to you later. I'm busy."

But as soon as Sammy left, I had an idea: why not push my relationship with Costello a little? "I've helped this guy all day, and now he comes in here and asks me for more." I sounded angry. "He must have made six hundred dollars in bond returns from cases I helped him with, and do you know what? He didn't do one thing for me. How do you like that?"

"What are you helping that Mork for?" That is, Costello was wondering why I helped a stranger and not him. He pulled out his wallet and tried to put two fifty-dollar bills into my hand. "Here, take this hundred. For all the favors you done."

"Keep it, Jim." I drew my hand away and stepped back as if trying to deny the moment. I was afraid someone might open the door and see him holding the money out. At the same time I told myself: *You're being stupid, this is what you were sent to Branch 57 for!*

"Come on, Terry. Take it."

"It's not necessary, Jim, you're a friend." My hesitance might even have been in my favor, since Costello probably would have been suspicious if I were eager for a bribe.

"Just put it in your pocket and shut up, will you?"

Don't do this, Jim, I thought, *can't you see I'm poison to you?* I had stopped regarding him as a fixer weeks ago, he was now a friend, and yet my fingers tightened on the money.

"Well, okay," I said and pushed the bills into my pocket. "Have a good weekend."

He waved and went out the door.

The rest of my filing seemed to take forever because my thoughts ping-ponged over whether to report Costello or find a way to return the two fifties. When I went down a short hall and turned to the block-long concourse linking the old courthouse with the new administration tower, a couple of prosecutors from the other Narcotics Court asked if

I wanted to go with them to Jeans, their ritual to end another week in the arena. I went along, but my heart wasn't in it.

In the 1980s, Jeans was the hub of the criminal court subculture. No one taking a peek inside the pale-yellow brick building would believe all the deals made there, or imagine the anguishing moments as defendants and relatives of victims sat at the tables waiting out deliberations.

The restaurant was larger than it seemed from the front window because the inside took a partial turn, like a lazy "L." The tables in the front third were covered with checkered oilcloth and the rest were bare, since the clientele liked things simple. Along the back wall were three tiers of liquor bottles kept only for decoration because the patrons seldom ordered anything more exotic than a martini. The bottles followed the long bar this way and that from the front counter to a tiny back passage where a warped back door needed a shoulder-push to close.

Jeans never encouraged off-the-street customers. On weekdays, the front door was locked at three p.m. and regulars came in through the back, near the kitchen. White-haired lawyers often played cards at the front table, where the natural light was best. Waitresses addressed the police officers, court clerks, and bailiffs by their first name.

Jeans was still open for street customers when we arrived, but it was already looking like a seedy private club. Some patrons were drinking beer straight from the bottle because they thought only sissies used glasses. As conversations floated around me, I kept feeling that these insiders could tell from my face or voice that I had just accepted dirty money.

After ordering a beer and grilled cheese sandwich, the least greasy thing on the menu, I wondered how I could even think of turning Costello in. He was real to me and would help me with problems, while the agents at the Chicago FBI office were only telephone voices I heard once or twice a week. They were so morally strict they could not comprehend that people in any courthouse moved about in a world of gray.

I kept trying to convince myself that since the hundred dollars I had taken wasn't payment for a specific favor, it wasn't really a bribe and so I would have nothing to report. As I dithered I kept glancing at the old-fashioned wooden phone booth just inside Jeans' front door. It was the sort of place you would expect a Capone mobster to be shot in. After a few minutes, I told myself that Costello had stepped over the line without any encouragement from me, and this made it my duty to set the law in motion against him. If I couldn't turn in a cheap hallway hustler, how could I think of going after Olson, Roth, Silverman, and others?

Stepping into the booth, I pulled the hinged door shut so no one could overhear. An FBI switchboard operator told me that my contact agents, Lamar Jordan and Bob Farmer, weren't around. So I dialed the U.S. Attorney's Office, but Sklarsky wasn't in, either. Maybe they were all busy in the field, or maybe they had come down with the disappearing itch known to afflict government employees on summertime "federal Fridays." For a moment I thought no one really cared what was happening in the courts. But with my next quarter I reached Assistant U.S. Attorney Dan Reidy.

"Costello just gave me a hundred dollars," I told him. "He said it was for past favors, but I haven't done any for him yet. It's my first bribe, if you can call it that."

"That's great," Reidy said, and set up a meeting for that afternoon across from the old Chicago Stadium, home of the Blackhawks and Bulls. I slipped out of the phone booth feeling excited for the first time since agreeing to go undercover.

Waiting for me in a white Chevrolet outside the parking lot where the United Center now stands were Reidy, federal prosecutor Scott Lassar, and an FBI agent originally from Texas, James Hershly. I climbed in and slammed the door. Costello's money had been in my pocket for nearly two hours, and I was eager to get rid of it.

Hershly told me to date the two bills and mark them with "TH" for Terry Hake, then he jotted his own initials and recorded the serial numbers. Those bills and all the other bribes I eventually would receive went into a vault at FBI headquarters as evidence in future trials.

With that out of the way, Reidy turned to me with an adrenaline gleam and said, "Let's hear it, Terry, I want everything that happened between you and Costello, word for word."

"When he gave me the money, I told him I didn't want it."

"Please repeat that," Hershly murmured, while taking notes for the team.

"I told Costello, 'Jim, it's not necessary, you're a friend.'"

They had an "is that all?" stare when I didn't add anything. So for nearly an hour I went over with them everything that had happened and didn't happen.

"Well," Reidy said finally, "at least they can never say you tried to entrap the guy. But in the future, Terry, just take what they give you. You have to go back and get him to acknowledge on tape that he gave you the money and that it was for something you did in court. Those favors he mentioned when he gave you the money could mean anything, you could have mowed his lawn or something. Take him to lunch on Monday and firm it up."

That meant wearing a wire for the first time, something I had been dreading.

Reidy must have sensed I was feeling a little guilty about firming up evidence against a friend, and assured me before I left the car, "By the time we're done, Terry, you'll be glad we're kicking them all out."

3

WEARING A WIRE

June 1980

By now I had an apartment in Evanston, a generally nice suburb adjacent to Chicago. Living by myself gave me a little more freedom for my undercover role. Three months earlier, Jordan had shown me in his light Southern drawl how to thread a tape through the Swiss-made Nagra, a commonly used body recorder for federal investigations at the time. Forget high-tech spymaster images. Anyone could rent a Nagra from an electronics shop, and who knows how often this one had been used and abused?

The Nagra's advantages were that the tape ran for two and a half hours of reasonably good sound, even when the recording was made under clothes. The device was four inches wide, five and three-quarters inches long, and one inch thick. The microphone was no larger than a pencil eraser, but the wire was long enough to tape it practically anywhere.

Standing in my flat at seven in the morning, I used a few strips of surgical tape to secure the mike vertically on my chest so my tie would cover the bump. Then there was the problem of hiding the three-thousand-dollar Nagra, which went into the pocket of an elastic band. No matter where you placed the Nagra it was too tight. Many undercover operatives kept it in the small of their back, but to me it seemed too easy for someone to put a hand on it.

After a little experimenting, I decided to wear the recorder under my left arm. But checking the contours of my shirt in the bathroom mirror, I thought I might as well be wearing a sign reading "Watch out, mole!" Off went the shirt and I tried again, this time with a T-shirt underneath. I felt a little silly as I moved this way and that in front of the mirror, but at last I became convinced the bulge would go unnoticed—as long as no one suspected me.

My next worry was about the machine itself. I had installed two new AA batteries, drawn the recording tape along its path, and turned the reel until the tape was taut. But there was no way to test whether I had threaded it correctly because the device had no playback. As I started my car, I thought about the way the tape had kept sliding under my nervous fingers and wondered what would happen if I gave the FBI more than two hours of blank tape? Well, it was too late now.

Thirty-five minutes later I was entering the courthouse with the peculiar feeling that everyone was staring at my armpit. Finding Jim Costello hustling clients in the stubby first-floor corridor as usual, and hoping I sounded like a prosecutor cooperating with fixers, I suggested, "How about we meet at the cafeteria for lunch?"

Costello might have talked like a high school dropout, but he was sharp in the cynical way ex-policemen often are. Suppose his delay in answering meant he could recognize my pose for what it was? Even if nothing happened to me or my family, that might turn Operation Greylord into a fiasco.

"Yeah, Terry," Costello said. "I'd like that. I'll see you up there."

After a court recess, I went through the annex corridor and rode up an elevator to the second-floor cafeteria. The large room resembled a glass and stainless steel waiting area, with just a soft background of voices even at busy times and its wide windows overlooking the gloomy Cook County Jail complex.

Costello and I moved from the stack of plastic trays over to the grill line. We both ordered cheeseburgers and fries. I switched on the Nagra as sweat crawled down my back. We took a seat and the always-talkative Costello hardly said a word. Since I had invited him, he must have been waiting for me to explain why.

"Hey, Jim," I said, "thanks for the hundred. Really, it came in handy over the weekend."

"Did you take your girlfriend out?"

"We had a nice dinner and went to a movie," I lied. "Thanks again."

"Don't mention it," Costello said.

"And for the lunches you buy me."

He made an "it's nothing" gesture, and the conversation died.

Hoping he could not sense my apprehension, I hinted that I was curious about the mechanics of payoffs. Since this was Costello's favorite subject, he soon recalled his first days in the building, when he learned he could buy clients by getting their names from court clerks and deputy sheriffs.

"Know how I found out? I went back and gave the guy ten bucks, like a tip. 'What's this?' he said, like I insulted him. 'Come on, come on,' he said, 'it's a third of the bond around here.'"

"The bailiff told you that?" I asked, to clarify the reference for the tape.

"Yeah, like it's written down somewhere. Jesus, a third. I'm the one with the law degree, I'm the one who does all the work, but he gets a third. But you make enough if you keep at it."

Trying to prod him into saying more, I hopped around subjects until I got around to a prosecutor who refused to drop charges against one of Costello's clients. "Hey, Jim," I said, "I'm sorry he gave you a hard time about SOL-ing that case." That meant having charges stricken with leave to reinstate.

"It happens. You don't always get what you pay for in this business. I'd rather deal with a judge, like those guys that keep going to Olson."

"That doesn't mean anything, Jim, he's just got lots of friends." That was the sort of thing I might have said when I had started out, before my eyes were opened.

"Oh, come on, Terry, don't be so dumb. Olson cares for only one thing, 'How much money have I got in my pocket today?' That's why those guys get all the cases from him. That's how I get my cases out of him—I go back there and pay him practically every day."

Oh God, oh God, please let me be recording this. "You're kidding," I said.

"I thought you knew."

"I've never seen you in his chambers."

"I wait until no one's around." My expression must have been too eager, because he backtracked. "Hey, it wasn't always that way. When I first started, I was starvin' down here. I saw Olson assigning cases to everybody but me. He was sticking it up my ass, knowing I'd come around sooner or later. I bust my balls, I'm as good a lawyer as those other guys; if they have to come across to get some justice for their clients, then I got to come across. It's only fair."

"Well, thanks again for the hundred."

"To tell you the truth, I kind of felt sorry for you," Jim said. "You been doin' favors for a couple of guys and they still don't trust anybody new. Most of them, anyway. But Silverman likes taking care of people starting out."

"Would Bob rather give me the money than the policeman?" This was my first obvious allusion to my supposedly being corrupt.

"Maybe, if he thinks the cop is honest. Why not? He's got to deliver for his client, doesn't he?"

Then we talked about problems new defense lawyers encounter, since Costello took it for granted I would be coming over some day, as indeed I would. He mentioned that Olson told one who was having trouble lining up clients, "Come down to my courtroom and I'll take care of you." The judge, Costello added, "is a ballsy guy. The shit he has pulled on the fuckin' bench!"

"What do you mean?" I asked calmly while tingling.

"Not now," he told me with a knowing toss of his head. Some prosecutors happened to be walking by. Besides, we had to get back to work.

As I was presenting cases before Olson that afternoon, my mind was going over my conversation with Costello so I could repeat the relevant parts to my contact agents if the recording didn't turn out, and I felt used up by the end of the day.

Once I was back in my apartment, I set my briefcase down and pulled off my shirt and perspiration-soaked undershirt, then ripped the microphone from my chest so I could feel like myself again. But I was still all tight inside, and my thoughts were still jumbled. I had betrayed a friend, I was turning my back on my profession, and I was finally on my way to doing something important. How could I get much sleep?

The next morning I drove to the wide parking lot by the lakefront museum complex and rendezvoused with FBI agent Lamar Jordan. Hardly saying a word, I handed over the Nagra and he opened the cover. Seagulls were squealing over the water as I watched his fingers.

"It's threaded wrong," Jordan said in his soft Southern accent. "The tape is supposed to be in front of this post, not behind it."

"It's no good?" I thought my worst fears had come true.

"You can't think of everything when you start out. I'll take it back to the office and see what we can do."

A few hours later Jordan cheerfully called me at home. "It's beautiful, Terry. Costello comes off loud and clear. We lost a little but we got just what we want. Keep it up, you're doing all right."

I hung up feeling as happy as when I made a perfect back flip from the parallel bars at a high school gymnastics competition. I was not giving Reidy what he wanted—Costello saying why he had given me the money—but the door to the closed world of corruption was unlocking.

A day later I found Jim at Jeans engaged in his most beloved pastime, plucking an olive and tossing the rest of a martini down the hatch. Naturally he was feeling sorry for himself. Even though he was doing well enough, he still thought he was a waif abandoned in the back streets of justice.

"I hustle and do what I can, but I'm not getting rich," he moaned in a confidential tone that was louder than most people's natural voice. His elbows had been on a table at Jeans for so long the sleeve of his new suit had soaked up gin and vermouth.

The restaurant was closed except for the courthouse crowd coming in through the warped back door. I had sensed for some time that I had to stop being passive, and now seemed a good time to act. So when Costello's self-pity got around to clients Olson was sending to him, I mentioned, "I hope there's something in it for me."

"Don't worry, Ter," he said, making my name sound like "Tare," "it just takes a little time."

At first glance Costello seemed like just a big man who took little care of himself, but once you knew him you might have noticed he was moderately nice looking. He recently had moved up a notch in his relationship with Olson, but instead of looking more secure he made himself ludicrous with his unwieldy hair and increasing lack of coordination at the bar.

He probably wanted me to keep up with him, but I was never much of a drinker. I made two beers last as long as the Nagra reels rolled under my shirt. Jim spoke about his days as a policeman. Whenever he was about to appear in gun court, gentlemanly Bob Silverman would go up to him and ask, "You know how to testify, don't you?" Then Bob would hand him one hundred dollars tucked in a folded newspaper.

"Every time Bob had a case, I went out and came back with a paper," Jim said. "The other cops must have thought I liked reading newspapers. What a character. But Bob's very proud of himself. He'd say, 'In my twenty-three years as a defense attorney, I never hurt any-body.'" If an officer or a prosecutor couldn't be bribed, Bob found ways so the person would not seem to have bungled the case, and he paid off everyone who had a hand out, from witnesses to the judge. "I mean, everybody gets stroked," Costello said, before downing another martini.

Some courthouse people listening behind our backs chuckled with recognition at Jim's approximation of Bob's mellow voice. After a little more rambling, he told me, "You know, some part of police lingo has been taken over here. When a lawyer wants to make a payoff, he'll tell the judge's guy to 'open the drawer.' That's straight cop talk, from how the district commander gets his payoffs."

"He doesn't really open a drawer?"

"Well, sometimes, but he doesn't have to, it's just a way of lettin' 'im know that money is being dropped wherever the hell the judge wants it."

"That's how Olson does it?"

"That God damned Olson, yeah, that's how he does it."

Before Greylord

Because I had the backup of the Justice Department, I was on my way to go further than Mort Friedman had when he headed the criminal division of the State's Attorney's Office in the seventies. Friedman even looked like an aggressive idealist, with dark hair and black-frame glasses.

Acting on his own, he saw a chance to attack the problem when a policeman told him an attorney named *Walt Fisher had offered him fifty dollars to lie on the stand in a drunken driving case. Fixers were protected by the common knowledge that prosecutors would never be crazy enough to encourage perjury. Friedman told the cop to go along with the offer and see what happened.

The officer gathered enough proof to put Fisher on trial, but the lawyer was acquitted and went on to be elected an associate judge by the hundred and seventy-five full judges in the system. All of them must have known of Fisher's dishonesty, but they liked him.

Another policeman later told Friedman that an attorney had offered him two hundred dollars if he would drop charges against a young woman who had seriously stabbed her female lover. The lawyer even climbed into the officer's private car and threw two one-hundred-dollar bills and a fifty-dollar bonus at the policeman's feet. The officer picked up the money and simultaneously handed him a subpoena to appear before a grand jury. But the lawyer testified that the officer had demanded the bribe, and that he had thrown the money at him to avoid being shot. The jury found him guilty and the Illinois Supreme Court upheld the conviction.

Friedman's third case involved the victim of a police shakedown. The man had been in an apartment when officers confiscated ten pounds of marijuana and nearly forty thousand dollars. Three detectives told him that if he shut up they would make the search appear shaky, but that if he told the truth they would "trunk" him.

Friedman persuaded the man to go into court wearing a tiny radio transmitter. Unaware the officers had lied, the judge dismissed the case. There is nothing a reputable person hates more than being considered dishonest. When the judge learned about the wire, he called Friedman a publicity hound and threatened to find him in contempt. His outrage forced an Illinois Supreme Court review of Friedman's conduct.

The majority opinion held that he had been misguided and warned against any further presentation of false testimony without judicial approval. Although Friedman kept his law license, he was ostracized even by honest lawyers and judges. His one-man attempt at exposing bribery had only left a chill in the system. He gave up prosecutions and was hired as the chief attorney for the state police. He became not only a friend of mine but also an inspiration.

The final stage of Greylord would reach the junction of the courts, city hall, and the mob, an interrelationship that explains why corruption had become so entrenched in Chicago. An example was the shocking acquittal of mob killer Harry Aleman, the impetus for our sweeping investigation. There was as yet no proof the judge had been paid off, but the fact that criminals could fix one of the biggest local trials of the decade meant something had to be done quickly. Cook County State's Attorney Bernard Carey, a former FBI agent, brought his concerns about the case to U.S. Attorney Thomas Sullivan.

They cautiously started by approaching a couple of corrupt lawyers they had learned about from drug and syndicate gambling investigations. Both attorneys were willing to give them a few names, and one helped build a case against a policeman and a bagman. But he refused to violate the shyster's code by going against someone in the legal profession.

Not yet envisioning a full-scale assault, Carey and Sullivan transferred to federal court all significant state narcotics cases involving attorneys suspected of being crooked. This forced Bob Silverman and our other targets to drop clients who were about to come before untainted judges. But that was as far as the authorities could go, and all they had to show for their efforts was a couple of hundred pages of notes, court transcripts, and unverified FBI reports. Everything was kept in disorder inside a plain cardboard box.

Then came the "Abscam" operation, basis for the 2013 movie *American Hustle*, in which convicted perjurer and cheat Mel Weinberg introduced to Washington, D.C., society federal agents masquerading as representatives of a wealthy Arab sheik seeking legislative favors. Eventually six Congressmen and a senator were convicted of bribery despite their cries of entrapment.

Soon afterward, Sullivan met with FBI Director William Webster, a former federal judge, to consider whether anything like that could be attempted in Chicago. After all, the unified Cook County court system was too large for anyone to keep a watch over it all. There were three hundred and thirty-four judges, nearly twice as many as any other circuit court in America, and the growing backlog was being handled by five hundred assistant state's attorneys, some barely out of law school, as I had been. It didn't take a great defense lawyer to win acquittals, just bribes that went unnoticed by underpaid, overworked, and underprepared assistant prosecutors. And now we were seeing corruption breeding corruption.

Sullivan suggested to Webster that they use the files in that cardboard box as background for going after specific targets. The FBI director was a reserved academic and troubled by what was happening in the halls of justice. Abscam had whetted his enthusiasm for long-term stings, and he answered, "I don't see why we don't try it." But the House of Representatives might use any serious slip-up in the Chicago project to slash the Justice Department's budget.

Not long after that meeting, Sullivan's chief of special prosecutions, Gordon Nash, knocked on Reidy's door and handed him the box with no more explanation than "Here's the beginning of an investigation into judicial corruption." That was how Reidy came to draft our strategy.

As it turned out, I was the second mole in the operation. There were many good agents already working in Chicago, but authorities wanted someone who had never made a local court appearance. With their survival instincts, corrupt lawyers develop a memory for faces.

Abscam prosecutions were still in the news in March 1980 when attorney David Victor Ries arrived in the city's canyon-like legal district and rented space at 2 North La Salle Street, where Bob Silverman had his offices. Ries had come from Detroit, so he was a new face, and he had an Illinois law license. Nothing seemed out of the ordinary as he handled cases in the Traffic Court Building in a former warehouse a few blocks away.

The Justice Department now needed a name for the investigation. "CoJud," for "Corrupt Judges," was too close to what it was about. "Operation Fly Catcher" had been used for another kind of probe in Delaware. Then, sitting around their office on a slow day, supervisor Bob Farmer and agent Lamar Jordan choose a name at random. Since Farmer owned a few quarter horses, he suggested looking over the race results. Jordan glanced at a horse's name in the back pages of the *Chicago Sun-Times* and said, "How about 'Operation Greylord'?" The name had magic.

Ries continued strapping on a wire every morning before going to Traffic Court, but he just wasn't picking up any evidence because the lawyers were cool to every outsider. That was when Dan Reidy and the others realized they needed someone already working in the Criminal Courts Building halfway across the city, and drew up their long list of one.

4

THE FIXERS

June 1980

Judge Wayne Olson would rush through his call by dismissing the majority of cases so he could finish before two p.m. The frequent dismissals and suppression of evidence in his court were helping violent street gangs extend drug distribution by murder and intimidation through low-income neighborhoods, but he had his afternoons off.

A judge's chambers should be a sanctum of quiet dignity, but Olson's were more like an airport terminal with traffic when seen on fast-forward. Because he usually left the door open when he withdrew between his morning and afternoon calls, the people who might be traipsing through at any moment included clerks in shirtsleeves, attorneys in suits, police officers in blue, and bailiffs in black. Other court workers breezed in to find files they had misplaced or to use the private washroom rather than one marred by graffiti down the hall, which served as a pre-trial meeting place for defense lawyers and their lowlife clients.

Occasionally a defendant taking a shortcut to the clerk's office behind the chambers walked in and wondered why a judge was there in a swivel chair. Comfortable amid the chaos, and looking and sounding like the late comedian Rodney Dangerfield, Olson would ignore everything not directly concerning him, even quarrels among attorneys or staff members.

Why did he want to leave early every day? Like a coach more interested in popularity than winning, he would take his staff and some fawning lawyers to Jeans or another restaurant with a bar. When they entered, the attorneys flanking him were like scavenger birds encircling a rhinoceros for the privilege of plucking food from between his teeth.

Despite Olson's show of good humor, he could be rude, sarcastic, and ill tempered. If the state judicial disciplinary commission had been effective, he would be a bartender instead of wearing a robe. The former train conductor and polka band drummer would boast that as a private attorney he had paid off every judge he ever appeared before. At the age of thirty he lost a run for the state senate, and his unfulfilled heart remained in politics rather than the law. But after he was elected to the bench, something happened in 1964 that ended his hopes of going any further than a preliminary hearing court.

He and his drinking buddies had landed in a place named the Alibi Inn. At closing time the Democratic Olson and one of his friends started squabbling outside with a sixty-year-old man who said he was going to vote for the Republican presidential candidate. Olson claimed later that he saw a pistol in the man's hand and pushed him in self-defense. Whatever the truth, the older man fell back and cracked his head on the pavement. Prosecutors called it involuntary manslaughter. A court reporter once told me that a colleague had to take a witness's statement eight times before the witness got his story straight. "Straight" meant in Olson's favor. And so the county grand jury declined to return an indictment.

Why were such judges kept on the bench? In Chicago, politicians decide the candidates, and the people are asked to vote from long lists of names meaning nothing to them. Many voters just choose names reflecting a certain nationality or that "sound nice."

In an ideal world, judges wouldn't even have to run for election, but Chicago has never been accused of being an ideal world. Judgeships were awarded to people who could deliver the most votes for the Party slate— Democratic in the city, and Republican in the outer suburbs. There also was a rumor that judgeships could be bought for thirty thousand dollars or more. Not all the judges who were given their robes by the machines were looking for payoffs, but many of the honest ones were naive or gratefully blind to what was going on, which is a kind of corruption in itself.

My introduction into the fixer's milieu had taken longer than we expected, but at last I was able to start directing events my way. From my conversations with Costello, I picked up that of all the judges in the system he hated Wayne Olson most. Jim maintained a hazy fantasy in which he would have been a man of integrity if it hadn't been for "that Swede son of a bitch," forgetting that there isn't much of a step down from being a crooked policeman to becoming a crooked lawyer.

Until recently Costello would place Olson's bribe with a clerk. But because Mike Ficaro, head of the state's attorney's criminal division, had some fun shuffling the clerks around in June to encourage lawyers to take their bribes to me, Jim decided to make his payoffs to Olson in person. The transactions were not always simple. Such as when Olson was on the phone in his chambers and Jim found a young lawyer was waiting at the door to talk to the judge.

Costello wondered how he could deliver the money before his case came up. As he told me at a restaurant that summer, a deputy sheriff walked in, momentarily blocking the young lawyer's line of vision. "I just fuckin' whipped out that money and Olson grabbed it, and I was out of there like lightning." And so Costello put another drug dealer back on the street.

I forced a laugh in pretended admiration and asked, "How do I start selling cases down there? Or is it worth getting involved in something like that while I'm still an ASA?"

"Don't do it, Ter. Don't take money from anybody you don't know. Believe me, they'll hurtcha. You're too nice a guy for that. Get to know them good first."

"How can they hurt me?"

"Just take my word for it."

As he went on, I wondered why he was spending so much time trying to help me. Although I kept suggesting that I might be "dirty," I couldn't change my Boy Scout appearance and soft voice. I seldom speak coarsely, and I rarely used profanity while undercover because I didn't want to put off any jurors listening to my tapes. Who knows, maybe my drawbacks as a mole were an advantage in the long run. Perhaps in some corner of Jim's mind he thought he could relive his long-ago innocence through me.

In that rambling conversation with me, he got around to saying that the deputy sheriff who ran the Narcotics Court lockup had sent him the case of a prisoner found with seven hundred dollars. "I charged the client six hundred and eighty-one dollars for my fee, and I gave one hundred of that to the lockup keeper."

"Wait, wait, wait," I said, "you charged him exactly six hundred and eighty-one dollars? Isn't that a little strange? Why didn't you round it off?"

"The theory behind that is leave 'em with a few bucks. Remember that when you go private. Don't empty their pockets. That's not class."

A passing waitress refused to give Costello any more martinis. Jim shrugged it off and made a mock pass at her. Then he wiggled some money at me from under our table. "Hey, Ter, take this and have a nice dinner with your girlfriend."

I glanced at the denomination as I put it in my pocket. "You don't have to give me a hundred," I said for the tape.

"Don't gimme that, you been a super guy. Believe me. I made six hundred today, you know what I mean? This hundred—that's bullshit. Terry, either I take care of you or it goes to somebody else's pocket. Don't worry about it."

He was so tipsy it was a struggle for him to get up, so I asked if he wanted me to drive him home. Costello made a dismissal gesture that so upset his balance he dropped back into his chair. "I gotta take a piss," he groaned.

"Can you go through the kitchen?"

Unable to get up by himself, he sat back and looked down at his clothes. "I got my best suit on," he said. "I paid a lot of money for this suit. It's from Capper & Capper." Not even bladder strain could stop Jim from looking at me with soulful eyes and sounding like a commercial.

He towered over me as I helped him to his feet, and he reached the tiny washroom in time. Soon we were walking across the parking lot in an afternoon breeze. I talked him into giving me the keys of his newly waxed Ford Thunderbird. "Always buy black cars," Jim would tell me from time to time, "they're classier."

A few blocks away, Jim slumped again into his guilty phase. "Look at you," he mumbled as I drove, "comin' to work every God damned day in a six-year-old piece of junk." Actually, my Plymouth was eight years old. "Why don't you get yourself a real car? Uncle Sam don't know it, but I make more than two thousan' a week. I mean, I'm making so much money it's ridiculous."

I still couldn't believe he was earning that much regularly, but I turned the radio down for the benefit of the tape. Costello didn't use the word "bribe"—speaking directly was practically blasphemy among fixers—but he told me he had to pay off the cops. Still slurring and making aimless gestures, he reached under the center armrest and startled me with a thirty-eight-caliber revolver. "What do you think of this?" he asked, while waving it in my face.

I nearly lost control of the wheel, that's what I thought of it. A gun in the car I could take, but a gun in the hands of a drunk was something else again. This also was my first visual reminder that crooked attorneys could be dangerous.

"Whoa, Jim," I said, steering through Western Avenue traffic while keeping the corner of my eye on the revolver, "don't you think you should put that thing away?"

"I keep this here for protection 'cause my clients live in some pretty bum neighborhoods. If I ever get stopped and the cops find this, all it takes is a hun'red bucks and I'm on my fuckin' way. The point is, Ter, money can do anything." The revolver kept wobbling in front of my face.

"Jim, I get nervous around guns."

"I jus' wan'ed to show it to you."

"You did, and I'm impressed, now would you please put that thing away?"

He clumsily shoved the gun back and said, "A lawyer's always gotta be prepared. Remember that."

Half an hour later we were in his far South Side home, where the basement had been remodeled into a bar and party room. While still describing life in Traffic Court, Jim opened a beer for each of us, as if he needed another drink. He said that whenever a client gave him fifteen hundred dollars to secure an "NG" (not guilty), fifty dollars went to the "copper" bagman who worked in the courtroom, two hundred to the judge, and fifty to the perjuring officer. That left the prosecutors "all Morky-dorky. They don't know what the hell is goin' on." Indeed, I knew the feeling.

Costello assured me that many of the judges had their price, but you had to know how to reach them. For example, he gave the police officer assigned to the courtroom of Judge Al Rosen one hundred dollars from a client charged with drunken driving, but Rosen found him guilty anyway. "That Rosen, know what he says to me afterward? 'Motherfucker, if you want your "not guilty," you come to me.'" Costello guffawed at the memory.

I never learned whether that particular officer was a bagman for the judge or just a rainmaker. Rainmakers are officers, court clerks, and lawyers who ask for money to fix a case but don't inform the judge, who may be upstanding. If the client is found guilty, the rainmaker says that for some reason he couldn't deliver the bribe and hands the money back. Rainmaking is unethical, but the law at the time was not all that clear about whether it was criminal. This ambiguity would haunt us years later.

Relaxing in his recreation room, Costello said that when he wanted to fix a verdict in Traffic Court he didn't need to go through Joe McDermott, the lawyer who "wires up [rigs] the cases." I asked if McDermott was one of the "miracle workers," the nickname for certain Traffic Court lawyers who seldom lost a case. Rumor had it that all were fixers.

"Let me tell you," Costello responded with a tap on my arm, "a miracle worker is just anyone that comes up with the bread."

As our conversation was winding down, I looked for a way to pull out. "Say, Jim," I said, "is there anything I can do for you? You know, help steer cases—"

"Naw, I don't wan'cha go out on a limb."

"Well, it's getting late. I have to go all the way to Evanston."

Having passed through self-pity and guilt in his intoxication, Costello dipped into the maudlin level as I reached for the door knob. "Ter, you been super to me. I don't forget guys like that."

His wife, Martha, agreed to drive me ten miles back to my car in the courthouse parking lot. Martha wasn't a bad-looking woman in her mid-thirties, but there was something cloying about her as if she imagined that by a lot of drinking and a little flirting she could be eighteen again. During the ride, I also received the impression from what little she said that her marriage was falling apart. I didn't know if Jim's drinking was the cause or the effect.

July 1980

By the end of July I had grown tired of waiting for "Silvery" Bob Silverman to make the first move. With my new confidence I told the officer working in Narcotics Court, "Hey, listen. Bob's case—we're not going anywhere with it. I'm going to SOL it [dismiss on leave to reinstate]. He's a pretty sharp guy—you know his methods. It'll just wind up getting thrown out anyway."

No doubt suspecting I had been reached, the policeman gave me a weary "Do what you want."

Word got around to Silverman and, judging from later events, he must have felt that now he owed me one.

Costello came to me a little later and spoke about a client whose auto was about to be sold at a police auction because of drugs found inside. Jim handed me fifty dollars—my first official bribe—and I appeared before Judge Olson to say the state would not oppose a request that the car be returned to its owner. Like so many cases in that building, the hearing had been a sham. In the hallway, Costello let me know that "Wayne got his."

Eventually things were happening so fast that my FBI control agent, Lamar Jordan, was having me meet him in his car almost every morning to pick up my tapes and any money I had taken the day before. Our usual location was a parking lot where the Adler Planetarium, Shedd Aquarium, and Field Museum of Natural History share a little greenery at the lakefront. There we would discuss what I had done the day before, what I had tried to do, and what I hoped to accomplish in the next few days.

"How is your girlfriend taking things?" Jordan asked one morning. "You're spending a lot more time in bars now. Is she complaining about it?"

I could read a message in those rock-hard eyes: You probably told her, didn't you? "Cathy doesn't mind. I still take her out. She knows I haven't changed." Behind this seemingly offhand remark I was lobbing back: Yes, I told her, but don't worry, no one else will know.

Then I drove away so I could be in the courthouse to watch the action around Olson's chambers before his call began. The same half dozen attorneys would drop by Olson's chambers every day to check on their cases or make a payoff. Most of them were in their early middle age, well dressed, and had a professional sociability, but I got the feeling they did not like one another all that much. After all, they were competitors in a crowded field. A couple of them had already begun that day's drinking.

The most frequent visitor to Narcotics Court was attorney Richard Stopka, a former policeman with pale skin and a round face. Since Stopka came from a Polish family, the predominantly Irish, Italian, and Jewish lawyers in the fixers' club grumbled that he had "no class." Costello told me Stopka was receiving most of Olson's cases because he was paying the judge a third of the bond money returned to him as the lawyer's fee. Jim clearly thought the judge shouldn't play favorites—unless the favorite happened to be him.

As this was going on, the old benches in that cavernous courtroom were filling up. Narcotics Court never drew a cross-section of humanity. The more affluent dealers were usually indicted for additional crimes and appeared elsewhere, leaving the poorest ones on Olson's call. Before the doors opened, some paced nervously in the corridor and occasionally one would burst into an erratic dance to work off tension. Once the public was let in, some would be slumped in the benches still obviously on a high. But most sat back and trusted their lawyer to get them off. Sometimes mothers diapered their babies on the benches.

Attorneys leaving the judge's chambers would come down the aisle between the benches with case folders and call out the names: Lewis? Vargas? Preece? A man or woman would get up with a glazed expression and stumble across the knees and feet of defendants waiting their turn.

Handling an average of a hundred and fifty cases between nine in the morning and two in the afternoon, it was no wonder Olson enjoyed hearing a joke, even when it was in bad taste. Then at the end of his call he would walk into his chambers, put his black robe on a hanger, and talk to his bailiff or some attorney about his family. He was proud of his daughter in law school but less so of his son, a policeman. Then the judge would spend a few hours in bars with anyone who cared to join him. Whoever went along was assured of a good time but often wound up paying the entire bill.

One story Olson loved to tell was about his days as a lawyer, when a company hired him for cases involving its illegally heavy cement trucks. At the time he was also working as a police magistrate. Olson would charge the company half the amount he had saved it, then give the judges half of what he had received. But then a new jurist demanded more.

"So I filed a motion to transfer the case," Olson said, "and do you know what reason I listed on the motion? That the bastard wanted more money! The judge almost shit in his pants, but he transferred the case anyway," allowing him to pay off a less greedy judge. "Then a year later I became the chief judge of the district. That meant I was his boss, and I assigned him to nothing where he could lay his hands on dough. So the moral of the story is: Never kick your janitor in the ass because some day he might be your landlord."

The whole building we worked in had a things-are-not-as-they-seem character once you came to know it. A clerk in the Narcotics courtroom down the hall from Olson's made side money by selling phonograph records from a stuffed filing cabinet that should have been used for court records. And a deputy sheriff connected with a clothing store discounted three-piece suits for new attorneys.

Even the avarice that ran the place was deceiving. Fixers—and fixers who became judges—lived for the emotional highs that only money could bring them. "Let me tell you," Costello once told me, "when you get on the other side, all you do is drink." Or take drugs, as I learned about two crooked attorneys. Or gamble.

On Friday nights, Jeans became a little Las Vegas. With the doors locked, the courthouse people—black and white, those just starting out and those near retirement—would turn a table on its side so they would have a surface to roll the dice against. "Come on, Little Joe," a player might call out as lawyers, police officers, and judges knelt around him, some in four-hundred-dollar suits.

After every toss, the money changing hands included bribes that had been used to send criminals back onto the streets. A few players would throw the dice while holding a lucky penny or a little toy animal, and some chanted "Baby needs a new pair of shoes" as one-hundred-dollar bills descended like autumn leaves. The city's violence rate was soaring, and yet this was where the attorneys and judges could be found.

That summer my friend Mark Ciavelli left the State's Attorney's Office for a defense practice with another competitive young lawyer, *Frank Cardoni. He came from a politically connected family, was the son of a wealthy surgeon, and was looking for a fast track to affluence. Frank wanted to keep handling cases before Judge John Reynolds' felony preliminary hearing court in a North Side police station and needed Mark to represent clients transferred from there to other judges. I wished Mark had chosen someone else to work with. Cardoni was pleasant enough, but I heard that he was "dirty."

Now that Mark and I no longer worked together, we didn't see much of each any more. In a way I was glad, because this meant that around him I didn't have to act as if I were selling cases. And although I had told Costello that I was not seeing Cathy much anymore, because I did not want him to intrude on my personal life, we saw each other often now. Our times together were about the only way I could untwist my two selves.

August 1980

Judge Olson was talking with some attorneys at an Italian restaurant on a humid August Friday when I started to leave three hours into the session to keep a date with Cathy. By then everyone else was pretty drunk. In fact, Olson was feeling so good he hurled a glass across the room and shouted, "*Finito!*"

Some ideas were playing around in my head as I studied the judge, then saw Costello sitting at a table oblivious of everything. For weeks "Big Bird" had been complaining that Olson was giving other lawyers cases that should have gone to him. What if I brought the two of them a little closer? Then I could watch money-hunger lock them together.

Sidling up to Jim, I said, "Olson's in no condition to drive, so why don't you give him a ride home? Maybe you can discuss some things on the way."

Costello wasn't much more sober than the judge, but he nodded, pulled himself up, and walked over to Olson, and soon these two big men waddled out in mutual support. I wondered whether they would talk over percentages during the drive.

Five days later Costello came over to me in a restaurant as pleased as a cat who has learned how to open the canary cage. "You're looking at the new Richard Stopka," he crowed, with a good-natured glow.

"What do you mean?"

"Remember last Friday when I drove Olson home? I paid him a hundred dollars on a case and asked him how he wanted to work it from now on. He starts complaining that Stopka only kicks back thirty percent. So he says, 'If you're willing to give me *half* of any bonds or drug cash I return, we can make anywhere between five hundred and one thousand dollars a week.' So I said screw the Pollock. And know what? Richard didn't get a single case off Olson today!"

Costello was only interested in becoming Olson's number one boy, regardless of how little money he might make in the partnership. I was sure the arrangement was in trouble from the start, but what I said was, "That's good, Jim, I'm happy for you."

5

MONEY TRAILS

Late August 1980

When I told my contact agent Lamar Jordan about the new development that night, he was only mildly interested since Greylord wasn't concerned with hallway hustlers like Jim Costello. But both of us would have been jumping for joy if we had known that by establishing a steady payoff in Olson's chambers, Jim had unknowingly made possible the most dramatic element of our investigation.

Not that I realized this a few days later, when Jim and I were having beers at a restaurant and he complained about his wife. "Martha drinks like a bitch," he said, so upset he must have been unaware he had substituted another word for "fish."

We also talked over judges we liked and didn't like, attorneys who were often drunk in court, and a lawyer called "Trick Baby" behind his back because his mother supposedly had been a prostitute. The topics got around to a supervisor in the State's Attorney's Office who, Costello said, "should have been indicted" for all the things he was doing, but he wound up being promoted to the trial courts. This led us to two defense attorneys who had asked Costello whether they should buy Olson a set of golf balls with his name on them in appreciation for all the clients' money they were making off his rulings.

I excused myself and went to the tiny men's room. With one elbow an inch from the wall and the other elbow an inch from the flimsy black door, I removed the Nagra tape and threaded a new one over the reels. When I came back, Costello got around to talking about when he was an assistant prosecutor before the other Narcotics Court judge, Arthur Zelezinski. "Am I glad he's honest, Ter," Jim said. I knew what he meant, but he explained anyway. "The only way attorneys could fix a case in his court was by going through me. There was a big heroin bust I managed to get thrown out."

How big, I asked for the wire.

"Let me put it this way, Ter, I made a down payment on my Thunderbird."

He added that Zelezinski had outlawed hustling at his courtroom and was content with living off his judicial salary. "You can bet that when *Olson* gets his paycheck, it goes right to the bank."

"Wayne's living off payoffs?" I asked.

"Sure he is, and it's all unreported income."

"Wayne must be getting at least fifty thousand dollars a year on the side, huh?"

"Fifty thousand? Yeah, sure."

"You know, that's a pretty good method you told me about 'opening the drawer.'" My dialogue seems painfully obvious to me now, but I was new at the game and I had to keep up the momentum while simultaneously thinking of all sorts of things.

"It's common knowledge, that's the signal. Ever see the clerk with the sheet of the SOLs and wonder why so many were stricken? Now you know."

The waitress came over, and we had a tug-of-war over the bill. "Please, Jim," I said, "let me pay, you've been very good to me."

What Costello was outlining for me was only a sliver of what was happening every day. With the insight of what took me months to develop, let me walk you through a typical day in the giant Criminal Courts Building as it was in the early 1980s. For Judge Maurice Pompey, the day would begin when Deputy Sheriff Lucius Robinson—his driver and bagman—picked him up at his home in a large red Lincoln with a white vinyl top. On the way, the two would chat about anything other than work. Then they would park in the judges' lot adjacent to the courthouse and enter the somber seven-story gray building.

They would say a few cheerful words to the guards and go into a small, lever-operated judges' elevator in the back. Pompey would go to his chambers and put on a black robe from the closet. He would sit behind the bench in front of defendants, their friends, and witnesses to dispense prepaid justice.

While this was going on, lawyers would go to Robinson in the back of the courtroom and slip him envelopes stuffed with cash or hand him a newspaper and say something like, "You might like the article on page five." There would be several hundred dollars for a favorable ruling on a case coming up in a few days. Robinson would put the envelopes and the entire newspaper into Pompey's briefcase when the chambers were empty. Robinson would not mention details of the payoffs until he and Pompey were on their way home.

Now let's suppose you were a visitor to the courthouse. You would wait in a long line at the metal detectors just behind the revolving doors in the modern annex, then cross over to the concourse at your right and be in the main building, constructed during the Capone era. The first thing you would see would be the shoeshine stand that lawyers patronized for good luck before their opening and closing arguments. Next you would walk by a wall covered with call sheets listing the day's courtroom assignments. Turning left, you would pass through large interior black columns of neo-Babylonian design and serving no imaginable purpose. Beyond these were the wide brass doors of elevators to take you upstairs to the felony courtrooms.

Once there, you might come across a pair of attorneys speaking casually in the corridor. Suppose one pats the other on the back and shakes his hand. That could be a parting gesture or a bribe to be passed on to a judge. Or a lawyer drops by in a judge's chambers and talks with the bailiff while His Honor is away. The lawyer might be there to tell a joke, or he could be dropping money into an open drawer. Some judge's clerks made sure they knew exactly how much was put in because they would be getting a percentage. But fixes were never definite. Judges gave money back in "heater cases," ones receiving so much public attention the jurist feels pressured to decide according to the evidence.

As part of the bribery ritual, judges seldom took money directly. Thomas Maloney—who would become the first American judge ever convicted of taking bribes in murder cases—stood by on the sixth floor one day while an attorney handed bagman Lucius Robinson an envelope containing two thousand dollars, with the understanding that Robinson would pass the money on to him. This way, the lawyer could truthfully say he never gave Maloney a bribe. The bagman could lie and say he kept the money for himself, and so he never took part in actual bribery. And Maloney could say he was never bribed.

Robinson, a tough black man with street smarts and incisive movements, kept his share in a tin file-card container he called his "goody box." Some court clerks stashed their bribes in cans under their desk just a few feet from the witness benches. Anyone could see the cash there, if they thought of looking.

Now that I was gradually moving into the inner circle, the argot I had overheard for months began to make sense. Bribing a prosecutor was "saying hello," and if someone wanted to know whether a case was fixed he would ask the defense attorney, "Have you seen the judge?" Most of the defense attorneys now thought I was "okay," meaning I could be approached.

But how smoothly the bribery went on depended on the personalities involved. For example, I could feel the electricity each time Olson and Costello were together. There was something that made them regard each other with a reined-in hatred, a combination of opposites and similarities. Something explosive was bound to happen between them. Although I didn't know when or where it would be, I hoped to be there when it did.

Just then a friend from Loyola University's Rome campus asked me to attend his mid-week wedding near San Francisco. There was no way for me to back out without making him wonder why, so I agreed to go. But I prayed that nothing would happen between Olson and Costello while I was gone. Once again, I asked Cathy to come along.

The bridegroom picked us up at the airport and drove us to a friend's home in one of the ornate Victorian "painted ladies" on a hill. I fell in love with San Francisco even though my luggage was lost at the airport, the August weather was cool and damp, and I put my back out lying all night in a sleeping bag on the floor.

When I returned I learned that contact agent Lamar Jordan had been trying to reach me for days. Federal prosecutor Dan Reidy, the stocky keeper of the box, had come up with an idea so daring that it could transform the entire Greylord operation. Jordan didn't offer any hints over the phone, but he urgently asked me to meet him in a place where neither of us would be recognized.

The next day, Friday, August 22, 1980, I drove to the YMCA in suburban Glen Ellyn and met him on the racquetball court. I was eager to learn why I had been called, but Jordan said, "Let's play." We slipped on plastic goggles and padded gloves, then bounced the ball off the walls as if trying to kill it. During a break, the powerfully built Mormon FBI agent told me the government wanted to listen in as payoffs were being made.

"But they don't trust me enough yet to let me get close," I said.

"You won't be there. We want to plant a hidden microphone in Olson's desk."

I was astonished. "My God, can you do that?" The entire justice system rested on the assumption that there must be no interference with a judge except for flagrant misconduct.

"We don't know yet," Jordan said. "Dan's idea came from the regular payoffs you helped set up between Olson and Costello. There is nothing in Illinois or federal law that exempts judges from electronic surveillance. The problem is that it will make us look like bad guys unless we can show there is no other way of obtaining the evidence. We also have to make a case for whether what we hope to accomplish is worth setting a precedent that no one is going to like. Congress will probably think it violates the separation of powers. But the way we see it, we're just doing our job of going after extortionists. It'll be more than just a legal decision, you understand."

Translation: there were politics to consider.

"So we need hard evidence," Jordan added. "Each case Olson refers to your friend Costello should be documented. You also will have to get the facts on every case you think has been fixed by any lawyer." Was I hearing right? "We'll try going after them all."

That surely slowed my game. "But that could be fifty of them, and I'm only close to Costello."

"We're counting on you to get what we need, Terry. We've got to have the strongest case we possibly can, and we know you can do it."

But Jordan didn't know how I would gather that evidence, and neither did I. Even so, I felt great as I drove back to my apartment. This wasn't just an FBI sting operation anymore, it was an assault on an entire court system that had become infected. The government had finally found a viable approach by defining a new criminal class: judges who could be pinned down on racketeering charges.

Yet when I arrived for work Monday I discovered that Narcotics Court prosecution supervisor Ed Hansen had routinely transferred me across the hall to Judge Zelezinski's court. Hansen said this might be only for a week, but I had seen temporary assignments last months. What could I possibly pick up in the courtroom of an honest judge? On the other hand, how could I protest without letting on that the FBI was planning to turn Olson's desk into a giant mousetrap?

In a panic, I called Dan Reidy between hearings in Zelezinski's court. When I told him about the transfer, he said, "You've *got* to get back in with Olson. Don't say anything to Hansen; see if you can go over his head."

So I went back to Mike Ficaro. But this time I wasn't like a beginner asking for a favor. Rather than sit down as he suggested, I remained standing and demanded that he transfer me back. "I can't say more than that," I added.

Mike caught the hint but knew better than to ask anything. "Just do your work with Zelezinski and I'll see what I can do," my roly-poly mentor said.

"You've got half a dozen other ASAs you can put in there."

"I've been helping you all along, Terry, maybe in some ways you don't know about. There is only so much I can do. Besides, if I even tried to step in, someone might get suspicious. Just accept the assignment and wait it out."

The very next day my fears were confirmed. Over a beer, Costello bragged about making more than thirteen hundred dollars in referrals from Olson that day. He had reached the level he had dreamed about and was planning to buy a twelve-thousand-dollar Oldsmobile right off the assembly line. Jim also dropped a mention that attorney Peter Kessler* "owned" the Auto Theft Court of Judge John "Dollars" Devine. This was the sort of thing I should be working toward developing further, but I felt banished from all the action just when I was on the brink of giving the FBI what it needed for clearance to bug Olson's chambers.

September 1980

Ficaro kept his promise and I returned to Olson's court in early September, relieved to learn that my anxiety had been unfounded. Nothing had changed except that some new people were visiting the judge's well-worn chambers to fix cases, including bagman Lucius Robinson. Now that I knew about them, each had to become a target for us. But I would shake their hands, pretend I was enjoying their small talk, and casually ask if I could do anything for them.

As I was having coffee with Costello in the cafeteria of the courthouse office annex, he said he had just tried to give money to Olson but the judge refused to accept it. "He wants to bag me," Jim added as if anyone could understand slang he made up on the spot.

"What do you mean?"

"We had it all arranged, I'd give him his money every Friday in his chambers for the cases he referred. But now he says, 'Why don't we just do this at Jeans?' That motherfucker. Wayne's hoping I lose track so only he knows how much I owe him."

Damn! Damn! I kept thinking. Bugging Jeans would be out of the question, if only for the noise, yet without recorded conversations it would be impossible to prove that Olson was part of the defendant referral bribe scheme.

But Olson was such a volatile character he changed his mind sooner than I had imagined. That Friday afternoon, September 12, I saw Costello walking out of the judge's chambers with some papers in hand from unrepresented clients Olson had just assigned to him. "How much?" I half-whispered although no one was around. With a smile, Jim held up the five fingers of his free hand and said "Plus." During the break, he celebrated by sending out for pizzas for the twenty people who worked in the two Narcotics courtrooms.

Two days later, Olson was reprimanding one of the sleazier-looking defendants for missing an appearance when Chicago policemen Bill Stump and Tony Opiola saw me sitting off to the side. "Excuse me, Mr. State's Attorney, can we talk to you?" Opiola whispered.

I knew the suited officers from their frequent appearances as arresting officers. I left my seat and followed them to the wide vacant area behind the benches. The men explained that after six years they finally had found enough heroin on *Celeste Bailey to send her to prison for six years. "We really want to nail her ass," Stump told me, "but we think the case has been fixed."

"How do you know?" I asked.

"You know her lawyer, Cy Yonan?" Cy had gained a reputation for having cases thrown out before they could go to trial.

"I say hello to him in the halls sometimes."

Actually, I knew Yonan a little better than that. Costello always called him "that motherfucking Jew," but he was from an Assyrian Catholic family that had emigrated from Iran. Dark-featured Cy came on so strong with his courtroom aggressiveness that I was surprised to learn he could be personable when he chose to be. Earlier that month,

Costello said that Cy had always paid him off when he was an assistant state's attorney, "but now that I'm on the other side, he seems to have lost his ability to say hello."

Officer Stump told me, "A cop came to us and said Yonan's ready to be nice to us if we don't say everything that happened when we're on the stand. First it was to be six hundred bucks and we said no, then he said a thousand."

As innocently as I could, I asked, "What can I do?"

"We don't know," Opiola answered. "We just thought you should know that we're clean. We're going to testify to exactly what happened, and if that woman gets back on the street again you'll know somebody got paid off."

When the case was called that day, Yonan presented a motion to suppress the sixty-three grams of heroin found on his client. Without changing inflection, Olson ruled that the two officers had made an illegal search and that the drugs could not be used in the trial.

The one thousand dollars refused by the arresting officers had to have gone somewhere, and I was sure Olson was promised all of it. Some corrupt judges are as selective as sharks but others, like Wayne Olson, are more like carp with gaping mouths gulping down everything they can.

The outraged officers looked at me for a way to save their case. From behind me, Opiola shot into my ear: "Appeal the God damn thing." From the side, attorney Yonan was looking at me cynically. What should I do? If I overplayed my role as a prosecutor on the take, the officers or another ASA could report me.

"Your Honor," I said, "because the suppression of the evidence has altered the circumstances, I request a continuance to consider appealing this case."

Yonan winced, realizing he couldn't read me yet.

"Motion granted," Judge Olson replied. He went through his desk calendar and set the case for three days later.

As I walked out of the courtroom with the officers, Opiola asked, "Are you going to appeal?"

"I'll do whatever I can," I said. "Don't worry."

I knew it was time to develop my own tactics for gathering evidence against each lawyer or judge separately as the circumstances allowed, starting with Cy. But I had to handle a number of plans at the same time.

CY YONAN

During a recess on the day the officers asked me to appeal, Olson took the unusual step of calling me into his chambers. Up to this point, he had not said a word to me that directly implied he was corrupt. Now he felt sure enough about me to drop the pretense. I closed the door and asked, "Judge, what is it you want?"

"I just wanted to have a talk with you to straighten things out," he said from his swivel chair. He sounded like a businessman in a cold business. "From time to time a young prosecutor wants to score brownie points and hangs onto a case. That's understandable. But this Yonan crap is small-time stuff, Terry, and you know it. I don't see why we don't drop it right now. It won't be any reflection on you if you do not appeal it."

Never sound too eager, I reminded myself. "I can't drop it, I'm getting pressure from the cops and my supervisor."

Olson's tone hardened as he said, "Just to make sure I understood the situation perfectly, I phoned *Larry Higgins about this thing." That was one of the most important criminal attorneys in the system. "Larry's a friend of mine and he agrees that the search was improper. You can look it up yourself, People versus Seymour."

"That's not how I see it," I said. "The cops went over with me just what they did, and everything was legal."

"That's a lot of shit," Olson snapped. Then, apparently realizing he had been too emphatic, he tried to sound as if he were merely offering advice. "I mean, I didn't call you back in here to relive the thing. You know how I like throwing out everything but really good cases, the jail is overcrowded as it is. You've put a scare into that woman [Bailey], she knows that next time she won't be so lucky. If you decide to appeal, I really don't give a shit. Do we understand each other?"

"Sure. But I want some time before I make a decision."

"That's fine. Whatever you say."

Olson had made himself clear, all right, but out of habit he did it in such a way that our conversation meant nothing on my tape.

Later that day I agreed to drop marijuana possession charges against two of Costello's clients. After the first, he stuffed a fifty-dollar bill in my suit jacket pocket and said, "You're a super guy." After the second, he playfully shoved another fifty into my empty cup as we stood in a coffee line at the cafeteria. "Jim!" I said. Dozens of people could have seen us. But to him, life in the courthouse was only a game.

As I played along, I dropped only weak cases or ones where the defendant had played only a minor role, but I still hated seeing them walk free. Sometimes they smirked as if to say, "You and me are in the same business." But they were not necessarily off for good. I kept the FBI informed so that the defendants could be approached later about providing evidence against their lawyers to avoid being brought up on federal counts.

On a day I dropped charges against two more of Costello's clients, he slid a hundred and fifty dollars into my pocket in the hallway. As we had drinks at Jeans the following day, he dropped a fifty-dollar bill into my lap for dismissing two more cases.

In six weeks, Costello had given me five hundred dollars. And I wasn't the only one on the payroll that he kept in his head. I saw him give a lockup keeper one hundred dollars to get into a cell and solicit clients before another lawyer could reach them. Jim handed other deputies fifty to sixty dollars for referring drug defendants to him. He dispensed money easily because he saw himself as a public benefactor and a great guy.

Another time I was at Jeans with Costello, I mentioned that Olson had now twice called me back to his chambers to dissuade me from my plan to appeal his decision in the Celeste Bailey case.

"You got to understand that Yonan's a money man," Jim said. "Tell you what, I'll talk to him for you."

"Tell him I'm 'okay.' You know." "Okay" meaning that I took bribes for favors.

When the case was about to come up, Officers Stump and Opiola came looking for me. "Look," Opiola said, "we really want this woman to do hard time, we don't care what pressure you're under."

Yonan seemed just as apprehensive about the Bailey case when he spoke to me briefly in the courtroom. He was relieved when I told him I would ask for a continuance. What they could not know was that this would give Costello time to talk to him about bribing me.

After the continuance was granted, Costello wasted a beautiful September afternoon and evening by keeping me with him at the far end of Jeans long bar, and afterward we went to an Italian restaurant. The night seemed endless since I was only there to keep up my appearance as an ardent disciple, especially since I wasn't picking up anything on tape that I could use. As we slowly spooled our pasta, Costello assured me that if I went into private practice I could save money by using his office and phone number until I was set up.

As I finally was about to leave, Jim raised his glass of wine and slurred, "No, no, don't go yet, I wanna propose a toast."

"To what?"

"Here's to money!" Our glasses clanked.

While Jim might have been dreaming of pinkie rings and a Mercedes, Cy Yonan, my new target, apparently spent the following weekend anguishing over whether I was crooked or not, since he had to be careful about bribing a prosecutor. He came back that Monday willing to take a chance.

The strikingly dark attorney was easy to spot in any crowd, with his out-of-date thick sideburns almost reaching his jaw. I saw him step into Narcotics Court during a hearing and give something to Costello. Although Cy passed me as he was entering and leaving the courtroom, he didn't say a word. But not long afterward, Costello came over and casually remarked, "I just saw your man and he gave me a hundred to give to you, if you know what I'm talking about."

"I know."

"I'll see you later about it."

As we rode the elevator alone to the cafeteria that afternoon, Jim explained what had happened. "I told him, 'Cy, they're gonna appeal that thing.' He says, 'I don't think Terry's gonna appeal it.' I says 'Gimme a hundred to give to Terry,' and he did."

As the elevator doors slid open, he slipped me the one hundred dollars while we walked over to the cafeteria line. He liked me so much he felt he had to keep me corrupt so that we could be in the same game.

"Thanks, Jim," I said, "you're a friend."

6

THE BRASS KEY

October 1980

Silver-haired "Silvery Bob" Silverman was smooth and friendly, but the respected defense attorney could turn icy when making sure his clients stayed out of prison. Silverman had been convicted of bribery in 1963 but was acquitted after the state appeals court ordered a new trial. Like Midas, he now protected himself by contaminating with gold virtually everyone he touched.

Bob was just the opposite of his brother, Mitchell, a circuit court judge of unquestioned principles. Mitchell was sponsored by admired U.S. Senator Adlai Stevenson and received a one hundred percent approval rating from the American Bar Association's Judiciary Committee. Although no one would say so, the general feeling was that Mitchell would have risen higher if his brother's shady reputation had not stood in the way.

Bob was a man of average size who was just starting to lose his youthful handsomeness. He liked to give the appearance of being just a regular guy, going to as many Chicago Cubs games as he could and donating his services to indigent clients. He would come to court with his usual tan and wearing a plaid or ultra suede sport jacket, open shirt, and casual slacks rather than the expensive suits most lawyers wore. He was that sure of himself.

Another thing that set him apart from most of the other criminal attorneys was that he never brought a briefcase to court. From time to time he would take an empty envelope from his pocket and make a few notes on testimony. That was because he did his best work talking to judges and bagmen outside the courtroom.

Since fixers could not advertise in the yellow pages, they used a variety of ways to notify potential clients that they needed their services in a hurry. Such as the way Silverman came to represent Ken Eto, a Japanese-American who used mob enforcers to protect his gambling set-ups.

A man approached "Tokyo Joe" Eto one night and said he was interested in buying seven hundred and fifty thousand dollars' worth of heroin. Eto, as he later related, became suspicious and strung the man along. After meetings with the man a few times, Eto received a telephone warning from Silverman. Through contacts with "dirty" police officers, the attorney had learned that the supposed addict was an undercover drug agent trying to set him up. Eto supposedly was so grateful he gave the fixer twelve thousand dollars and retained him for future business in court.

There was little wonder why Silverman would glide from court to court as if nothing could reach him. From time to time I wondered how many favors I would have to perform before he would steer business my way. My answer came in mid-September, when he showed up in the corridor outside Narcotics Court to express his appreciation to me for throwing out the case of a middle-class woman arrested with amphetamines. Since he didn't bribe Olson, the best he had expected was probation.

"Thank you for your consideration," he told me in passing, in that low voice Costello loved to imitate.

"It's nothing, Bob, your client has no record, and she's got a good family," I tossed off. "It's just possession, anyway. Why hold onto these small-time cases, that's what I feel."

"Costello says you're a good man."

"I try to be fair." My tone was intended to mean one thing to him, and another to anyone nearby.

I kept thinking Silverman might be circling around me before making up his mind about me. He approached me a few days later before the court clerk called out the case of a low-level syndicate member. "You know, Terry," he began in his lullaby voice, "this isn't a great case you have." Indeed, there seldom is a drug arrest in which a top defense attorney can't find something wrong. "I'm not going to embarrass you by asking you to let it go. Why don't you look it over? I just want you to know I'm going to file a motion to suppress. If Olson rules against me, that's all right."

He left with a faint, classy smile and I knew I would be wasting my time opposing the motion: the fix was in.

Now that Silverman had made the first move, I made the second. A few days afterward, I started working toward his trust by dropping all four of his cases in Narcotics Court. He was bound to know that I expected something in return.

As much as I wanted to get something on Bob Silverman, I had to develop new schemes while still doing favors for Costello and dismissing a few cases for Cy Yonan. As with a circus act, I was spinning plates on sticks and seeing how many I could keep in the air. That included getting Yonan to confirm his bribe to me, since Costello had only acted as a bagman for him. With my tape running under my clothes in the rear of the courtroom, I thanked him for the "gift" and asked whether the money was just for the appeal or for two cases coming up.

"Just the appeal," he said.

I tried to keep my expression blank, but running through my mind was *Cy, you idiot, I've got you now*. Although I hadn't been competitive in high school, I was now developing a killer instinct.

Yonan gave us more evidence to use against him with the case of *Lou Bickford, a street corner pusher stupid enough to enter the courthouse with marijuana in one pocket and a tin foil of cocaine in the other. Sheriff's Deputy Jim Metavilas found the drugs while routinely searching people when they came through the metal detector. Metavilas' Greek family had provided him with a strong sense of right and wrong. Since there was no way to bribe him, the money had to go to the person at the next step in the process, me.

Yonan entered the prosecutors' small office along the side of Olson's Narcotics Court and was blunt, since I was alone. "I want you to find some legal reasons for dropping the case," he said.

"It was a perfectly legal search," I parried.

"There are always legal precedents, Terry, do you want me to look them up for you?" This came almost as a threat, as if he were saying: If you don't play ball, you won't get any more money from me.

"Okay, I'll tell Metavilas that we don't have a good case," I said.

"You better."

I should have been glad Yonan was trying to pressure me, but I was afraid that Metavilas, unaware of the undercover investigation, would suspect a fix and report me to authorities. Then the microphone might never be planted in Olson's chambers. But since so much of what was going on in the building went unreported, I decided to see if I could make Metavilas overlook what he would sense was a bribe.

At a break, I went over to him near the revolving doors in the annex corridor and asked if he could spare a minute. As we walked toward the elevators, I let him know that "we're going to have some trouble with that arrest you made." One of the hardest parts of volunteering as a mole is playing bastard to good people.

"Nobody had trouble before," Metavilas said defensively.

"We just don't win many cases against Yonan."

"Cy's a real trip, that guy."

"You know how Olson is. He doesn't go by the law. The rulings depend on which defense lawyer is on the case. He gives his friends the benefit of the doubt, and Yonan is one of his friends. Do you see what I mean?"

"If you think the case won't fly, fine, that's your job," the deputy said. "Did you see Bickford's rap sheet?"

"Then I'll dismiss the case, it'll save us all some time," I said, as if not listening to him.

As I started to walk away, I heard Metavilas mutter, "They all do it," meaning crooked prosecutors. Then he gave me his own kind of warning. "One of these days it's going to go the wrong way with all these dismissals, and somebody's going to wind up bitching."

"Well, they don't."

"Maybe someone should tell TV reporters what's going on in Olson's court."

"What would be the point, Jim? Things just go better this way. You'll see."

He must have felt terrible, but how else could I convince Yonan that my office was for sale?

Nothing happened until mid-October, when Yonan gestured for me to step into an empty office. My heart was thumping in expectation. We had barely cleared the doorway when Cy turned to me with three hundred dollars in his fist.

"Thanks, Terry," he said. "You're doing a good job."

"It's nice to know I'm appreciated."

"See you next time," he said as he left.

Next time!

As soon as I could, I phoned my contact agent Lamar Jordan. But this was seldom simple. Jordan never let me call him or Dan Reidy from my office because there would be no way of knowing who might overhear me. The few times I had used the courthouse phones, I had to be sure no one was around. Occasionally I would grab Olson's phone when his chambers were empty.

But most of the time I walked down the concrete front steps, crossed the boulevard that runs down South California Avenue, climbed into my car in the large lot, and phoned from a gas station a few blocks away, then hurried back to be in time for my next case. The first few times I did this, the inconvenience was part of the excitement, but now it was wearing me down.

"I got Yonan in the bag," I told Jordan from the gas station. "He gave me three hundred for dropping Bickford."

"Good work, Terry, you're getting to be an old hand at this," he said. That was as much of a joke as you would get from the dour Jordan.

"Is this the hard evidence you wanted?"

"We'll see."

The agent helping him, Bill Megary, soon called me to a McDonald's a mile from the courthouse. In his car were two other men in white shirts, gray suits, and with short haircuts. Their assembly-line appearance might as well have been a billboard proclaiming "FBI!" I learned that one of them, tall and slender Ed Tickel, went around the country doing court-approved bugging.

We went to the Criminal Courts Building when all the jurors were gone and there were just the black-uniformed guards at the revolving doors, a lone reporter calling in a story from the large first-floor press room, and the gossiping cleanup crew. We looked over Olson's court, Branch 57, to make sure no one was still around, then Tickel stopped at a door to a courtroom undergoing renovation. He drew a tool that looked like a small screwdriver from his pocket and in seconds the entire lock assembly fell into his hand.

Tickel dropped the metal into his coat pocket and said, "That's all I need." You could see that he loved his work. I stood there not realizing it was all over until the FBI agents headed for the doors. Once we were outside, Tickel handed me a plastic case no larger than an audiocassette. Inside was a wax wedge. "If you can borrow a key to one of the locks in Branch 57, you can press it in this and make an impression," he said.

"That's all you need?" I asked in disbelief.

"With that and this lock assembly I can make a master key for the entire courthouse."

During a recess two days later, I told a Narcotics Court deputy on Costello's payroll that I had locked myself out of my office. "Okay if I borrow your keys?" I asked. The deputy handed them over without question.

Feeling like a spy, I went to my office, locked the door, and nervously sat at my desk. But I couldn't get the plastic case open. *Hurry up*, I told myself. The keys dropped to the floor, and when I picked them up I realized I didn't know which one opened Olson's chambers. That meant copying all three.

"Hake, you in there?" the deputy asked as he banged on the door. To avoid his seeing me from the little window, I bent over to the side of the desk as he said, "Hey, I want my keys back, I gotta go to the lockup!"

I was afraid the deputy was going to break the door down. But I was able to make my final impressions in the wax, shove the kit into my drawer, and unlock the door. "Sorry," I said, "but I was on the phone."

"Jesus Christ, Hake," the deputy grumbled and grabbed his keys back, "have some consideration for others."

The following day I turned the wax over to Megary, and he sent it to Tickel at FBI headquarters. A week later, Megary handed me a master key at our regular morning meeting near the planetarium.

Almost trembling with excitement, I hurried to the courthouse before any other lawyers arrived and slid the shiny brass key into Olson's lock. But the key wouldn't turn, no matter how hard I pressed or wiggled it. Jordan said they would rework it at headquarters, but I never heard anything more about the key. And that, I'm sorry to say, was the end of my spy adventure. We never learned whether I had failed to make a proper wax impression or the mistake was done in making the key.

But that didn't interrupt the preliminary work for the bugging. On a late September evening, the muscular Jordan showed up at the Criminal Courts Building, as crooks might say, to "case the joint" and determine the best time to install a hidden microphone. We both thought ten p.m. would be ideal, since juries seldom deliberated past nine-thirty and yet a couple of men looking like lawyers and moving about at that time might not draw suspicion.

So much for logic. We entered Olson's empty courtroom and saw that the door to his first-floor chambers was open. Janitorial workers from the entire building had gathered inside for their nightly break—of all places in the building. We could hardly believe what was going on. It looked like a convention of maintenance men and cleaning ladies. We casually asked a few questions such as what time they got off, and turned back.

The next afternoon I was walking through Olson's empty courtroom to see if I could come across something that might help the bugging. This was at four-thirty, two and a half hours after his last case for the day. Before I could reach the judge's chambers, a wrinkled janitor suspiciously walked over to me and asked, "What are you doing?"

"I forgot something in my office."

"Okay," he scowled. "Only reason is, I heard there were some guys in here last night."

"Oh?" I asked, unnerved.

"Some nosy assistant state's attorney and his buddy snoopin' around."

"Who was it, do you know?"

"Just some guys bein' where they shouldn't," he said with a shrug.

So that was how we learned that the courthouse after dark is like a small town in which any event leads to gossip and speculation. The eventual break-in would have to be made earlier to avoid alarm, even at the risk of increasing the number of people who might see it.

Since everyone obviously would have to do more homework, I kept trying to pin Costello down on just where the payoffs were being made in Olson's chambers. But drunk or sober, he was never explicit. His opinion of the judge was also unclear, since it was more variable than the weather. "Wayne's a funny guy," he told me over drinks. "He's like Jonah and the whale. Know what I mean?"

"Yeah," I said, not having the slightest idea what he meant.

"He'll take your money one day, and he'll kill you the next. He's always telling you, 'You ain't got me sewed up.' I never want to lose my fuckin' grip on him. Half what I make off him I give back—that's *half*! But if I don't, I lose him to those other guys. Know what I mean?"

"Sorry, Jim, I better go."

"Say, Ter," Costello rasped, "if you see Olson, tell him I'll have an envelope for him on Friday."

"Friday? Yeah, sure, I'll tell him."

By then, my records showed that Costello claimed he had paid Olson more than fifty-four hundred dollars in the three months since he had started talking to me in late June. That didn't include all the money Olson was getting from the other attorneys who regularly appeared before him. According to Costello, Olson boasted that he was worth a million dollars, with most of his money put into investments.

Yet by now he was tired of the relatively small bribes he was getting from drug dealers. Olson wanted to grab the big money being passed around in Divorce Court in the downtown Richard J. Daley Center. But he wanted to leave Narcotics Court with an appearance of dignity. So he wrote to the chief judge that he was shocked—shocked!—to discover that certain lawyers were soliciting clients in courtrooms and the hallway. He added that such conditions were "terrible" and he therefore wanted a transfer. Of course, Olson was the one allowing it to happen and filling his pockets. As Costello said, that guy was "ballsy."

I was further alarmed that Olson was planning to take November off to bask in the Florida warmth at his Marco Island condominium. This meant he might be transferred out of the criminal courts before Washington could get around to authorizing the electronic surveillance. And we couldn't just switch the judges' names on our application, since no one else was flagrant enough to take bribes in his chambers without using a bagman. Could it be that Operation Greylord, so long in the planning, might miss its biggest opportunity by only a month?

Until the listening device could be planted, I would have to continue going wherever Costello went, like a puppy at his heels. To him, my presence must have seemed like proof that he was magnetic. He also was bribing me so much he couldn't keep track of it all. Once, for example, he told me he was putting fifty dollars in my pocket for dismissing a case, yet when I pulled out the bills I counted sixty. When I asked him the next day about the extra ten, his eyes lifted from their drowsy look and he asked, "Was I that drunk?"

The bribery between us now took on a casual air. One time we were standing idly in the courthouse concourse, a part of the annex corridor set aside for any TV crew covering a major trial, as we waited for a policeman to pick us up for lunch. One of Jim's clients, who should have been in court on a narcotics charge that morning, showed up half an hour late with his wife, a toddler, and a baby. Jim hollered out that a bond forfeiture warrant had been issued for him, but that I had informally agreed to set up another hearing for that afternoon.

"See, I told you that you can trust me," Costello reminded his client. "Have lunch, then go to the room at the end of the hall at one-fifteen. Be there early, make an impression. Okay?"

The client nodded appreciatively and left with his family.

The tardy defendant passed from my mind, but Costello was still thinking about him as we drove to a restaurant. "Tell you what," he said, "why work on the son of a bitch's case, Ter? Just pitch the fuckin' thing and I'll give yuh something. Is fifty bucks all right?"

"You got it," I said.

At the restaurant, Costello waited for an officer we knew to use the men's room, and then tugged a fifty out of a wad of bills. "Thanks," I said, and took the money.

When I dropped the case in court, the defendant's wife hopped around the bench in happiness and Costello seemed invigorated.

By mid-October, Jim had given me nine hundred and fifty dollars in ten transactions, along with a gift of a new coffeepot "for being such a nice guy." Even the coffeepot went into the FBI's evidence vault.

Since Jim had given me so much money, I had to lie about where it was going. From time to time I would tell him I had bought such things for my small apartment as a sofa and a television set. If he ever visited my place, he would have thought everything had been repossessed.

"You also need a new car," he would say about my eight-year-old Plymouth Fury. "You got to look sharp in this business."

Of course, Costello wasn't the only one I had drinks, lunches, and dinners with. Once around this time I was alone with Judge Olson at Jeans. He abruptly told me, "This really isn't any place to talk. I think there's a federal investigation going on."

This doubly startled me: first that Olson suspected something was up, and that he now considered me one of the good ol' boys he could talk to about corruption.

"There's nothing you can put your finger on," Wayne said. "Play it safe, Terry, don't talk to anybody in the halls. I heard that some black FBI agents are posing as defendants in the bullpen. Costello hustles back there, so you might warn him to stay out if he doesn't know it already."

"I haven't heard anything."

"You probably wouldn't. The feds are supposed to be doing a mail fraud investigation on checks sent to hustlers from bond slips."

"So it doesn't affect you?" I asked.

"Naw," Olson said, "but we have to be careful, just the same."

The next time I got back to my FBI handlers, I asked them whether the rumor was true. It was and it wasn't. An investigation into lawyers who illegally solicited clients in the courthouse corridors had been authorized but it hadn't started yet. I was glad of that, because I didn't need a parallel effort to undermine what I was doing. But how could Olson have known about a probe even before it even began? Even now, I can't answer that.

Although I still kept pretty close to Costello, I avoided sounding pushy by working questions into our general conversations. That meant I sometimes went to his home far from the courthouse just to talk to him and his wife and, once, to help him rake leaves.

I kept trying to pick up what the fixers might be thinking of me. I had been assigned exclusively to Narcotics Court for four and a half months, twice as long as usual for an assistant state's attorney (ASA), and I could feel a mild paranoia setting in. I could almost hear lawyers wondering whether I might be a plant, but evidently no one gave me a second thought.

One of the newly assigned ASAs was a friend from my early days in the building, the former Alice Stein. We had met when she was in special prosecutions and I was a law clerk for Mike Ficaro. She was attractive and friendly, someone to banter with in the corridors or the court library. Alice was just as pleasant now that she was married to defense attorney Barry Carpenter, who worked in the misdemeanor courts at police headquarters, then at 13th and State Streets.

The narrow office we shared off Olson's courtroom had a comfortable informality to it, with empty pop cans here and there, and the back wall taken up with memos and reminders. We worked at a small table and a couple of desks, sometimes carrying the phone around with us as we talked, so it might be found on a desk, a filing cabinet, or the sill of our opened window.

Since Alice would never have anything to do with someone corrupt, she must have considered her husband's hallway solicitations a permitted area of toleration. But one day she leaned over in a chair and let me know what must have been on her mind for days. "Do you know your friend Costello is a hustler?" she asked. Since that was obvious, she must have been trying to hint that he was a fixer as well.

"He's all right."

"Why do you hang around that slimebag?"

"What do you mean by that?"

"I don't mean anything. I'm just saying he's a slimebag."

I could see in Alice's eyes what she really wanted to say, that slime has a habit of spreading. I quickly changed the subject, but our conversation bothered me for the rest of the day. How many honest lawyers and judges were having doubts about me? That was one part of my undercover role that troubled me. I could be losing more than just friends. I might be saying goodbye to something in myself that might never come back.

The next day was routine. I worked as usual out of the long closet-like prosecutors' office, presented several cases before Olson and, during breaks, joked around with fixers in the courthouse snack shop. But all during that time, I was darting my eyes and straining my ears for something that could go into my FBI reports or might advance me in the underworld of graft.

When I got back to court, Yonan nudged me and said, "You know the young lady you're working with?"

"Alice?"

"Her husband called me about my office. He wants to rent space."

"Well, if he's married to her, he must be a pretty good guy," I said.

But behind my words was the thought that if Barry Carpenter wanted to rent space from a fixer, he might not be as "clean" as Alice thought he was.

7

DISCLOSURES

Mid-October 1980

Maybe it's because court behavior is so confining that judges and lawyers often use their automobiles to express themselves. Or maybe it's because they want everyone to know they have moved up. Take Costello and his beloved black Thunderbird. Or corrupt Judge Alan Lane, whose car bore the vanity license plates PNGJW, representing the fixers' code for "Plea of Not Guilty, Jury Waived," which would let a corrupt judge hear a case and not a jury.

Then there was *Gary Walter Street. Sunlight bounced off all the gold that the athletic-looking attorney wore around his wrist and neck, he wore European-style suits, and he cruised around in an aqua Mercedes-Benz. Rather than pull into the employee lot across from the courthouse, he preferred one north of there so his car and its GWS license plates would cry out: Look everybody, Gary Street is here!

Gary was one of the lawyers I had been keeping track of because he frequently went into Olson's office, but for all I knew everything was legitimate. And yet on the autumn afternoon that Alice Carpenter had cautioned me about Costello, Street gave me the first scare of my undercover career.

Instead of a suit, I was now wearing a sport jacket in the style of fixer Bob Silverman. Judge Olson had just denied a motion to suppress the felony drug evidence against a pusher, giving Gary the option of working out a plea agreement with me. Since his client had an arrest record, a trial would mean prison. Gary was hoping I would agree to probation.

As he sat at my desk looking like a magazine ad, I wondered whether to act normally or use a knowing tone. Acting tough had worked with

Yonan. So I secretly turned on the tape recorder and indifferently said, "I'm going to see that your guy gets what he deserves."

"Come on, Terry, it won't kill you to ask for probation."

"He's got to take some pen time."

"Prison, is that all you know?"

"That's it, Gary. Now, if you don't mind, I have other things to do."

While I headed for the doorway, trying to scare Gary, he reached for my arm and missed. Instead of grabbing my bicep to spin me around, he inadvertently latched onto the tape recorder just under my armpit. Horrified, I wished I could disappear. He jerked his hand back as if he had been hit by static electricity and asked, "What do you got under there, Terry, a gun?"

"Oh, no," I said, relieved that he hadn't guessed, "it's a back brace. Last August I was at a friend's in San Francisco and had to sleep on the floor, you know? It was cold and I got this terrible backache." My story sounded so phony that I kept adding to it. "So I've been wearing this brace during the day, and it helps, but my back still gives me problems."

Gary nodded politely. *He bought it*, I thought with a rush.

As I returned to my desk, with my hands cold and sweaty at the same time, Gary seemed as relaxed as ever. He began telling me about his own physical problems as if I were hanging on his every word. Then before leaving, he wrote down for me the name and number of his masseuse.

I was so shaken that when Judge Olson asked me to join him for drinks at Jeans that afternoon, I locked the tape recorder in the trunk of my Plymouth and swore to myself that nothing like that would ever happen again. But of course it did.

In the hallway outside Olson's courtroom the following day, Costello wanted to stress a point in our conversation. As he poked my chest, his hand brushed against the recorder under my shirt. His expression didn't change, but a *My God!* exploded in my mind. An ordinary attorney might not have suspected anything from the bulge, but Costello had been a policeman.

"See yuh later, Ter," he said as I fought to keep my expression from betraying me.

"Yeah, nice talking to you." The perspiration was falling drop by drop onto the small of my back. Where was he going, to tell everyone the heat's on? There had to be something I could do, and it had to be done now.

Since painters were working on our office alongside Olson's court-room, the ASAs assigned to narcotics cases were temporarily using an even smaller office. So I went into its cramped washroom and kept the door shut with my foot. I threw off my sport coat, my tie, my shirt, and my undershirt. With trembling fingers I wrenched off the tape holding the microphone wire and yanked the Velcro fasteners from their elastic wrap. I was sure the rip could be heard down the corridor.

I shoved the recorder, the holder, and the wire into my charcoal gray briefcase and quickly redressed. Next I went over to the sergeant's desk in Narcotics Court and asked him to lock my heavy briefcase in his file cabinet, freeing me to go looking for Costello with empty hands.

Jim was easy to find as he recruited clients, with his Brillo hair like an island above everyone else. As usual, the humanity in the hallway between the two Narcotics Courts smelled of alcohol breath, sweat, hair spray, lawyer cologne, and processed hair.

"Hey, Jim, I'm a little disappointed in you," I said in what I hoped was an ambitious, materialistic voice. "You didn't say what you thought of my new sport jacket. I bought it at the Hart Schaffner & Marx warehouse sale. Looks nice, doesn't it? What do you think?"

I held the sides of the jacket out as if he might be interested in checking the label. In doing so, my shirt stretched across my chest without a telltale bulge.

"Yeah, it's nice, Terry," Costello said without a glance

At the end of the day, I called FBI agent Bill Megary, who was slowly taking over for Jordan as my go-to person. He knew what he wanted because, as a lawyer, he got all of the legal background of the fixes without needing explanations. I told him that I needed to stop wearing the recorder for a while. Two near-misses in as many days were too much for me, and I was exhausted. But Bill psyched me up to wear a wire again, reminding me how incriminating things were happening every day.

FBI agents are specially chosen and trained for undercover work and the double life it requires. But I was being depleted by all those secret meetings with federal agents, slipping away to make phone calls, putting in full days at court, watching a dozen suspected fixers throughout the day, and then going around with them until nearly midnight, only to do it all again the next day.

In less than five months of palling around with the corrupt, I probably drank more than I had in my entire life. I wondered how my contact agents could understand that moles like me lived in a world that becomes increasingly unreal because of all the mental switching back and forth we have to do. My body and brain held out on Mondays through Fridays, but they gave up on weekends, the only time I could be myself. One Friday night, Cathy and I went to her sister's condo for dinner. We turned on the television for a movie, and five minutes later I was asleep. Another time Megary showed up at a meeting place and found me asleep behind the steering wheel.

As for Costello, he was becoming unglued on his own. One of my most embarrassing experiences with him came that October at a fundraiser for *Judge Henry Gordon. Costello had invited me to the fundraiser only to have a friendly face around, because he hated the judge. "Gordon is a kink," Jim told me, meaning a graft-taker. "When he was a prosecutor he tried to sell the Criminal Courts Building. You know Judge *Willis in the suburbs? Willis would sell his mother's teeth, and Gordon is below that, because Willis is a super guy and Gordon isn't."

From the suburban banquet hall we went to a Costello drinking spot that was so close to his home his car could probably take us there by itself. We sidled up to the bar, and Jim started to drink off one of his black moods. For no reason that I could tell, he turned on a nicely dressed, fairly good-looking woman in her early forties a couple of stools down. Maybe she reminded him of his wife.

"Look at her," Jim said to me, "a fuckin' drunk. Hey, bitch, why don't you go home?"

"Not so loud, Jim," I whispered. Being with Costello was so humiliating that I wished I could have left him there, but I never knew when he might tell me more about "kinks." He should have been ejected, but the bartender liked big tippers. Jim signaled for more drinks and put one hundred dollars in tens on the bar. Noticing that I was scratching at a food spot on my tie, he muttered, "Quit worry'ng about that fuckin' tie, will yuh?"

"This is brand new, Jim," I said. "It cost me ten dollars."

Costello scooped up the money he had just placed on the bar. "Buy a new tie," he said, and dropped a ten-dollar bill into my lap. "Buy a new tie . . . Buy a new tie . . . Buy a new tie . . . Buy a new tie." At each repetition, another ten dollars floated to my lap. There was now fifty dollars, Costello's half of some dope dealer's one-hundred-dollar bond after the rest went to Olson.

"Go ahead, take it, take it," Jim said. "Now take off that piece of shit."

I slid off my tie with a little reluctance because I rather liked it. Costello bunched the tie into a ball, tossed it to the bartender, and told him to "throw that fuckin' thing in the garbage." Despite Costello's laughter at himself, he was bitter about something and I felt sorry for him.

We had to be in court on opposite sides of the criminal justice system the next day, so at ten-thirty p.m. he paid the tab and threw me the change to complete my new-tie fund. The next day I turned over to the FBI as possible bribery evidence the entire amount, fifty-three dollars and forty-five cents.

On the Friday before Halloween, I drove from the midtown courthouse to the lakefront museum campus near downtown. I was expecting a pep talk from Megary about getting whatever evidence I could until Olson's chambers were bugged. Instead, all he said was that he was taking me downtown to see Dan Reidy from the federal prosecutor's office.

As cool winds blew from a gray sky, we were soon caught up in a traffic snarl but made it to a ramp leading down to a parking garage below the modern federal complex on South Dearborn Street. My first realization that something secret was going on came when Megary quietly told me to "get down. On the floor."

I couldn't help feeling a little foolish scrunched under the dashboard as the metal door of the garage rattled up. After Megary drove past the attendant's office, he told me, "Okay, you can get up now."

We entered the large, black freight elevator and slowly rose to the mysterious twenty-eighth floor. Since the public elevators go only to the twenty-seventh, even most federal workers were unaware of this place. The doors slid open and I saw a large storage area with bare light bulbs illuminating the dusty concrete floor.

Chuck Sklarsky was waiting for me, along with Dan Reidy, with his brown hair and contrasting red mustache, and Scott Lassar, who greeted me in a gravely monotone. "What's this all about?" I asked them.

As I took a plastic chair amid the clutter of the concrete storage floor, Reidy told me that all the preliminary work for installing an electronic listening device in Olson's chambers had been cleared, and now the Chicago office was ready to apply for permission from a federal judge.

"Just apply?" I gasped. From all this furtiveness, I had assumed the equipment was already in someone's black bag.

"Apparently you don't know how things work," Reidy said. "Nobody's said 'No,' they're saying 'Let's look at it.' That's practically a 'Yes.' Don't worry, we're making this a priority."

He handed me an inch-thick copy of the reports detailing information from my phone calls and the tapes I had been handing over. "We want you to go over this carefully," Reidy said. "Make sure it's accurate and see if you can add anything."

I went through the loose photocopied pages and found myself mumbling, "Wait . . . What's all this about Traffic Court?"

"You're not the only one working undercover," Reidy explained. The other work was being done by David Victor Ries, the FBI agent who had set up a phony Loop law office before I came on.

"Why didn't you tell me I'm not alone?"

"Terry, we've never done anything this secret before," said Reidy. "From the beginning, we decided not to treat it like just another sting. Information is being given out only on a need-to-know basis, and you had no reason to know about Ries."

He then let me in on some of the behind-the-scenes action. For months after receiving the box of unrelated files that had formed the starting point for Operation Greylord, Reidy and Lassar considered—and rejected— nearly forty variations of a written proposal needed for the undercover operation. The first sixteen pages were always the same—they outlined what was then known about bribery throughout the court system.

"Those first sixteen pages were designed so the Justice Department would look at them and get as sick as we were," Reidy said. Initially the Justice Department approved only a restricted effort to target fixers/lawyers in the municipal courts built into the Traffic Court Building.

Agents were allowed to rig only drunken driving cases because the police department was in such a sorry state that Superintendent Richard Brzeczek said he could spare only one trustworthy officer to work with federal investigators to arrest undercover FBI agents, and that man refused to turn on his fellow officers. Taking other officers of proven integrity away from their assignments would have drawn too much attention.

Without police cooperation, undercover FBI agents tried getting arrested for drunken driving early in the morning, when traffic was light and there was little danger of harming anyone. But they discovered that officers didn't want to make arrests just before the end of their shifts, because of the paperwork they would have to fill out.

This led to a brainstorm. Since many FBI agents were attorneys, why not have one pose as a corrupt lawyer in Traffic Court? That was why David Ries was brought in from Detroit. So that was how the initial phase of Greylord evolved, by a series of false steps pointing to the right direction.

"What if Olson moves out of Narcotics Court?" I asked the case supervisors. "I worked like hell to make my contacts there. I can't go through all that again somewhere else without someone catching on."

"Don't worry, we're making this a priority," Dan said. Well, that phrase was getting to sound familiar.

Going over more of the reports they handed me, I stared at one showing that an FBI agent who had been conducting a preliminary surveillance inside the Traffic Court Building had noticed Deputy Clerk Harold Conn strolling arm in arm with Chief Traffic Court Judge Richard LeFevour and slipping money into the judge's pocket. This was before LeFevour headed all the municipal courts in the city, the largest division in the circuit court of Cook County.

Seeing my surprise at the LeFevour report, Dan said, "Now you know how high we want you to go."

So they expected me, someone untrained and still with little experience, to help them bring down the judge in charge of all the city courts! I had never even worked in his building.

"We haven't found anyone else in the criminal courts to help you," Reidy continued. "It looks like you're going to have to do this by yourself. If it's going to be too much of a strain, or there are personal considerations, just tell us. You're not in so deep now that you can't pull out. No one would be the wiser."

"No," I said. "I'm doing all right." The words must have sounded tired and maybe a little uncertain.

It took me half an hour to ink in adjustments here and there in the reports, which would be part of the package seeking authorization for the bugging. As I handed the pages back, I felt a little apprehensive.

These allegations were against perhaps twenty policemen, lawyers, judges, and even an assistant prosecutor I had thought was honest. How many others were out there? "Suppose the judge who authorizes the bugging tells someone?" I asked. My throat had dried up.

"Don't worry," Dan replied. "This will need the approval of the chief judge of the federal courts for northern Illinois. He doesn't have any contact with anyone named in here. This investigation is going to be airtight. We have no choice but to assume he will keep the secret."

When I went home that evening, I had to keep reminding myself that the majority of officers, lawyers, and judges were honest—they had to be—and yet I could no longer be sure about anyone.

On Monday, I was sitting on a bench during a break in Olson's court when a familiar voice asked, "Hey, Terry, how about lunch?"

Standing in a doorway was my good friend Mark Ciavelli. The young defense attorney looked great in a tailored suit, a luxury he could never have afforded when he was an assistant prosecutor. Last May, I had hoped Mark would be interested in joining me in my undercover work, but I soon learned he was becoming too successful on the defense side to give everything up.

We agreed to meet at a nearby Mexican restaurant after my last case. Mark now drove a BMW—just like his new law partner, suspected fixer Frank Cardoni, and also like the judge they often appeared before, John Reynolds. The two of us sat at a small booth with piped-in mariachi music.

Before long I realized that Mark didn't just want to fill me in on a couple of weeks' worth of courthouse gossip. With his rapid-fire delivery, he was dropping hints that he wanted me to resign from the State's Attorney's Office and join his law firm.

"It'll take a while to get used to the change of defending people instead of throwing them into prison," he said, as if I had been successful in doing that before Olson. "Another change, of course, is working with the judges. You know what I mean. I just gave two hundred to Judge *Jelnik on a criminal damage to property. It wasn't easy, you got to go through channels."

He continued speaking without a pause that would have let his words sink in. The shock drove everything else from my mind for a few seconds. Slowly the sounds around me came back, but there was no feeling in me as I heard them.

"He had five witnesses and the state had only the victim," Mark continued with whatever anecdote he had started. "Now, remember that I had a real good case, but Jelnik finds my guy guilty. I couldn't figure out what went wrong. So I asked around and someone told me Jelnik could be approached."

Please don't tell me this, I thought.

"So I file for a new trial and bring two hundred to Jelnik in his chambers. He takes the money and he vacates his guilty verdict. But I still got to get my guy off. Jelnik's been transferred to another court, and P.J. McCormick's going to hear it, and that's going to cost me at least another hundred."

It was an effort for me to speak after our orders arrived. Not so long ago Mark and I had started out pretty much alike, or so it had seemed to me. I must have been living in a dream world. When I blurted out my question at the table, I was no longer an undercover operative. I was back to being still too innocent to accept what I had just heard.

"Don't you think it would be better if you didn't pay the judges?" I asked.

"Come on, Terry, it doesn't work that way, you should know that by now. Sometimes my clients really are innocent and the cops run over their rights. You have to look out for them. There's only one way to get a fair shake, and that's not to leave anything up to chance." Chance, that's what fixers think of justice? "It's been going on so long, it's never going to change."

"Well, I suppose . . . " My voice had trailed off because I didn't have anything to say.

Mark later said Judge Reynolds would steer clients to him for a rakeoff, but not all that money stayed with the judge. Mark had seen court workers steal cash from Reynolds' desk, while clerks were stealing what they called their "lunch money" from cans that other clerks kept under their desks. Virtually everyone who had anything to do with the administration of Reynolds' courtroom had found some way of getting money from anyone who walked in, even a prosecutor who had taken bribes from Mark.

Not only in Reynolds' court but in courtrooms throughout the building a clerk who sized up lawyers well and knew what favors to perform might make ten thousand dollars a year in undeclared tips.

"You still haven't answered me," my friend said. "What about joining Frankie and me?"

As I poked at my food, I really couldn't think about anything. I had just discovered that I had lost my closest friend in the system to corruption, and I would never again be naive about anyone in this investigation. Something in me had been crushed.

PART 2

ONE OF THE BOYS

8

THE NEXT LEVEL

Late October 1980

I was so upset after talking to Mark that I headed for my parents' home in suburban Palatine rather than spend one more afternoon slugging beers with Olson or Costello. When I arrived, I didn't know what made me go there; I certainly didn't want to talk to anyone about what was on my mind. Maybe I should have made the FBI happy by informing them about one more crooked lawyer. But I didn't care about Greylord at the moment, and I didn't give a damn about all the bribing lawyers and the judges with blood on their hands.

Just a few months before, Assistant U.S. Attorney Charles Sklarsky had told me I might learn that some of my friends were among the scum. "Maybe your friends, Chuck," I had thought smugly then, "but not mine." How innocent I had been.

My mother knew something was wrong the moment I walked into the house and slumped into a living room chair. "It's all right," she said, without asking why I was so morose. She continued fixing dinner as if this were just another evening, but I knew she was waiting for me to let my feelings out.

"Mark's corrupt, Mom," I murmured from the chair. I started crying because I had lost a friend to the poison in the court system. "He's in it, too. Just like the rest."

"Did you hear that from someone else?" She always distrusted rumors.

"No, from him. Right from his own mouth."

"What are you going to do?" she asked.

"I don't know."

Because I hadn't worn a wire since my recent two close calls, there was no recorded evidence against Mark. But if I had had a microphone strapped to my chest, would I have turned it on as soon as he mentioned bribing a judge, and would I have handed the tape in? I still don't know.

I had trouble eating and sleeping for the next couple of days. I was about to make the hardest decision in my entire Greylord role, and I needed more time to think it over. Actually, I was imagining that I could postpone a decision indefinitely.

On Friday, three days after my Mexican lunch with Mark, I went to a Near North Side athletic club to play racquetball with agent Lamar Jordan again. I would have preferred an isolated location, but Jordan didn't mind. He was a fair player and was close to catching up to me in a hard game that left us both a little exhausted. When we went to his car for privacy, I finally told him what I had been reluctant to disclose all week, that my close friend Mark Ciavelli was now bribing judges so he could join the BMW set.

"You know," Jordan said, "this conversation could be just between us. It doesn't have to get written down."

"No, put him in the report."

"That means you'll have to go after him."

"Yeah, I know," I said. "If I have to, then I have to."

I was naive enough to think the worst was over.

Then about 5 weeks after his revelation in the Mexican restaurant, Mark asked me to go with him to see the Sugar Ray Leonard-Roberto Duran fight on closed circuit television at a movie theater. Although I had resolved to stay away from him, I thought why not, this would have nothing to do with my investigation. But I was wrong.

As soon as I climbed into Mark's BMW outside his Near North Side apartment, he told me about a suburban felony case where he and Bob Silverman, as co-counsel, had put in the fix. Then he brought up a case that would be coming to Olson's court. The police had seized about three thousand dollars and some PCP from his two clients. Mark mentioned that the officers were willing to lie down on the case in return for half the money they had confiscated. He and his law partner, Frank Cardoni, were willing to let the officers have some of the dealers' money, but not half.

To make them grumble less, Mark lied to them by saying a fixer friend needed to be cut in, but he really hoped to work out an arrangement with Olson. I knew where this conversation was going, and I wished

I could stop it, but he kept on. Mark had never appeared before the judge before, and he was afraid Olson might not return most of the confiscated money to him as his fee. Taking his eyes off traffic for a moment to study my expression, he said, "If you dismiss this thing. Terry, it will solve the problem and we'll all make money."

His words were no longer troubling me because I had unconsciously been distancing myself from him. We had once been friends, but Mark was now trying to make me a criminal. That made it easier for me to regard him as nothing more than just another crooked lawyer who was about to get what he deserved. So I said, "I don't want any money, I'll take care of the case for you because you're my friend."

"You're doing us a favor, you should get something."

"It's not necessary to pay me, all right?" I said with surliness.

"Why are you so sore?"

"I'm not sore, I just had a rough day."

We arrived at the theater late and the packed audience was hooting with every punch on the screen. I discovered that Mark and Cardoni had bought nearly a dozen tickets at seventy-five dollars each and passed them out to court clerks and bailiffs who might be useful someday. In the mood I was in, I wouldn't have enjoyed the fight even if it had ended in a fifteenth-round knockout. As it was, we headed for the doors when Duran refused to come out for the eighth round, saying *"No mas, no mas"*—no more, no more. Maybe he was just a quitter, but I left the theater thinking the whole world was phony.

Frankie Cardoni, looking as always like a ladies' man, was waiting for us at a pricey restaurant. He immediately asked if Mark had talked to me about the PCP case. I nodded, and he looked pleased. So they had it planned all along that they were going to bribe me. We left the place close to midnight, but Mark brought the case up again in his car. It was as though the only way he could trust me was by making sure I was corrupt, and not merely dropping the case out of friendship.

"Don't worry," Mark assured me. "The sun is gonna shine for all of us on this one."

"I still don't want any of the money," I said. "Just tell Bob Silverman I'm okay."

Mark had been using me, and now I was using him.

The very next morning I told Megary about the bribe offer. Then it was back to work presenting cases to Olson and watching fixers going in and out of his chambers. Sometimes they stood in line. They always exchanged pleasantries with one another, and often they went to dinner and out drinking together. But generally they distrusted and disliked each other because they were rivals for the same money and favors, and perhaps because they didn't care for reminders of what they had become.

This was made clear to me in the last days of October when dope peddler *Leon Hester had a problem with representation after missing a court date. His bond was raised to twelve hundred and fifty dollars to keep him from skipping the next one. When Hester appeared, I wanted to see if Olson would transfer this honey pot of a case to the bar association attorney as he was supposed to, and therefore receive nothing in return. But there was no doubt. Olson was not dealing with anyone for just one-third anymore. He was smelling six hundred and twenty-five dollars as his share if he gave the case to Costello for an even split.

I stepped over to the diagonal bench to announce that the state was ready to proceed, and Costello asked for a time out. While Olson called another case, Jim led Hester to the hallway to explain his services and fee—that is, to shake him down. After a few minutes, Jim complained to me in his megaphone whisper that he wasn't able to sign up Hester, and so he needed me to request a continuance that would give him time to pressure the drug dealer into coming up with more money.

"The cop has the lab report on the drugs in his hands," I told him. "What excuse can I give without being obvious?"

"It's okay, Ter. We'll think of something."

When Olson called the case again, Hester said, "Your Honor, you gave me to Mr. Costello here, but do I have to take him?"

"What do you mean?" Olson asked, annoyed that someone should question one of his arbitrary decisions.

"Mr. Costello wants too much money." That is, for the more than twelve-hundred-dollar bond money, Jim was proposing to do the same things he would have done for the usual one-hundred-dollars bond.

"Obviously you are not properly communicating with counsel," the judge burst out. "I'm going to continue this case for one month."

The policeman in the case was glad to go home because he had worked the midnight shift and needed sleep, and Hester went off to find the bar association attorney for that day, Jay Messinger. I could tell this because Costello was walking toward me with a steady step instead of his usual lope. This showed that "Big Bird" had some plan in mind.

By now I had recovered enough from my two close calls to be wearing a recorder again, but no longer near my armpit. And I didn't trust it in the curve of my back, where the bulge would show when I bent down. I was keeping the pouch where I had more control, right behind my belt buckle. That hide-in-plain-sight location was safe under most circumstances, since men stay clear of the groin.

"Terry," Jim said, "go tell Messinger you're going to take this fucker's case to the grand jury so I can keep him. Can you do that for me?" Costello felt that Messinger was unlikely to follow Hester's case through an indictment and a trial. Bar association attorneys worked for the cash bonds and, like hustlers, made more money from dismissals or knocking out cases on motions to suppress the evidence.

"No problem, Jim." I did not tell Jim, but my supervisor had already told me to indicate Hester.

I found Messinger conferring with Hester in the back of the courtroom and told them of my intention to seek an indictment. "If you want to talk about this anymore, see me in my office," I added.

After a few minutes, Hester entered the long, narrow office I shared with two other ASAs, something unusual for a defendant. "Man, why you jackin' me around?" he complained. "Why you callin' a grand jury, I don't even have a record."

"You weren't ready for the hearing," I said. "You refused to hire the lawyer the judge recommended to you."

"Mr. Costello?"

"This is a serious felony charge, and you've already forfeited your bond once. There will be no more delays. We are not playing a game here, Mr. Hester."

"I'm tellin' you, all that guy care about is money. He don't give a shit about me."

"That's your problem," I said. "Now, please excuse me, I have to leave."

Hester followed me into the hallway, then exchanged grimaces with Costello. A moment later they walked away together with their heads lowered as they discussed finances. In a few minutes Jim almost pranced over to me and said, "I signed him up! This is going to be the easiest six hundred I ever made. I'm getting the case called again this afternoon. Get this—since the arresting officer is gone for the day, I'll demand a trial. With no witness, you'll have to drop the case!"

I had to admire the quick flexibility that fixers developed to stay in competition. Before I could reply, Costello clapped a hand on my shoulder and added, "Don't worry, Ter, we're all going to make money on this one."

Another ASA working in Narcotics Court that day was Frank Speh, a quiet man who would stay home on weekends to watch television, and in court he was incorruptible. Not that this stopped him from becoming friends with Costello, who managed to have him go to places with other lawyers and look as if he were having a good time. Jim once explained the difference between Speh and me. "I taught *Frank* how to be a man," he said, "and I taught *you* how to steal."

So when Hester's case was called for trial that afternoon, Speh raised his head like a deer whiffing a scent. "This case was continued just this morning," he whispered to me. "Something's wrong here."

Since I had to appear honest for my colleague and yet dishonest for Costello, I told Olson, "Your Honor, I would request a continuance in the matter. The arresting officer has left for the day."

Everyone but Speh was in on the game, and Olson played it well. He looked over the file, frowned in concentration, then responded with the illusion of fairness, "Motion to continue denied."

"Then Your Honor," I capitulated, "in the absence of my witness, I respectfully dismiss the charges against Mr. Hester."

"All right, case is dismissed. You're free to go, Mr. Hester."

There was no surprise on the defendant's face. He got what he had paid for, several times over.

Two days later Olson was practically singing on the bench in anticipation of his month-long vacation in Florida. All week he had been inviting court workers and lawyers to the party he was planning for Thursday.

Nearly two dozen clerks, sheriff's deputies, lawyers, and friends crowded into the booths and around the tables at Febo's, at 25th and Western. The Chianti and the cheerful prattle were getting to Costello. He foghorned to Olson's clerk, "Hey, Frankie, what the hell does Terry have to come over to my house for? I paid you so much money *you* ought to be the one raking my leaves!"

Frankie turned red. They were surrounded by fellow thieves, but Costello had violated the one taboo by openly mentioning bribes. Laughing at his own joke, Costello told us he had dropped twenty dollars on a clerk in the court of honest Judge Zelezinski that morning to get a file on a defendant, then discovered that the man had a bond of only thirty-five dollars. With the other fixers glaring at him with tightened jaws, Costello slapped the table and chortled at himself.

Judge Olson was also drinking more than usual. Actually, the word going around the courthouse was that Olson could have been one of the great drinkers of the criminal courts but held himself back because of his family, and maybe because of the memory of that fatal bar quarrel he had years ago.

As waiters bustled around us, a court clerk mentioned that he was looking over houses for sale. The judge joked with his friendly abrasiveness, "So, how much money did you pocket today? You know, you guys make more money under the table than I do."

The silence that set in was even deeper than when Jim had made the same sort of *faux pas* moments before. We didn't know whether to laugh or be shocked.

"Well, you're the one with a Florida condo, Wayne," one of the fixers said, to lighten the mood and redirect the conversation.

"You guys are welcome to come by any time you're over there," Olson said, adding, "It's great fishing."

After our plentiful and delicious dinner was over, our waiter stepped up to Olson, as the leader of the party, and handed him a brown plastic tray with a bill for more than six hundred dollars. The judge kept stalling by telling one anecdote after another, obviously waiting for someone to pay it. His bemused expression told us that this had really been our party for him, only we didn't know it until now. Glances circled the table in a six-way standoff. Somebody had to give in, and it couldn't be me because I was a lowly assistant prosecutor. And it wouldn't be one of the clerks, who were bribed only five dollars at a time. That narrowed the field down to the defense attorneys, who were uneasily wiping their hands on napkins or brushing bread crust from their silk shirts in hopes a colleague would make the grand gesture. After a ripple of nervous laughter at the awkward pause, Costello and another attorney said something to a third lawyer, and that man reluctantly drew out his American Express card.

But the day was far from over. As we were starting to leave, Olson, a little unsteady from the wine, said, "Let's go to Jeans." He wanted to get drunk on more intimate ground on his last night before vacation. So at eight forty-five p.m. we piled into our cars and drove back to the courthouse neighborhood.

Once there, Costello had some more wine and half a dozen martinis until he was in a haze. By now I could tell his alcohol content just by the sound of his voice. When Assistant State's Attorney Mike Kress approached us on his way to say goodbye to the judge, I could feel negative energy radiating from Jim. I don't know why he hated Kress, but it was more than just dislike.

"Get out of here, you motherfucking Jew," Costello snarled.

"The hell with you," Kress snarled back, "I'm saying goodbye to Wayne."

Costello pulled off his glasses and tossed them on the table as a silent threat, but Kress said, "Fuck you, Costello!"

Moving between them, I told Kress, "You have to ignore Jim, he's had a little too much. You better leave."

As Kress walked to the shabby back door, Costello called out to his back, "You God damn cocksucker!"

Judge Olson stood up and said, "Don't you talk to my friend like that."

"What the hell d'you have friends like that kike for?" Costello asked.

"Jim, you're an ass," the judge said.

Costello understood that to mean he would never be anything but a hallway whore, which everyone knew, including Costello himself. I could hardly believe it when the one-time tough street kid and cop grabbed the heavyset judge by the wrist and shoved him against some chairs.

Regaining his balance, Olson said, "*Never* touch me again!"

"Screw you," Costello said and plopped down. As Olson kept shouting and flailing his arms at him, Costello pretended to be indifferent to the tirade although his face was flushing. Then he said, "Why don't you just shut the fuck up?"

Olson seemed about to explode with the kind of rage that had already killed a man, but you could see he was holding himself back. Instead of throwing a fist at Costello, he contemptuously snatched a glass of wine and poured it down Jim's expensive white shirt.

"Big deal," Costello said and looked around at his fellow lawyers. "Look who's the ass now." He pinched the sodden front of his reeking shirt and flapped it a few times to dry it.

Having failed to make Costello angry, Olson grabbed Jim's expensive eyeglasses off the table and hurled them against the wall.

We all knew what Costello wanted to do, you could see it in his face. But lawyers do not manhandle judges, so Jim wrapped his large hand around a decanter and flung it all the way to the other side of the restaurant. The bottle sailed over three tables before it shattered with a spray of wine and glass.

Several lawyers had to rush in and separate the two men. As Olson was being yanked back, he sputtered at Costello, "I'm calling Chief Judge Fitzgerald tomorrow. You'll be thrown out of the courthouse and I'll make sure you never come back!"

"What the fuck do I care," Costello muttered.

"Come on, Jim," I said and took his arm. "Everything'll be all right. Hey, I'll drive you home."

My immediate thought was that I didn't want Jim to kill himself driving recklessly halfway across the city. But I also thought I was seeing the end of Operation Greylord, because Costello had been my only link to Olson. But the judge put his hand on my shoulder, and I had to make a decision—whom should I give up? Should it be Costello, who was my closest friend in everyday life at court, or Olson, the most important target so far in my undercover work?

With the short rasps of a heavy man who has overexerted himself, the judge told me, "Don't bother to drive that bastard home, Terry."

"But he's too drunk—"

"Serves him right," Olson said. "You have to work in my courtroom, I don't want you to be with him. I've already told Costello. 'I like this kid so much that I don't want you to corrupt him. If you do, I'll kill you.'"

That caught me by surprise. How could I do anything else but stay inside the restaurant and let Costello drift from my undercover life? But I kept the back door open and watched Costello pathetically stagger alone toward his prized black Thunderbird. His marriage was falling apart, Olson had renounced him, and now I was turning my back on him. As I let the thin black rear door close, I knew Jim would soon be leaning on his car and fumbling through his mass of keys.

"Christ, look at the place," said Carl, the bartender. "What the fuck's the matter with you people? Terry, you're the sensible one, can't you keep them settled down?"

"It's all right," Olson said beside me. "We always hated that son of a bitch Costello. I don't know why in the hell we let him hang around with us. Don't worry, you're like a son to me. I'll take care of you."

My God, I wondered, what had happened? Instead of witnessing the demise of Greylord, I had just been dragged by the collar to the next level.

The next morning was Halloween, and the third anniversary of my being sworn in as an attorney. I awoke with a terrible hangover, and my apartment seemed to be rocking. I had a headache, and I didn't want to finish dressing or shaving. But I forced myself to drive to a meeting near North Avenue and Wells Street to give FBI contact agent Bill Megary my latest tape. Since it had run out before the drinking session at Jeans ended, I filled him in on the split between Costello and the judge.

"The whole point of bugging Olson's chambers is to prove the steady payoffs," I said, "but Olson claims he's getting Jim banned from 26th Street."

Megary didn't even blink. "Things like this don't last long," he said.

"But they hate each other."

"Yes, but they need each other. You'll see."

He was right. When I saw Costello less than an hour later, he was squinting to see without his glasses, his bustling spirit was gone, and his hangover was worse than mine. I thought he would ignore me for forsaking him, but he actually was glad to see me in the hallway. He clamped his hands on me with an expression of bewilderment and panic, then pulled me closer to his bloodshot eyes.

"I gotta talk to you," he growled. "What the fuck happened last night?"

"You don't remember?"

"Would I ask you if the fuck I did?"

"You and Wayne almost got into a fistfight. Don't you even remember him throwing your glasses against the wall?"

"Jesus, so that's what happened to them. I hate it when I'm like that. This is Friday, isn't it? That means I owe Wayne a thousand bucks from bonds he assigned me. What the hell am I gonna do?"

Maybe there was a way to salvage the situation, after all. "You know, Jim, he's going on vacation today," I said. "You better get in there and pay him. Otherwise he'll brood about it for a whole month and wish he had the money."

"Yeah, you're right," Costello said after a little reflection. "I owe you one, kid." He straightened his suit. "Do you think I look all right?"

"Not really."

"So what the hell."

Then he walked into the courtroom.

In just ten minutes he was seeking me out. "Thanks, Terry," he said. "I went in there and said, 'I guess I fucked up last night.' That was when I handed him the money. And Wayne says, 'Yeah, but you were cute.'"

"Right then and there?"

"Right then and there. So we're okay again. Christ, I was worried."

Greed had saved Greylord, and not for the only time.

9

THE BLACK BAG

November 1980

The bugging authorization was finally signed. So while Judge Olson was vacationing in early November, FBI contact agent Bill Megary sent me to spy upon the movement of courthouse employees no one paid much attention to: the court clerks, janitors, and women working at the switchboard directly behind Narcotics Court. "We want a profile of when they arrive and when they leave, how they get to work and how they get home," he said. That way we could find an opening within their intersecting routines to plant the bug.

Megary could stay relaxed and think clearly no matter how confused or uncertain I was, but I wondered how I would be able to keep tabs on everyone since I didn't want to be caught loitering as I took notes, and I still had a full roster of defendants to prosecute. I kept wondering how often I could excuse myself for the washroom or claim I wanted to talk to one attorney or another before someone caught on.

I went outside the courthouse and stood out of the way in the parking lot to memorize the license plate numbers of the cars that two of the switchboard operators drove. On the day of the bugging, an FBI surveillance squad would follow the autos, and the bus that the other switchboard operator took, to see if any of them turned back because they had forgotten something. The agents would also trail the conscientious judge filling in for Olson, Phillip Sheridan, when he left for home. The judges' parking lot could be seen from a window in Olson's court, and Sheridan would be the easiest to shadow since he drove a station wagon rather than a fancy car.

During these preparations, I took Megary on two tours of the building to draw up a basic floor plan. On one of those days, a Saturday, we stumbled around the dank basement for hours while straining to hear if any custodian came down. But there wasn't much evidence that janitors ever went in the basement. We had to walk through a puddle of water from a burst pipe, brush past cobwebs, and watch out for rats. When we left the basement, fellow prosecutor Linda Woloshin came out of weekend bond court and looked at me peculiarly because I was there on my day off.

Act casual, I told myself. "Hi, Linda, meet Brian McFall," I said, using Megary's cover name. "He's a lawyer from Maryland and wanted to see what the courthouse is like while he's in town."

"Hi, Linda," Megary said with his light East Coast accent, and shook her hand.

"See you," she said to me, without wasting a second thought on us.

Lying was easier for me now than it had been just a month before, but I was apprehensive about eventually taking on major corruptor Bob Silverman. After a couple of weeks of doing unasked favors like a would-be protégé, I was still unable to guess what the fixer might be thinking about me. I always felt safe around Costello, Olson, and Cy Yonan. But with Silverman, I sensed actual physical danger. From his contacts with the mob and crooked cops, he had influence at every level of the justice system.

One morning I saw Bob getting out of the one-seat shoeshine stand in the concourse. Having your shoes shined by an old black man everyone called J.C. was considered good luck just before opening and closing arguments. But I had never had my shoes shined there, partly to save money and also because I didn't want to be thought of as ambitious. But as Bob stepped down, he motioned to me and said, "Why don't you get up here, Terry."

My shoes didn't need polishing that badly, but this was no time to jeopardize a potential friendship. Self-consciously, I climbed into the chair with a pretended carefree attitude. Bob talked to me all the time J.C. brushed and buffed, then handed him five dollars with a lordly gesture, no doubt confident that he now controlled one more prosecutor.

Eagerly I phoned FBI agent Lamar Jordan with the news. "I finally got into Bob Silverman's pocket!" I said.

"Fantastic!" he replied. "How much did he give you?"

"He bought me a shoe shine."

A protracted stillness ended with a "Shit!" Only then did I realize how silly I had sounded. "If Silverman ever does pay you money," Jordan said, "I'll take you to lunch."

Washington, D.C.

Although my progress with Silverman was slower than the FBI would have liked, things were finally moving quickly against Olson and his entourage of fixers. Chief Criminal Court Judge Richard Fitzgerald, one of the few people who had been notified about Operation Greylord, stayed late in his office one evening to sign an authorization for me to tape conversations with Costello and Cy Yonan for ten days. This formality would let us use those tapes in state court if something went wrong and the federal prosecution had to be abandoned.

Instead of reporting for work at the courthouse the next morning—a cool, windy day a little before Thanksgiving—I drove to O'Hare International Airport on as close to a cloak-and-dagger assignment as I have ever gone through. A ticket to Washington, D.C., had been purchased in my name even before Megary notified me that FBI Director William Webster wanted to talk to me. Making my flight more mysterious was that Assistant U.S. Attorney Dan Reidy was sitting directly in front of me, but I was under orders not to acknowledge him in any way. Even when we landed at National Airport, I was not allowed to look for him.

As I opened the cab door I was thrilled to say something I had wanted to say ever since I was a boy: "Take me to the Justice Department, Tenth and Pennsylvania."

As we neared the steps I could see Dan waiting for me. FBI supervisor Robert Walsh shook our hands just inside the lobby and drove us around the Capital. Seeing the white monuments for the first time, I indulged in a fantasy in which the FBI director would swear me in as an agent right there in his office.

In the Justice Department cafeteria, Dan and U.S. Attorney Thomas Sullivan, who had flown in the day before, briefed me on what to say and, mainly, what not to say. I was to answer as succinctly as in court. Then I was ushered into a conference room and was face to face with Webster. The square-jawed man motioned to a chair and began with, "What's going on in Judge Olson's chambers, Leo?"

It felt odd to be addressed by my FBI code name, Leo Murphy.

I told Webster that Costello had given me eleven hundred dollars in various payoffs. "Costello, by my calculation, has said he has passed about seven thousand dollars to Judge Olson since late summer. Another attorney, Cy Yonan, so far has given me six hundred and fifty dollars for fixes."

"Your understanding is that there are other lawyers making payoffs to Olson?"

"Yes, but I don't know how much Olson is receiving from them."

"Do you think Costello is telling you the truth?" Webster asked.

"Yes, sir. I think so. Everything I have seen and heard backs up what he has told me."

I could see the caution in Webster's face. This investigation was bound to make national headlines, and Congress no doubt would accuse him of trampling on the separation of powers even if things went well. He could put up with all that, but I'm sure he did not want the Bureau to be embarrassed by a failure.

There also was another reason for his pondering. Webster had been a federal judge in St. Louis, and the hesitancy in his voice told me he had reservations about violating the sanctity of a judge's chambers. He needed to share our certainty that the unprecedented bugging was absolutely necessary.

When I finished, all he said was, "Thank you, Leo. You're doing a good job. We'll be in touch."

For the moment, I did not care that the subject of my becoming an FBI agent never came up. I was elated at just meeting the director. But flying back to Chicago, I thought over "We'll be in touch" and wondered whether that meant his support or not.

The day after my return, my ASA friend Alice Carpenter agreed to have lunch with me and Costello, although she never liked him. Jim called out a few words in Italian to the waiter and spoke to us about the days when he was an ASA in a suburban court. He said there was a regular schedule for bribes then: four hundred dollars for dismissing felony cases, one hundred for dismissing battery charges, and seventy-five for dismissing shoplifting. Caught unprepared, I flipped on the recorder just below table level and asked a few questions for future jurors.

"Say, Jim," I said, "what was the price for UUW (unlawful use of a weapon)?"

"Hundred and fifty. Me, I like gun cases. Know why? Guys with guns always come up with the money."

Alice was glowering at him, but Costello seemed incapable of understanding that anyone would get upset about something that had been going on for generations. I sat back and wondered when the bugging authorization would come down.

Infiltration Day

I received my answer on the morning of November 26, the day before Thanksgiving. Agent Lamar Jordan gave me a call at home and drawled, "We're going into Olson's chambers this afternoon."

"What?" After weeks of impatience, I could not believe the moment had arrived.

"Justice [Department] says go. You know what to do."

I was so excited it took me two tries to hang up the phone. What a great time to eavesdrop. When Olson returned from vacation on Monday, attorneys would be banging on his door to fix a month of cases they had not dared to try rigging with no-nonsense Judge Sheridan.

I drove to the courthouse that crisp morning with a sense of purpose. By now I knew all the rhythms of the court world and could use them to steer more payoffs to the judge's chambers. I spoke first to Costello and then to Yonan, offhandedly telling them I had decided not to take any more cash because I wanted to look clean when I left the State's Attorney's Office for private practice, which was part of the FBI's plans for me. The reason for telling them this now was that it would force them to pay the judge in his bugged chambers and not me.

As a pretext, I pinned my decision on the recent election of popular Mayor Richard J. Daley's son Richard M. Daley as Cook County State's Attorney, and said it would take time before I could trust the new administration. Yonan wished me luck and added, "If you want, you can use my phone until you're set up, and I'll give you all my misdemeanor work until you can get started." Then he shoved one hundred dollars into my hand anyway. "Don't worry about it," he added, "I'm making money."

Yonan's gesture went unnoticed by people walking by, but not by the police sergeant assigned to Olson's court. From thirty feet away, John Janusz had sensed that I was being bribed and he wanted a cut even if it meant hinting at blackmail. When I went to the cafeteria upstairs, the tall, middle-aged officer with wire-rimmed glasses moved in line next to me, and I felt as if I were being watched by a vulture. "What's that guy's name you were talking to?" he asked, knowing full well it was Yonan.

I answered as I paid for a Coke and turned away. Janusz followed me and said I should buy him a cup of coffee.

"Are you out of change?" I asked, meaning: why should I buy you coffee?

"Do you know in three weeks it's going to be my fucking birthday?" he asked. "I sure hope everybody remembers it. Cy Yonan, boy, that fucker's doing all right. He has another case coming up. You'll be handling it, won't you? You know, my sight's pretty good now that I have new glasses. Hake, where are you going after work, to the bank?"

Compared to Janusz, Costello was suave, and I was glad when I was finally able to shake off the greedy boor.

That afternoon most of the courts closed early so everyone could get a head start on the holiday weekend. By four p.m. only Olson's replacement, Judge Sheridan, and the three switchboard operators remained around Branch 57. As I loitered in the concourse just off the hall, I knew that the "black bag" people were standing by impatiently.

Just as the three women left the room housing all the courthouse telephone wires, two agents dressed as repairmen entered the building. No one questioned them even as they opened the unlocked door to the switchboard room. Everything was going well, but no one could do anything further as long as the judge remained at work.

Come on, come on, I thought. Sheridan took his duties seriously and stayed in his chambers to finish all the details. At last the door opened and I could hear his footsteps on the marble. I went to the nearby phone bank and dialed the FBI radio room. Using the code name for Sheridan, I said, "Phillips just left."

My message was radioed to the surveillance team assigned to follow the judge to ensure that he was not coming back to work. Then I walked to the parking lot across the boulevard on California Avenue and climbed into my car. Following instructions, I drove to a supermarket a mile away to meet Megary and phone the FBI again. That's when things stopped going as planned.

While I waited for the dispatcher to get back to me, I could hear exasperation as he spoke to agents on another line. The team that was supposed to follow the judge could no longer see his station wagon.

I returned to the store parking lot and told Megary, "They lost him. What are we going to do now?"

"That depends," he said. "Do you think Sheridan will come back?"

"Probably not."

"Let's go ahead, then."

Megary went inside the store and made the call to start planting the bug. Minutes later the two bogus workmen brought their tool kits into Olson's chambers. By then I had switched to Megary's car. Inside was an attractive female FBI agent ready to pose as my girlfriend. Our plan was that if anything went wrong, I would rush in with her and claim I had forgotten something. The two of us would then somehow create enough confusion for the two black bag experts to slip away.

But as Bill drove us down the working-class side streets around the courthouse, there was an unsettling quiet on the FBI radio. Not total silence—every now and then a click or a bit of static told us the radio was working—but I edgily thumped my fingers on the armrest.

"Don't worry," Megary said, "no messages just means that everything is going well."

Then we heard: "We arrived at Mr. Chambers' residence and no one is home."

This meant the break-in experts had entered the chambers without encountering anyone. In the unnerving quiet, I could picture the men removing a panel in the switchboard to splice wires, and then crouching at Olson's desk to install the tiny microphone. But I kept thinking of everything that could go wrong. Suppose they had forgotten to lock the door? All it would take would be for one cleaning lady, one janitor, or one fixer to happen upon them.

An hour passed as we killed time by zigzagging across streets surrounding the courthouse, then two hours, then nearly three. We didn't ease the tension with small talk. Megary was good at waiting, but I wasn't. I was so tense my muscles were aching. At last the stillness was broken by a test message—"One, two, three."

The female agent looked at me but didn't know what to say. Provided all went well for the next few months, we were setting criminal justice history. But if for some reason the operation fell apart before we could get evidence from the chambers, all of our work would be just a stack of reports on a shelf in Washington as if nothing had happened. Unless, of course, the fixers caught on.

The black baggers, notified by agents in the radio room that their test had been received, said, "We're going to leave Mr. Chambers' residence now. Let's get the turkey ready."

"Now what?" I asked Megary.

"You go home, and tomorrow have a nice holiday with your folks. Starting Monday, we're all going to be busy."

My tension was replaced by exhaustion, but this time it was a good kind of exhaustion, like sinking into a cloud.

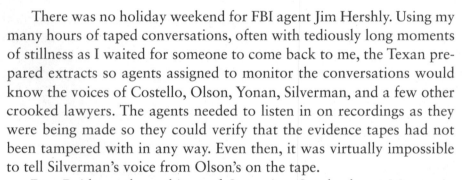

There was no holiday weekend for FBI agent Jim Hershly. Using my many hours of taped conversations, often with tediously long moments of stillness as I waited for someone to come back to me, the Texan prepared extracts so agents assigned to monitor the conversations would know the voices of Costello, Olson, Yonan, Silverman, and a few other crooked lawyers. The agents needed to listen in on recordings as they were being made so they could verify that the evidence tapes had not been tampered with in any way. Even then, it was virtually impossible to tell Silverman's voice from Olson's on the tape.

Dan Reidy, as the architect of Operation Greylord, put Megary in charge of the listening post in the downtown FBI offices and told him to turn off the equipment whenever the conversations were about official business. That would keep us from being accused of violating a person's right to privacy. Megary also instructed the monitoring agents about code phrases I had picked up, such as when Costello would say "open the drawer."

Early on December 1st, Jordan met me at the planetarium parking lot and gave me a transmitter no larger than a pocket calculator, activated by screwing in a small rubber antenna. "Use this to signal us when someone is going into the chambers," he said. The device was unable to send any verbal messages, but its beeps would be picked up by an agent in a car parked near the courthouse. Three beeps, Code Black, meant a target was entering the chambers. A single tap on the button, Code Red, was a Stop! because the fixer was leaving or there was trouble. Two beeps, Code Green, and the agents should resume monitoring. The agent in a car on the street about two hundred feet from the side windows of the courtroom would radio these codes to the listening room ten miles away.

Shortly after I arrived that morning, Yonan seemed pleased with himself as he told me that he had persuaded an officer to change his testimony to make a drug arrest seem illegal. As he went into Olson's chambers, I reached into my pocket and pressed the button three times. After pretending to do a little busy work, I wrote down Cy's name and the time on a file card from my pocket so the conversation would be attributed correctly. The men spoke away from the desk, but the large reel-to-reel tape machine in the FBI offices recorded enough to be used in court.

Seeing that the door to the judge's chambers was opening, I signaled Code Red. Yonan left the chambers and went over to say a few words to his client on one of the benches. When the case was called, Olson declared the search illegal, I didn't protest, and the drug dealer was let go.

Cy later hurried up to me as I was leaving the courthouse on a break. "Hey, Terry," he said, "aren't you forgetting something?" He pulled out his wallet.

"Forget it, I'm cooling it. Seriously."

My pose must have increased my credibility, because Cy handed me the cash with a grin.

Instead of having lunch, I returned to the door outside the judge's chambers. Olson was talking to a lawyer whose voice I couldn't recognize. The fixer complained that he was glad Wayne was back, since the State's Attorney's Office had won every case tried before his replacement.

"I'll fix that," Olson said.

10
LISTENING IN

December 1980

Jim Costello asked me about Cathy again. We were having lunch, and he was feeling good because he had persuaded a drug dealer to sign over his five-hundred-dollar bond for a legal fee while the bar association-assigned attorney was away from the courtroom for a few minutes. Whenever Jim was happy he wanted to become a part of your life.

But by now I was in so deep I needed to keep my personal life separate from my fixer pose to maintain my edge. If you let your two lives merge, your responses get confused and you find yourself being uptight when you should relax, and making slip-ups when you should be on your guard. But as I lay awake at night, I thought over all the possibilities that I had refused to consider during the day. Even if there would never be retaliation for what I was doing, I didn't want to force Cathy into pretending that she liked these sleazy lawyers, and I didn't want to ruin her future law career once my role was found out.

"You don't talk much about her anymore," Costello said over pasta. "You bust up or something?"

"Cathy's a nice girl but I'm not ready for anything serious, you know what I mean?" I was lying, of course. The truth was that in the nine months I had known Cathy, I felt more comfortable with her than with anyone else in my life. Even more than that, I needed her as a way of keeping myself together. "I go out with her now and then, but that's it. I'm trying to find a way to break it off nicely."

"Did you know I had a few cases before Cathy's dad when I was a cop?" Costello said about her father, Judge Will Crowley. "He was a good man, not like Olson. Too bad he died. He had a good family, I bet. I'd really like to meet her."

"Maybe sometime," I said, meaning never.

"She sounds like a nice girl. I'd be on my best behavior. We could go to a nice restaurant or something and have a few drinks." I especially didn't want Cathy to see Jim when he was drunk.

As for why Costello was so insistent, I think he misinterpreted the distance I kept between us and thought I was ashamed of him. That must have cut deep since of all the lawyers and judges he moved around with, I was his only friend. Even in my crooked pose, I was the only one not out for whatever he could grab, and he was continually seeking assurances that I at least accepted him.

Seeing he was getting nowhere with his hints about meeting Cathy, Jim forked up more spaghetti and changed the subject. "Hey, Ter, what are your plans when you go into practice?"

"I'm looking for an office, maybe like yours but on the North Side."

"Make some money first, Ter. Come down and work the hallways until you get started. You can keep everything you need in your car. You hustle for little bonds at first, and then you develop a line and can really plant the fear of God into the bastards." He meant defendants.

Judge Olson came by and cheerfully signaled for a glass of wine. "First drink in six weeks," he boasted as he lowered his bulk next to me. He had sworn off alcohol the night of the party when he and Costello were nearly at each other's throats. Now they were closer than ever because the money was good for them both.

I put down my share of the tab and gave Jim a parting slap on the shoulder. Whatever the judge and the fixer had to say to each other, I knew they wouldn't say it while I was around.

While I was tied up monitoring the comings and goings at the bugged chambers, Alice Carpenter was handling the prosecution of what we were calling the park bench case. Attorney Jay Messinger was representing a man arrested when police found eleven packets of heroin in foil at his feet. The man claimed that as he had been sitting on the bench someone dropped the package on the ground as a squad car pulled up.

Messinger breezed into Olson's chambers on the morning of December 5, the only time I ever saw him go in there. Thanks to the tiny microphone under the desk, it was as if he and the judge were talking right in the FBI offices. What you are about to read is the conversation just as a jury eventually heard it, leading to Messinger's two-year prison sentence:

> Olson (a little cautiously): "They found the tin foil in his pocket?"
>
> Messinger: "No, not in his pocket. They found it under the bench."
>
> Olson: "Yeah, but they're [the police] going to say they found it in his pocket."
>
> Messinger: "They'd better say they found it under the bench."
>
> Olson: "Well, in the first place the cop has got every right in the world to look under the bench if he wants to."
>
> Messinger: "Yeah, but the cop says he saw the guy put it there."
>
> Olson: "That's the trouble with the average [prosecution] lawyer around here. He puts on the copper, and the copper testifies to a lie, which I know is a lie. I've been here for twenty years, okay? Now, the scales of justice went like that [he must have made a gesture of a heavier weight, representing the police] and there's nothing over here [probably gesturing for a lighter weight, the defendant]. You gotta put the guy on and say, 'Sure, I had a lot of cocaine,' or whatever the fuck you want. 'It was in my pocket and he took it out of my pocket.'"
>
> Messinger: "Put it on that way?"
>
> Olson: "Put it on: credibility. I'll believe you."
>
> Messinger: "It's not what *you* believe, though. I mean, I gotta give you something to hang it on. I'll argue the search was illegal."
>
> Olson: "That's fine. But if I hear something from the cops I don't know about, and I don't declare the seizure illegal, you can ask for a preliminary hearing. I'll find no probable cause on the ground that they can't charge this man with that because there were fifteen people around. It could be any of them [who dropped the heroin there]."
>
> Messinger: "Okay."
>
> Olson: "Okay, that's the worst that will happen."
>
> Messinger: "All right. He is supposed to give me money. I've got the bond, which is yours. It's about three hundred, but I might get a little more."

With the mention of money, Olson's voice became more personal. "Well, put it on. Sometimes you can't tell. We'll see how things develop. It might turn out to be an easy throw."

Messinger left the chambers and the case was called minutes later. Olson threw the evidence out according to the script the two of them had worked out, although none of us knew then what had gone on in the chambers. Seeing me coming back from the grand jury room, Alice Carpenter told me she was certain the park bench case had been fixed.

When I asked with a pretended innocence how she knew, she said that Messinger had been in Olson's chambers and "that preliminary hearing was an act."

"Forget it," I advised. "There were a lot of people around when the cops found the drugs, Alice. The case isn't all that cut and dried."

She scowled at me, and I could tell she was wondering if the plague had spread to me, too.

By now I had helped gather evidence against Costello, Olson, Mark Ciavelli, Cy Yonan, and Jay Messinger. I felt probably as ready as I ever would be to go after the biggest and potentially the most dangerous fixer in the system, "Silvery Bob" Silverman.

BOB SILVERMAN

Agent Lamar Jordan had told me not to accept bribes while Olson's chambers were being bugged because the FBI wanted to drive as many fixers as they could into that small room to make payoffs. In just four days, Megary's team had recorded seventy-five separate conversations. Some of the phrases were couched so well they seemed like repartee until added to other conversations. Because the agents had to turn off the recorder whenever the discussions concerned legitimate business, in time there were three hundred thirty-seven starts and stops.

On December 8, while the world was stunned by the murder of John Lennon in New York City, my former friend Mark Ciavelli poked his head into the prosecutors' office in Narcotics Court and asked me, "Mind if we step outside for a minute?"

Even though I had made the decision to not give Mark a free pass after he tried to bribe me, I still needed to force my hand to reach under my suit jacket and push the switch on the tape recorder. My only consolation was that Mark had already given the government evidence against himself by talking about the upcoming PCP case to Olson in the judge's chambers.

As soon as we hit the corridor, Mark shoved cash into my hand. I stared at him, not knowing what was going on.

"Compliments of Bob," he said, as if I should be pleased.

"This is from Silverman? Through you?" I asked for the tape as I put the bill in my pocket without looking at it.

"I told Bob you're really our kind of guy," Mark said. "He goes, 'For God's sake, why didn't he say something before?' I says, 'Well, you know Terry, he's quiet.'" Silverman then told him to give me the hundred for the case I had dismissed for him on the nine-thirty a.m. call.

"Thanks," I told Mark. "Say, how much is it?"

"An ace." One hundred dollars.

Well, well, I thought, *Jordan owes me a lunch!*

Although I was dismayed that Mark played bagman as well as being a fixer, putting him in as deep as anyone else, I was elated at the bribe. Even if we snared no one else but "Silvery Bob" in all of Operation Greylord, my undercover work would have been worth it. Silverman's shadow fell on every court in the system, and if left alone he could easily corrupt five judges for every one we threw in prison.

Silverman could also be the most sinister of our targets because of his contacts among crooked cops and drug-ring enforcers. This bribe meant I was no longer a kid just snooping around. From now on, there would be a danger that I might get too close to that potentially violent vortex of Chicago corruption, where judges, the mob, and city hall insiders merged into a single force powerful enough to set hit men free. It was a world where strange things can happen and witnesses sometimes disappeared.

That all-important payoff had taken just two minutes, but for the rest of that day it dominated my thinking and I could hardly pay attention to my busy load of preliminary hearings. I also had to confirm the bribe on tape as soon as I could. After thinking over what to say so that I wouldn't seem to be trying too hard, I turned the Nagra on and caught up with Silverman gabbing cheerfully with the lawyers waiting at the elevators. With fake nonchalance I quietly said, "Bob, I got that C-note from Mark. Thanks, thank you very much."

Would he say anything to acknowledge it? Instead, he said something even better.

"I'll match that right now. As soon as we're alone, because I have another case coming up on the eleven-thirty call, which you can dismiss."

"Mark's a super guy," I said to keep the conversation going despite my bewilderment at how easy this had been.

"Your friend's a gentleman," remarked Bob, the gentleman of fixers. "Thinking of going into private practice with him and Cardoni? Why don't you stick around where you are until Olson is reassigned" to Divorce Court, at his request. "The working conditions are so beautiful. I mean, you've got a judge who's the sweetest guy in the world. Do you know he's going to be my partner when he leaves the bench?"

"Some people mentioned it, but I thought it was a joke."

"No, we really've been talking about it," came his creamy deep voice as we stepped into an elevator. "But he's more interested in fucking around in Florida. I figure he's good for six months a year here. He'll move into my office downtown, but he's got five years before he can retire with a pension."

"I thought he was older."

"Wayne was born old."

We left the elevator, and Silverman took me down an empty corridor. Without specifically mentioning the one-hundred-dollar bribe, he said, "That thing is going to be lonesome." He handed me another hundred dollars just to make sure I stayed conveniently corrupt. "Take care of yourself," he added in farewell.

My heart was pitter-pattering as I watched him walk away. *My God*, I thought, *I did it, I did it!* We now had him on racketeering conspiracy.

Contact agent Lamar Jordan was so excited when I called him about the bribe that he drove to my apartment that afternoon with a Nagra device that had playback capability so I could listen to the tape with him. "This is enough, isn't it?" I asked when I turned the Nagra off.

"Maybe," he said in his Southern drawl. Maybe? "You weren't supposed to take any bribes until we remove Olson's bug."

"Mark shoved the hundred in my hand. What was I supposed to do, shove it back? How in the hell would that look? And didn't I need something from Bob's own mouth? You heard him, he's the one who suggested matching the first hundred."

"You really should play things like you're told."

"Lamar, you have to trust my instincts."

"You know what we told you."

I was fed up with this damned if you do/damned if you don't situation. Since I wasn't a sworn member of the FBI, the agents were refusing to trust my judgments. These agents, who had never served in corrupt criminal courts, wanted me to be just a walking listening device, a robot.

"You know, Lamar," I said, "I'm the undercover agent out there. It's taken us seven months to get this far, and we just can't count on Silverman talking money in Olson's chambers. You have to give me a little leeway in making decisions on my own. There are all sorts of cues I've got to pay attention to, and they don't come off on tape. Sometimes I have to take calculated risks."

"Just so you know where we stand," he said. "I don't want you to take any more money from Bob unless he hands it to you, like today."

Yet in spite of Jordan's dour expression, he seemed to be agreeing with me. He just didn't want to make a formal departure from the company line. If contact agents did that, all untrained moles would be going off on tangents.

He rewound the tape and grabbed his coat. We shook hands and said goodbye as if this were the most ordinary meeting we ever had, but once I closed my door I felt like throwing a party. I had grabbed a little freedom of movement for myself and knew that since Silverman now trusted me, other fixers would start falling in line. And so they did.

BRUCE ROTH

Criminal attorney Bruce Roth was a sharp dresser with lightning reflexes, and he always made a good appearance in court. He visited Olson's chambers the next afternoon to talk over the arrest of a drug dealer accused of curbside service in a high-crime neighborhood. In some ways the materialistic Roth was a good man, but he specialized in drug cases and was seen hanging out with flashy cocaine dealers. His own cocaine use was widely discussed around the halls.

His latest client was a dealer who had scaled a fence when he saw the police closing in on him, but they caught him in a gangway. The arrest was as tight as they come, so Roth entered Olson's chambers to loosen it.

"Who are the coppers?" the judge asked while Megary was listening in on the conversation being taped on the reel-to-reel in the FBI office.

"They're not cool," Roth replied, using the code phrase for people who can't be bribed.

"Does their report say anything about binoculars?"

"Absolutely not." Roth sounded thankful.

"He's been arrested before?"

"Once before, by the same guys. I beat them on that case."

"That's an important fact to bring out," Olson said. "Put on a motion to suppress."

"Motion to suppress?"

"See how things turn out. We'll do the best we can."

"All right," Roth said with a shuffling sound as he apparently stood up. "I got five hundred. How's everything going? You look happy."

"At my age," said Olson, "I'm glad to be here, pal."

The following day, Olson made Roth look brilliant. Once the case was dismissed, Bruce went to the vacant back half of the huge courtroom to take care of business. While I signaled a Code Black, Roth entered the judge's chambers. There he mentioned in passing that the judge was right in transferring to Divorce Court. "Some of those cases involve a lot of money and property," he said. "The sky's the limit" for bribes.

They went on to discuss various court people who could and could not be bribed. Chief Criminal Court Judge Richard Fitzgerald was honest, for example, but Judge Alan Lane was, as fixers would say, "dirty."

Then Megary must have tingled as he heard Judge Olson say, "I love people that take dough. You know exactly where they stand."

"Sure," Roth responded, "that's the only way to do business."

Roth was soon walking down the courthouse steps with his newly freed client, who we would eventually learn helped him obtain drugs.

A few months later, a guard escorted Roth down an elevated walkway in the gray County Jail behind the courthouse. A cell door opened, and the fixer paid an unannounced visit to *Henry Sutherland, who was awaiting sentencing for a vicious rape. Without mentioning names, Roth said he had been sent by a very influential person. Sutherland understood—it was Judge Alan Lane, who was about to sentence him. Roth told Sutherland that his lawyer was ineffectual, and that the conviction could be overturned for a price.

To avoid speaking of money, as we know from an Attorney Registration and Disciplinary Commission opinion, Roth held up a sheet of legal-sized paper on which he had written: $10,000 OR TEN YEARS. Later that day one of Roth's pals called Sutherland's girlfriend and said that if she didn't come up with the money she would never see her boyfriend on the outside again.

But Sutherland was panicking at the size of the extortion demand. A friend intervened and had the case assigned to another judge. Sutherland was eventually retried and acquitted. But slowly our evidence was mounting against Lane, the judge who had the audacity to put the fixer's code PNGJW (Plea of Not Guilty Jury Waived) on his vanity license plates.

JAMES COSTELLO

The federal agents had to rely on my conversations with Jim Costello to fill in blanks as we gathered evidence against various targets. But now that he had served our purpose of introducing me into the underworld of bribery, we needed to document his bribes to Olson as if he were just any other fixer.

Costello had been telling me for months about his kickbacks to the judge, but we still needed taped confirmation from Olson's mouth. That was important for a RICO-racketeering conspiracy conviction.

I was no longer signaling the comings and goings in Olson's chambers with the transmitter. So much evidence was pouring in against members of the bribery club that Bill Megary and Dan Reidy told me it was clear that the lawyers seldom went in just to tell a joke. The federal court now allowed us to record all conversations. But I still had to write down the times on note cards for later identifications. I was relieved when I handed the transmitter back, since structural steel, radio traffic, concrete, and other interferences kept fouling up my signals. As an example, we may have missed some damning evidence when I pressed a Code Black as a crooked lawyer was entering that little room, but the FBI listening room received only a Code Red, stop.

On the tenth day, the bug picked up a fee-splitting conversation between Costello and Olson.

"What have we got in the kitty?" Olson asked Jim.

"We got eight hundred."

"Huh?" Olson asked in surprise.

"Eight."

"How come I wrote down twenty-three hundred?"

"What! What are you talking about?" Costello said. "I figured seven hundred eighty-five, I counted it. I don't know how you can have twenty-three hundred figured."

"You had eight or nine cases yesterday," Olson said.

"Let me look in my book."

After a pause, the two of them bickered over the appearance of a drug dealer who had posted five hundred dollars bail months before but failed to show up in court, so his bond was ordered forfeited. When the pusher was arrested again, Costello put the hustle on him and represented him for two minutes. Olson improperly reinstated the bond as if the dealer had never skipped. That meant the dealer could sign the five hundred dollars in bond money over to Costello for his fee. Jim thought the entire amount should be his since he had hustled the case on his own. But Olson felt differently.

"I resurrected the bond," the judge said, almost shouting.

"What!"

"You don't think I resurrected that? Jeez, man, holy shit! You want to see me un-resurrect it?"

Although I couldn't know at the time what had just been said, I saw Jim stomping out of the chambers. I reached him in the hallway and asked what had happened.

"I cannot understand Wayne," Costello said. "You know what he said? He said 'I'll stick it in your fucking ass.' That Olson is a greedy motherfucker. I'm scared of that man, you know what I mean?"

The quarrel over a few hundred dollars was just what we needed to prove a conspiracy in Olson's referring cases for kickbacks and then selling his rulings. Every word that Costello had told me over the last few months about his financial arrangement with Olson was now admissible in court because we had their confirming conversation on tape. So we at last had a RICO conspiracy case on Olson because of his greed.

The following day, Costello and I were talking over pasta again. He had decided to compromise on what he owed the judge and ask him to accept an even one thousand dollars. He pulled a white envelope from inside his double breasted suit and waved it under my nose. "One thousand bucks right here," he said. "I just don't know if I'm going to pay him today or make him sweat a little and give it to him tomorrow," Friday, Olson's regular payoff day.

"Tell him you can afford only one third of what you owe," I suggested. "You know, the taxes will kill you." Any such evidence would be great to play for a jury.

"The way my life's been going, taxes are the least of my worries," he said.

As I handed my latest private tape recordings to Bill Megary outside the planetarium that afternoon, he looked uncomfortable with what he was about to say. He started by telling me some things the hidden microphone had picked up. Then he went into the troubling subject:

"Somebody was talking to Olson about you trying to get into the FBI a while back."

A chill raced through me. "Who was it, Silverman? Yonan?"

"He was standing a little away from the desk. We couldn't identify the voice."

"Mark knows I applied more than a year ago, and maybe some ASAs do, too."

"Are you worried about it?"

"I don't know. What did he say?"

"He was talking about the possibility of a shakeup in the State's Attorney's Office, then he mentioned that you applied for the FBI. That's all he said."

"How did Olson take it?"

"We don't know. There was a bunch of noise coming from the hall."

After a pause, I asked, "What do you think I should do?"

Megary thought it over and said, "Watch Olson closely for the next day or so. That's all you can do."

He didn't sound worried. But, then, his life wasn't the one on the line.

11

SUSPICIONS

Late December 1980

While most courthouse workers were in a holiday mood, I stayed tense over whether Judge Olson could detect that something was going on. Even if he did, the bribery continued as openly as before. I saw Costello drop twenty dollars in fives into the wastebasket of Olson's clerk, and another time the judge threw out three of Roth's cases as if the evidence didn't exist. Since Wayne would soon be going to the Elysian Fields of Divorce Court, what did he care whether anyone complained?

Although my friend and fellow assistant prosecutor Alice Carpenter loathed corruption, she couldn't help liking the talkative and usually entertaining judge. When she suggested that we give Olson a tie for Christmas, I shopped around and bought him a navy blue silk one for fifteen dollars. We split the cost, and I billed the FBI for my half. At the end of the day, Alice surprised me with a fruit basket for the holidays. That made me feel bad because, with all the things that were happening, I had not thought of getting her anything. It brought home the reality of all the friendships I would be losing.

Alice's husband, defense attorney Barry Carpenter, was as tall and thin as Ichabod Crane, and could be funny at unexpected moments. He once walked into a restaurant where Costello was describing how he had set up a meeting with a defendant's girlfriend to discuss a case and wound up in a motel with her. When Jim suggested that Barry meet him for lunch some time, Carpenter said, "Ohhh no—I might wind up in a motel room with you."

Such moments were especially welcome in a somber courthouse where fates were decided behind every door, but few places showed more holiday spirit. Large wreaths were hung over jury boxes, and most guards, cafeteria workers, judges, clerks, and attorneys spent December 23 and 24 wishing everyone a merry Christmas.

On Christmas Eve, Cathy and I exchanged gifts at my apartment after a Chinatown dinner. I gave her diamond earrings, and as a gag gift she presented me with a spy book. I actually picked up some pointers from it. One was that, when there are rumors about you, talk them over with the people who may be suspicious rather than let the gossip become entrenched.

January 1981

When court ended one day, Bill Megary let me watch the action, if you can call it action, on another wire in the ten-by-twenty-foot listening room at the rear of the FBI offices downtown. I went past a door marked RESTRICTED and saw that there really wasn't much to look at, just thousands of dollars in recording equipment on shelves, a gray metal table, and a couple of chairs. An agent with earphones was keeping a log at the table and making notes on the conversation. I couldn't hear anything and just saw the large reels slowly turning.

One thing becoming clear from my work and the bugging was that anyone in the system could be a bagman—not only judges' clerks and fixers like Costello but sometimes the judges themselves. When FBI agents and I went over the tapes in preparation for court, we heard Judge Olson telling an attorney that another judge might acquit two men on battery charges but that he "will bitch at me for [conveying] less than a grand." When the lawyer apparently handed over additional money, Olson did not see any cash for himself. "What am I," he complained, "chopped liver?"

The day of that conversation, January 5, 1981, Bob Silverman asked me to look over one of his cases because "I haven't had time to study it." That meant he had not put the fix in with Olson yet. As he was using the phone in the Olson's chambers while the judge was on the bench, I told him that this would be no problem. "Okay, Terry," Bob said with a knowing smile.

As I left the room my walking slowed because of a nagging thought. Silverman had been so grateful that he might be willing to hand me money then and there. Why not let the agents at the listening post hear me accepting a bribe right in the chambers? As I went back in, Silverman was going through a wad of money. Surprised to see me again, he said, "Terry boy, what's up?"

"We're going to dismiss it, Bob."

"I know, I already talked to the copper." He slipped a fifty-dollar bill between the pages of a memo pad from Olson's desk and handed it to me.

"I think I'll go put this down on a new car," I said, imagining Megary's thrill as he listened in with his headphones that very moment.

One week later, while I was still having doubts about whether the fixers fully trusted me because of someone's remark about my FBI application, another assistant prosecutor caught up with me in the rear of the Narcotics Court. "Terry," he said in a hushed tone, "there's something I think you ought to know."

My insides churned. *They've found out*, I thought.

"I just thought you'd want to know that they're calling you 'Terry Take' behind your back."

"Who!"

"Just people. What you do is your own business, but you might want to watch yourself."

I was glowing inside but pretended to be so angry that I swore.

Over the next few days I asked around and learned that felony review supervisor Sandy Klapman, who knew nothing of my undercover work, had smugly given me that label after I asked him to change a one-hundred-dollar bill. Only fixers and courthouse bribe-takers carried multiple one-hundred-dollar bills.

So through an oversight I had joined the list of people with courthouse monikers, along with "Silvery Bob" Silverman and Judge John "Dollars" Devine. But the nickname was also further proof that honest people like Alice Carpenter and now Klapman were distancing themselves from me. For months I had been adding fixers to my friends in the building, and now I saw that only a fixer would be my friend.

At the time, I was still keeping close to Costello and letting him think I might open up shop with him someday. One reason I had grown fond of him was that his bad habits were so predictable, like a pet dog's. One early-January Friday, Jim dragged himself into court in a slept-in suit and with a hangover that wouldn't go away. I had seen that shabby look before, but this time he was panicking because he had only pocket change and couldn't meet Olson's weekly payoff.

"WhadamIgoingtodo?" he slurred into one word.

"Just keep hustling," I said.

He worked the hall with more urgency than usual and managed to pick up five hundred dollars in twenties from a client. Within the hour, the FBI's reel-to-reel was recording the judge's drawer opening and closing.

New Ground

The assistant state's attorney's aspect of my undercover career was ending and I was facing life as a sham defense lawyer so that I could start handing out bribes rather than waiting for them to come to me. No one talked about it, but I knew this meant the operation might take another year to run, or even more.

Over a lunch of chicken and tortillas, Costello mused that I had finally learned enough to set up practice on my own. "Remember," he told me, "if the cops ever stop you for speeding—"

"I know, say I'm a lawyer, throw twenty bucks at them, and take off."

Looking me in the eye, he asked, "Did you learn anything else from me?"

"You taught me how the system works."

"It's goofy," he said. "It's all money."

Yet everything was in question now because Cook County State's Attorney Bernard Carey, a Republican who had helped create Operation Greylord, had been replaced by Richard M. Daley, a Democrat whose late father, Mayor Richard J. Daley, probably had a hand in placing half the current judges on the bench.

The son was an unknown entity to us, and he was given to consulting advisors about everything with a political tinge. In addition, the younger Daley and his brothers moved in the social circle of numerous judges, including Judge Richard LeFevour, the prime target of the municipal courts branch of Greylord. Daley even went to White Sox games with him. Suppose Daley considered the bugging illegal or unethical, a very real possibility. Suppose he thought the investigation would be politically damaging? Suppose he meant well but accidentally dropped a hint to the wrong friend?

So Dan Reidy held a strategy session with the U.S. attorney. They decided not to let Daley know what was going on until he seemed ready.

We were later pleased to discover that the state's attorney gave us his full support and always kept the information confidential. He even continued social contacts with targeted judges so that they would not become suspicious. That let us continue gathering evidence against ever more targets.

PETER KESSLER

One of them, Peter Kessler, was friendly enough but often represented prostitutes and pleaded a lot of clients guilty just to increase his turnover. The only things he seemed to care about were his family and money. Who would have imagined that of all the attorneys, clerks, and judges being snared by Greylord, he would prove in time to be our wild card?

Consider his background. Kessler was born just outside Warsaw during World War II. When he was a year old his father was killed in a German ambush. Peter, his sister, and their mother lived in hiding wherever they could as impoverished Jews in a country overrun by Nazi soldiers. When the war ended, they moved about with hundreds of other displaced persons until they could board a ship bound for America in 1949.

The family settled in Chicago's large Polish community. Peter's mother worked in a factory during the day, and at night she prepared dinners in her home for about a dozen fellow immigrants. In time, Golda Kessler opened a restaurant to make money to send Peter to college. He stayed honest as one of the attorneys the Chicago Bar Association sent to court, but in 1978 he felt that he wasn't receiving enough cases to support his wife and four children. So Kessler began hustling clients among shoplifters in Women's Court, commonly called whore court because prostitution cases were heard on the first call. From there, it was easy to build a practice by keeping judges friendly.

That started with Judge John "Dollars" Devine's disguised hints that his pockets were open. The dark-haired, disagreeable judge hurled insults at Peter in court and ruled against him every time until he wised up. Peter went along with the shakedown and kicked back the usual one-third of his bond referrals. Buying judgments was the next logical step. In time, he became as avaricious as the others, but he was no longer proud of himself.

Kessler usually worked out of the small courts in the old police headquarters but would go halfway across the city to the Criminal

Courts Building when the price was right. One day a policeman called the prosecutors' office and asked me to reinstate one of Kessler's cocaine possession cases before Olson.

Since the officer worked on the Far North Side, near my Evanston apartment, I had him bring me copies of the reports that night. As he reenacted the arrest in my living room, I could tell the case should not have been dismissed. When I refiled the case, Kessler told me his client would plead guilty if I dismissed the gun charge and sought probation for cocaine possession. Instead, I offered special probation for the cocaine charge, and two days in jail for gun possession. As for my reason, I mentioned that I hated guns and lied by saying the arresting officer was pressuring me for jail time.

Kessler refused my offer and presented a motion to suppress the evidence, instead.

Since Olson felt that he should have "paid his respects," the judge thought his ruling would teach him a lesson. Hardly letting Peter speak, Olson rejected the motion and left the outcome to me. Kessler decided to bribe me by sending Costello as his bagman.

"Boy, Wayne really stuck it to Peter," Jim told me in the hall. "Are you going to take care of him, or what?"

"Peter doesn't even know I'm involved [on the take], does he?" I asked.

"He knows, Terry. Look, there's three bills [three hundred dollars] he gave me. Peter wants the case recalled today and the gun charge dismissed. He's really hot on this. I know you're not helping out [taking bribes] any more, but can you do it just this once?"

"What do I get, a hundred and a half?"

"I'll give you two, I'll keep one."

"Let me think about it overnight because I took such a strong position just now, all right?"

"Sure," Costello said. As he walked away, he added, "Say hi to Cathy for me."

"If I see her." He was still testing me.

The next day I walked into Olson's chambers and asked that Kessler's hearing be advanced. Contact agent Bill Megary had just told me that the FBI would be removing the tiny microphone from Olson's desk in two weeks, so I wanted the fix to go down before then.

The judge was feeling good because he was about to perform a Narcotics Court wedding for a policeman who often testified there. Without asking why I wanted an earlier date, he picked January 20—the final day of the bug! Next I told Costello I wasn't going to take any more money from Kessler because I was starting to feel pressure from my bosses, and that he should speak to Olson about supervision on the gun charge, hoping this would be done in the chambers.

The Final Day

As soon as I came to work on January 20, I submitted my resignation from the State's Attorney's Office so I could start my own (bogus) law practice. Then I went about tying up as many of the loose ends of the bugging operation as I could before the microphone was removed that afternoon.

Costello paid a visit to Olson's chambers and said, "Judge, I'm trying to catch up in arrears." The desk drawer opened and closed. We later learned that Costello had dropped in two hundred dollars from bond referrals, then added a cash envelope from Kessler. But the judge evidently had been looking elsewhere and didn't notice it.

"There's something else in there," Costello said on the tape.

Olson probably turned around, saw the extra money, and somehow acknowledged it without a word. Then Jim left, and I walked in to discuss the sentencing stalemate in Kessler's case.

"Kessler and Costello want supervision," I said.

"Well, if there's a good reason for it, I'll give it," Olson replied, "but otherwise I'm not inclined to give him supervision."

Wasn't the fix set? I went out and told Costello what the judge had said about the gun charge. A few minutes later, Costello returned to the chambers.

"I can't take the heat on a gun," Olson told him. "What are we going to work out?"

"The weapon came from the family's business, he's got registrations for it," Costello answered. "He knows there's no fuckin' way he is gonna get it back. He isn't a guy that's running around in the street."

"Who represents him, you or Kessler?"

"Kessler."

"What's he gonna drop?"

"He dropped three [three hundred dollars]. That's what I was trying to tell you. That's what I gave you."

From the sounds, it seems that Olson looked into the envelope in his drawer. Then, raising his voice, he said, "There's only four hundred and fifty in there."

"There was five hundred!" Costello insisted.

"Tell Kessler to make his argument," said Olson, dismissing the difference for now. "Argue that his guy needs to keep a good record."

"Okay, fine, Judge," he groused. "Thank you very much."

After Costello left, I walked over and asked him, "What's up, Jim?"

"There was five hundred dollars in that envelope. I've had it with that guy, Ter. I know Wayne's given me a lot of business, but I just don't give a shit any more. He's trying to screw me around for another fifty."

At the time, I did not know what had been said to Olson but I saw another chance to have the two natural enemies incriminate themselves. "Jim, you've got to settle it with Wayne," I suggested, "you're losing track and he's losing track."

"He isn't losin' track, I can tell you that."

"Then you don't want him to have a laugh on you, do you? Why don't you settle it now and get it over with."

Costello agreed with a shrug.

At the hearing, Peter Kessler played out the scene just as it had been worked out. The judge put the defendant on supervision and retreated to his chambers with Costello at his heels. Their agreement to keep better track of the payments was one of the last of the twenty-five hundred and thirty-eight conversation segments recorded in the FBI office in less than two months.

After Olson left for the day, federal agents snuck into his chambers and removed the device. I celebrated by going to a restaurant in the Little Italy neighborhood on my way home and ordering an Italian beef sandwich. After all, although I was working for the FBI, my only income was still from the State's Attorney's Office.

My resignation would not take effect until February, but I kept showing up at 26th and California even though my heart was no longer in court work. I was in a transition phase since I had been telling fixers for months not to give me any further bribes. But the hiatus was far from wasted.

A Fixer's Education

Because I was going into practice on my own, Costello's tip was to "give Wayne a grand and you'll start getting some business." Bob Silverman graciously decided to show me how to rig a case, using as an example something he was handling for a man arrested for drug possession in an apartment leased by his girlfriend.

"If a lawyer can prove the person charged with possession does not have residency, the charges are usually dropped," he said in his mellow voice. "Now, this copper is a friend of mine. He gave me the police report yesterday," no doubt for a bribe. "The report nowhere states residency. The only way to prove it is from testimony by the cop, and the cop isn't going to know." Another bribe. "You got to check your case report. If something isn't in there, it doesn't exist."

"But the ASA can prove residency with gas bills and rent receipts," I said.

"Sure, but those can get lost on the way to court," for another bribe. "These are the things it took me years to learn." Then he added a pun: "*Quid pro* crow, as we used to say in Latin."

"And it makes it all the easier for the state's attorney to dismiss the case, too," I said to feed the tape running behind my belt.

"Of course it does. I wouldn't go to an ASA and ask for a dismissal if there wasn't a way out. Now he can step up to the judge and say 'Judge, we cannot establish residency.' Boom—case over. And nobody's caught in the middle."

Silverman asked to see my copy of a police report on one of the cases I was handling that day, even though it didn't involve him. I handed it over and he walked away. A little later he gave it back. When no one could see me, I thumbed through the pages and found a one-hundred-dollar bill tucked inside.

My taking his money made me more trustworthy, and Bob could be less formal with me. Within two days he found me in the Narcotics Court clerk's office and said, "I want to talk to you about something." He led me to the washroom in the judge's chambers and put one hundred dollars in fives in my hand for dismissing a drug case before the damning lab report came in.

But since Silverman had given me the payoff before I could get him to be specific on tape, I met him in the hall a few minutes later and told him the money was more than enough.

"It's my pleasure," he replied.

12

SWITCHING SIDES

February 1981

Because of the old rumor about my being a government operative I was having trouble making headway in the criminal courthouse, which I had once known so well. In my final days as an assistant prosecutor, I dismissed a case for Silverman and found myself holding one hundred dollars in fives after we shook hands. That was my fifth payoff from him, more than enough to throw him in prison when the time came.

There was no going-away party for me, I just made the rounds and exchanged handshakes with the honest and dishonest alike. But I wasn't forgotten. The "boys" surprised me with a belated goodbye party at a restaurant two weeks later. Costello gave me a few hundred dollars he had practically strong-armed from fellow bribers and told me to use it for a new car.

I soon missed the hectic schedule of my double life. Until authorization could come down for "live" (set up) cases, for the next few months I did little more than sit at home re-listening to my tapes and writing down every word to help juries follow them. Costello called me regularly, unaware of the tape recorder I had attached to the receiver. So that I might at least be seen in a suburban court, I persuaded my mother sit down with me once as if she were my client.

Unflappable FBI agent Bill Megary suggested that since the Olson bugging had gone so well, we might plant a microphone in the chambers of Judge John Reynolds because a crime syndicate burglary case was coming up. Reynolds was such a martinet that he was called "Black Jack" behind his back, after General "Black Jack" Pershing of WWI. He was a well-dressed, thin man of fifty who had taken an airline stewardess for his second wife. For at least two years Reynolds, the son and brother of lawyers, had been grabbing every bribe he could. To make the pickings easier, he rid his courtroom of all attorneys sent by the Chicago Bar Association.

That was how Mark's partner, Frank Cardoni, could receive more than one hundred thousand dollars from bond referrals in just a year and a half in his courtroom. In return Cardoni slipped a third of the money into such places as a golf magazine on Reynolds' desk, in the pocket of a suit jacket hanging in the chambers, in the judge's home, under the table in restaurants, and in the console between the bucket seats of the judge's luxury BMW.

In fact, Reynolds' BMW came from payoffs—along with a fur coat for his pretty wife, a country club membership, a Mexican condominium, and an apartment in Chicago's Gold Coast. With the opportunity of free travel from his wife's job at American Airlines, he took single-day trips to New York just to be fitted by his favorite tailor.

Unlike Olson, Reynolds told fixers to keep a detailed record of how much they owed him. Fond of paying cash for everything, he always made sure he had at least two thousand dollars stuffed in a "sock drawer" at home. Reynolds would later attribute his corruption to "mid-career burnout." Records showed that this methodical "burnout" contributed to the corruption of at least five attorneys and half a dozen court clerks.

Some say that lawyers corrupt the judges, but in Chicago it was often the other way around. The good-looking Cardoni was a bright and aggressive young man who was just two years out of law school when he started representing clients in the court at the police station at Belmont and Western. Reynolds taunted him with such hints as, "Did you just get off the Belmont Avenue bus?" and, finally, "So far, it's been like you've been kept on a scholarship, and now your scholarship is over. This is a business. Look around you, see how business is done."

Cardoni took the hint, and a from-one-pocket-to-another relationship deepened between the two men. Frank had lunch with Reynolds daily and dated the judge's daughter from a previous marriage. He also was the judge's guest on a Mexican vacation. The friendship was so lucrative that Cardoni needed a partner to handle all the cases, and that was how my friend Mark Ciavelli was seduced into corruption. Within a month of leaving the State's Attorney's Office, Mark was delivering six hundred dollars a week in cash to Reynolds on behalf of the new law firm.

· While Reynolds was on vacation, his replacement opened a desk drawer looking for napkins and found a stack of one-hundred-dollar bills from various lawyers. But even honest judges abided by the code of silence, and Reynolds was never reported.

One of Reynolds' clerks acted as a bagman. Most clerks were already making five to ten thousand dollars a year from lawyers wanting their cases called early or to see court files. Not trusting them, Reynolds ordered that lawyers never leave bribes in a drawer unless he was in his chambers, but sometimes he would leave money there himself—and the clerks usually would steal it.

I had left the State's Attorney's Office just as Mark and Cardoni were in the preliminary stages of representing minor mob figure Salvatore Romano, who had been caught trying to burglarize a suburban meat market. Since Romano was also a federal informant, the FBI saw a way of expanding Greylord when he and three accomplices hired Silverman.

The police report was so damaging there was no way Reynolds could throw out the case without having someone cry fix, so Bob decided to bribe the owner of the meat market into staying away from court. The price would come high. "I want a nickel apiece," Silverman told the four defendants, meaning five thousand dollars each. "But if I can't help you, I don't want your money." Investigators learned that one of the defendants, Glen Devos, said, "If this guy [the owner] gets any second thoughts, I'll kidnap the motherfucker."

An FBI agent went to Romano's home and gave him a Nagra recorder. The next day, the mobster's tape picked up a conversation in which Silverman spoke about letting Cardoni in on the deal. Later, Silverman asked Romano to visit the owner of the meat market, Tony Pedio. But since Romano was working for the FBI, he decided to stay away from him, leading to confusion.

Pedio showed up outside the courtroom and sparked a huddle by the four thieves. Then Cardoni arrived in his tailored suit and well-polished shoes. What happened next, pieced together from witnesses, shows how complex payoffs could be: ·

"Hi, Sal," Cardoni said. "What's all the crowd for?"

"The complaining witness is here," Romano explained.

"Well, get him out. Now!"

"I say we offer him a thousand dollars" to go home, Romano said.

"Make it two," Cardoni said.

Then he and Romano walked over to Pedio. Lying, Cardoni claimed there had never been a case in Cook County history in which prosecutors penalized a witness who refused to answer a subpoena. Since the arresting officers in the hallway didn't like seeing a victim so close to the defendant and his attorney, they broke up the conversation.

Before long, Romano and Silverman met again in the hallway with the other men charged with the break-in. Seeing how scared Pedio was, Romano walked over to him and said, "Take two thousand dollars and go have coffee."

"Money don't mean nothing," Pedio said. "What you guys did was wrong."

"Me and my partners, we're sorry."

"The cops—"

"They won't say nothing other than 'The man didn't show up, Your Honor,'" Romano assured him.

"They'll want to know why in the hell I'm leaving."

"So you got tired, you got fed up. Otherwise, we're gonna continue this thing for a year." That was always an effective threat because of the lost business that postponements usually caused. "Walk in the washroom with me and I'll give it to you."

"No, I couldn't."

Silverman stepped in and introduced himself, telling the victim, "Nothing would happen to you. I give you my word on that. I won't let it happen. If there's any kind of steam at all, you won't be in the middle." After all, Bob Silverman was an honorable man.

Whether out of fear or dismay, Pedio left the police station empty-handed. Showing more sensitivity than most fixers, Bob told Romano to drop by the man's shop and deliver the two thousand dollars. "You know how much sleep this guy must have lost because of what you guys did? Sal, no phone calls, no nothing. Just drop it off in an envelope today. Walk in and walk out."

Reynolds dismissed the case because of Pedio's absence, but the ASA moved to reinstate it. When the case came up again, Silverman and Cardoni conferred with the burglar mole in a hallway. "It's time to bring in [bribe] Reynolds," Silverman said. "I want you to give him a dime [one thousand dollars]. If you haven't got it, I'll lay it out now. I want you to kiss it off."

"I got a couple hundred," Romano said.

Bob asked Cardoni, "Whatta you got?"

"Two," meaning two hundred dollars.

Silverman counted Romano's and Cardoni's money, and finally his own, a total of one thousand dollars, while mumbling, "Shit, I don't want to make a fuckin' career defending these guys."

Minutes later Judge Reynolds refused to reinstate the case. Cardoni expected to keep half of the thousand dollars he had brought to the judge's chambers, but Reynolds took it all, and that was the end of it.

The entire sequence shows how invaluable an insider can be when investigating corruption, since nothing Reynolds did publicly would have sent up a red flag. So it was little wonder we were devastated when we learned that the judge was being transferred before we could set up a listening post in his chambers. I had even suggested secretly photographing the room for a floor plan before the microphone was installed. But we weren't going to let up on Reynolds. We were still at the muscle-flex phase of the investigation in which we thought nothing could stop us. But we had a lot to learn.

I made a routine call to Costello's home on a Saturday in late February. "Don't talk on this line," he said in a worried voice. "My God, didn't you see the *Tribune* this morning? The feds are investigating Narcotics Court. From now on, if we speak, we speak in person."

"Jim, what's going on?"

He hung up.

I went to my car and drove to a newspaper stand. The front page story shot through me: A federal grand jury, reportedly conducting a major investigation of how drug cases are handled in Chicago, has subpoenaed all records of cases handled in two Cook County courtrooms during the last four years. There were reports that the grand jury is seeking evidence that defendants in drug cases are illegally "steered" to certain defense lawyers.

The courtrooms were those of Arthur Zelezinski, who was honest, and Olson, now in Divorce Court. I was relieved the investigation had nothing to do with Greylord, but the snooping was bound to increase the suspicions of fixers and crooked judges.

So I angrily called Dan Reidy, the architect of the operation, and asked how the U.S. Attorney's Office could have issued the subpoena so soon after my leaving the state prosecutor's office. "Wasn't the U.S. Attorney's Office thinking?" I asked. "This is bound to bring the heat on me and everyone else. It's absolutely stupid."

"Terry, you're right," Reidy said, "you better be careful in the next couple of weeks. But we couldn't just stop work at our end, either. We needed those records for the Charles Wilson case." Wilson was accused of running a curbside drug operation with the tacit knowledge of ten Chicago policemen.

But I didn't give a damn. If there was a serious flaw in Greylord, this was it. Until that morning, all the corruptors had opened their doors to me. But by nature they were sharp and distrustful, and I was sure they would never treat me the same again, if only because I was the newest member of their club.

Costello called my apartment the next day to arrange a face-to-face talk. "I think my phone is being tapped," he explained.

All I could do was put his fears to rest and discuss weather, sports, movies, anything that came to my head to make sure we stayed friends. As soon as I could, I notified Bill Megary of the meeting, and he told me not to wear the body recorder at the meeting because the situation might be getting dangerous.

I was prepared for anything when I showed up at the Criminal Courts Building that Tuesday—except for what Costello had wanted me there for. He didn't pat me down, he didn't confront me; all he did was talk about his family problems. "We gotta go to my house," the towering hustler said. "That asshole dating my Jackie smashed two of my windows. I wanna file a report and get the fucker arrested."

His daughter's steady boyfriend had broken the windows of the house in revenge for Costello's drunken attack on his car, in which Jim slashed tires, shattered windows, and poured a package of sugar into the gas tank. In passing, Jim mentioned that he wasn't concerned about possible indictments against fixers. He explained that he had listed all his bond referral money on his tax returns, but I knew that wasn't true because he had given me rundowns on how much he was keeping back. He kept a lot of that money in a basement shoebox.

By now I was coming to understand the fixer mentality. The reason Costello wasn't scared by the new investigation was that he refused to realize his crimes might someday catch up with him, not when there were bigger fish out there such as Olson and Silverman.

We went to Costello's comfortable home and a police officer filled out a vandalism report. Jim tipped him twenty dollars for his trouble. About an hour later we drove to the district station to learn whether the boyfriend had been arrested yet. As I waited by the front desk, Jim went to the tactical unit and gave four officers two hundred dollars to split as an inducement to put the boyfriend behind bars. It never occurred to Costello that some people might do their job without a payoff.

Over the next two weeks I occasionally dropped by the courthouse to stay in touch and pretend I was busy even though I was still on what amounted to a government-imposed vacation. One day while I was waiting in a corridor to meet Costello for lunch, a half-familiar voice said something that for nearly a year I had been afraid I might hear: "Hey, Terry, I hear you're working for the FBI."

I turned and saw Jim McCarron, a defense attorney I had known from my work in the chief judge's office. *What does he know*, I wondered. "That's not true," I said. Everything around me seemed unreal.

"You leave, and a week later the subpoenas came down," he said. "Don't you think that's a coincidence?"

"I never gave it a thought. Who were you talking to?"

"Costello," McCarron lied, as it turned out.

"Don't believe what you hear, it's bull."

"Yeah," McCarron said.

I told myself that he must have been fishing. But not two minutes after he left, court sergeant Bob Shuksta came by and said, "I hear you're an undercover agent."

He was smiling, and I forced myself to grin back. "Some joke," I tossed at him. "Who's been saying that?"

"Drozd, he's telling everybody." The officer was referring to gang crimes investigator Robert Drozd.

"He's a little early for April Fool," I said. "Tell him I don't think it's so funny."

I wanted to run out of the courthouse, afraid I might have to act like a human pinball by bouncing from accuser to accuser to deny everything. But I had to dawdle in the hallway until Costello finished his cases. As usual, we headed for an Italian restaurant.

"You know, Jim, there's been some talk about my working for the G," I said as he drove.

"That's just crazy talk," he said. "We all know you."

There was some advantage to my boyish appearance. Just as I didn't look like a fixer, I certainly didn't look or sound like an undercover agent. "Drozd has been mouthing off. Know anything about it?"

"Nah. I heard McCarron went to see Fitz [Chief Judge Richard Fitzgerald] to find out if hustlers were going to get tossed out of the building. That's all."

"Some things aren't funny, you know." Since there is no FBI manual for moles, you've got to wrestle by yourself with each situation. I was shivering in the winter cold, and yet if I had been carrying a recorder under my armpit it would have been wet with perspiration by now.

"McCarron was just testing you, Ter. Hell, you know how it is. At 26th and Cal, you can start a rumor about anybody and it's all over the building before the day is out."

"Maybe we should start a rumor about Drozd and see how he likes it."

I kept telling myself the gossip would die on its own. But by now I knew a real fixer would never wait it out—such suspicion would put him out of business. So I called Drozd at home and told him as nicely as I could that he was being unfair to me as a young lawyer just starting on his own.

"I'm sorry, Terry," he said, "it was a joke. I didn't think people would really believe it."

"Lies are the only thing that people believe around here."

"Hey, it wasn't a lie, I didn't mean it."

I couldn't come down too hard because Drozd was a good cop. He and his partner, Mike Cronin, had made more arrests than anyone else in the gangs unit. Drozd was always joking around in his nonstop talking, even while making arrests, and he often said things just to be amusing without thinking about them.

When I called Megary about the rumor, I said, "You've got to do something right away to make it seem like I'm actively in private practice." It wasn't a request. I was so concerned about what the fixers and the honest court workers were thinking that I was losing touch myself. *They're going to see through it*, I thought.

Just then Alice Carpenter told me by phone that she had been talking to a public defender recently transferred from Traffic Court. Her voice changed when she added that there was a new rumor going around, this one about an FBI investigation in the municipal courts downtown. That could have referred to undercover agent David Victor Ries' work for Greylord. "Do you know anything about it?"

"How would I know anything like that?" I said, and changed the subject.

I couldn't tell whether Alice suspected I might be involved in the investigation, or was trying to warn me that the feds could be looking over my shoulder.

13

WEB OF CORRUPTION

Early Spring 1981

The courtrooms for traffic offenses and city code violations had kept their jerry-rigged look in an aging former warehouse for generations. Here was where most new judges were assigned, their robes and gavels just out of the box. Outside every room was a long line of middle-class and blue-collar workers impatiently waiting for an adjudication.

This was the domain of Chief Traffic Court Judge Richard LeFevour, who had turned many of the courts into schools for corruption and used his policeman cousin as a bagman. How Judge LeFevour accomplished this can be seen in the case of Judge Brian Crowe, a former U.S. Marine hearing drunken driving cases eight months after being sworn in. Officer James LeFevour stopped him as he was carrying his robe, name plate, and law books down the hall. James—called "Jingles" because of all the change he rattled as a nervous habit, and called "Dogbreath" out of earshot—slipped a piece of paper into the reassigned judge's pocket. Crowe thought it might be a phone message, but it turned out to be a one-hundred-dollar bill. "You son of a bitch," Crowe fumed, "don't you *ever* do that again!"

Crowe had just flunked Judge LeFevour's corruption test. From then on, despite all his intelligence and legal acumen, he was assigned to preside only over minor cases. But at the same time, Judge LeFevour was boasting at speaking engagements that his daily rotation of judicial assignments had ended an era of bribery. In reality, the courts were filling up with greedy judges until the high-towered red brick building mirrored LeFevour's contemptuous philosophy that justice was another name for plunder.

Piecing together reports from my work in the criminal courts on the city's West Side and FBI agent David Victor Ries' posing as a fixer in the municipal courts in the large Near North Side Traffic Court Building, the U.S. Attorney's Office was learning that Olson's greed was paltry compared to LeFevour's. The judge, in charge of all city courts, lacked Olson's congeniality and sense of humor but had a genius for administration.

The glacial, gaunt jurist was so pumped up with self-importance that he held a private screening of the 1981 film *Prince of the City* for fellow judges, lawyers, and State's Attorney Daley. At the end of the movie about New York police bribery and corrupt attorneys, LeFevour gave a sanctimonious speech about how dishonesty must be rooted out *if* it was ever found in Chicago.

One of the more chilling aspects of Operation Greylord arose from speculation about LeFevour's political connections from the days of the late mayor Richard J. Daley and Chicago labor leader William Lee. At Lee's insistence, LeFevour was considered a possible candidate for a federal judgeship but Mayor Daley, who wielded national influence, died before an opening became available. If the mayor had lived a little longer, or the opening came a little sooner, LeFevour would have been presiding over the eventual trials of lawyers he now had in his pocket.

Agent Ries by then was calling himself by his middle name, Victor, because of gossip that a "Dave" was trying to collect evidence in the Traffic Court Building, where he was learning that some judges were taking up to two hundred dollars to dismiss cases.

The corrosion didn't stop at bribes. Presiding judge LeFevour found a way to steal from the city as well. Warrant unit policemen Robinson McLain and Art McCauslin helped him pocket thousands of dollars in parking ticket fees that never reached the city revenue department. But McCauslin was upset that LeFevour never cut him in on the cash. "Whatever comes in this office stays in this office," the jurist insisted. "You make yours out there."

In the past, there were occasional ripples of reform. But no more. When magistrates Harry Kleper and Mel Kanter were dismissed for taking money to discharge defendants, they set up lucrative defense practices and made steady payoffs to judges. Then other lawyers wanted to follow their example, including Assistant State's Attorney Joseph McDermott, who crossed over to begin defending drunken drivers.

Kleper, Kanter, and McDermott became known throughout the court system as the "miracle workers" for seldom losing a case in Traffic Court. Traffic Court bribery became so pervasive that one bagman told a new judge, "If you're out there, you're going to make money, especially when we get control of the whole building."

That goal had been reached in January 1981, when Richard LeFevour was named chief judge for the entire First Municipal District, giving him control over more than seventy courtrooms in the misdemeanor branches of the city in addition to civil courts where the damages sought were under fifteen thousand dollars. He now controlled the largest division in the circuit court of Cook County, and this made him possibly the most important corrupt judge in the entire United States.

With his new position, LeFevour moved a few blocks across the river to an office in the modern glass and steel Richard J. Daley Center near city hall. He appointed his first cousin Jimmy as the "court liaison" in charge of misdemeanor courts. In their expanded roles, the two men even found a way to turn a momentary crackdown to their advantage.

A monthly newspaper called the *Chicago Lawyer* featured a lengthy article about hustlers like Kessler and Costello. The information had been gathered by defense attorney Keith Davis, a Lutheran clergyman who had embarked on a private moral crusade. Working with the Better Government Association, Davis showed how certain judges steered clients to fixers in minor branches such as Shoplifting Court. The chief judge of the entire circuit court system, Harry Comerford, told Richard LeFevour that the article was an embarrassment. Judge LeFevour promised to deal with the hustlers. But he did it in his own way by calling in "Dogbreath" and saying, "Jimmy, there is a lot of money out there."

Whether they then worked out strategy together or Jimmy just had an instinct for this sort of thing, the bagman rid all the hallways of hustlers to keep Comerford happy—and to show them what would happen in the future if they didn't start paying off the new head of the First Municipal District. Next Jimmy took a month-long vacation, leaving the attorneys with no conduit for passing bribes to Judge LeFevour. Their law practices suffered from so many guilty verdicts that they had wads of bills for Jimmy when he returned.

Now that bribery controlled the system, three lawyers working in the First Municipal District mapped out their territories. Attorney Edward Nydam, struggling against alcohol and drug problems, would work at

Branch 29 in the police station at Belmont and Western. Fixers Vincent Davino and Lee Barnett would hustle in the Women's, Auto Theft, and Gambling Courts at police headquarters. In return for these franchises, each man paid Judge LeFevour five hundred dollars a month.

Two other hustlers at police headquarters, Peter Kessler and Neal Birnbaum, then notified judges on the take that they should start delivering monthly kickbacks to the chief judge through his bagman cousin, Officer Jimmy "Dogbreath" LeFevour. Since Judge Thaddeus Kowalski was honest, he was booted out of Branch 29 and replaced with one of LeFevour's corrupt judges from Traffic Court, John Murphy. In April, Judge LeFevour collected his first twenty-five-hundred-dollar monthly payment from what was being called "the hustlers' bribery club," and he left six hundred dollars for "Dogbreath" as if throwing him a bone.

And so it was that in just four months, Judge LeFevour had transformed the haphazard bribery of various branches into a systematized network with a portion of every transaction going to him. No wonder Nydam, Davino, Barnett, Birnbaum, and Kessler became the new "miracle workers." Virtually all their cases were decided before trial.

Such was the situation when an outside judge, young Brocton Lockwood, agreed to wear a wire—in one of his cowboy boots. Lockwood was a muscular outdoorsman from Marion County, three hundred and fifty miles to the south. He had first come to the big city because downstate judges must do stretches in Chicago's Traffic Court every few years to ease the backlog. At the time, he didn't even know what a bagman was. Shocked by what he saw on his return visit in 1981, Lockwood called the Justice Department in Washington because he felt he could not trust anyone in Chicago. The FBI saw this as a great opportunity to gather evidence augmenting the limited work their agent David Victor Ries had been able to do as a crooked defense attorney in the same building.

After Lockwood's stint he returned home, but agreed to come back if he could be of any help. Ries flew down to Marion County and they worked out a cover story. The judge, who was in his mid-thirties, would introduce Ries to fixers as a former student at Southern Illinois University. Since setting everything up would take a while, Lockwood volunteered to take the Chicago time owed by all his fellow downstate judges in the district. Since he was recently divorced, he claimed he just liked the singles action in the toddlin' town.

So the judge boarded a train with his little daughter and took an apartment near the Traffic Court Building for an indefinite stay. Although the FBI would use several other moles in Operation Greylord, Lockwood and I were the only ones who gave up our careers for the investigation and remained in the trenches month after month.

By then, FBI agent Lamar Jordan had been transferred from the Chicago office and Bill Megary took over for him. He helped the lean young judge through his early undercover work much as he and Jordan had guided me, including frequent meetings in a parking lot at the lakeshore museum campus. They never told Lockwood about me, but I knew about him. We never met until after the Greylord disclosures made national headlines.

Even though Lockwood raised racehorses back home, he was not the adventure-seeker I was at heart. He was more laidback and admitted that he just might be a century behind the times, which was a good thing for us. Most of Lockwood's family were preachers or teachers. Despite his education, Lockwood was regarded in court circles as a hick because of his Southern Illinois lilt, but he was smarter than most of the shady lawyers appearing before him.

Even so, as an outsider he was unable to record conversations with many of the crooked lawyers and judges. At least he was successful in introducing Ries to a major bagman, gruff policeman Ira Blackwood, and to assistant city attorney Thomas Kangalos, in charge of prosecuting traffic violators. Blackwood had mob friends, and Kangalos was a hyperactive gin drinker who always packed a gun.

Lockwood had to force himself to lie, and he even read spy novels to get in the proper frame of mind. His high school acting training helped him pose as a sometimes boozy womanizer who needed a lot of cash to keep up with his newly single lifestyle. Kangalos, like the devil on a mountaintop, showed the judge all the corruption he could share in. When Kangalos gave him his first bribe, the judge was still afraid that Greylord might backfire and he would wind up in prison, or worse.

Much of what Lockwood, Ries, and I picked up separately had to be painfully pieced together for patterns to emerge. Among the things this showed was that under LeFevour's judge rotation system, corruption could mask as reform because violators were assigned to courtrooms rather than to judges. This is how it worked: Mel Kanter, a miracle worker nicknamed "Candyman" for always carrying hard candy in his pocket, would hand bagman James LeFevour a list of pending cases when they met in the building at eight o'clock each morning. Jimmy then brought the names to his cousin, and Judge LeFevour would assign to those courtrooms one of the jurists who had passed the corruption test. At the end of the day, Kanter thankfully gave Jimmy an envelope containing one hundred and twenty dollars for each case: one hundred for Judge LeFevour and twenty dollars for Jimmy. Everyone was happy.

And yet there was something potentially destructive about the relationship between the cousins, and it went back a generation. Their fathers had been Chicago police brothers who disliked each other so much they didn't speak to one another for four or five years. Jimmy was born first by five years, and his father never rose above patrolman yet knew every bookie downtown. But the future judge's father rose to district commander. When Jimmy's father died, he moved in with Cousin Richard's family and stayed until joining the army.

Jimmy saw action in Korea and joined the Chicago police, but Richard was honorably discharged from the Marines for a boot camp injury. He married the daughter of locally celebrated newsman Buddy McHugh of *The Front Page* era and began his social ascent. McHugh once wrote an article disclosing that Jimmy's dad had been a bagman for a police captain. The socially inferior Jimmy mistook this as a personal insult and seethed ever after.

Richard used his gift for public speaking to work the precincts. The family name was originally French but his forebears came from Ireland, and Richard enjoyed the Irish-American tradition of mingling with politicians. He muscled people to make sizable contributions to the Democratic Party, always making it clear that he was doing it on his own and not on behalf of his family. Reaping what he had sown, Richard was elected a judge.

Once in control of the municipal courts, Judge Richard LeFevour watched over the judges under him with his deep-set eyes and a gaunt look that reminded Judge Lockwood of an archetypical funeral director. The presiding judge's reputation for "vacuum cleaner pockets" did not stop at cash. He arranged to have a steady supply of new Cadillacs by dismissing thousands of parking tickets racked up by the drivers of cars leased from a well-known dealership. In addition, wherever Judge LeFevour went, even to Europe, someone connected to his court paid some of the bills.

Several months after Judge Lockwood entered Greylord, Judge LeFevour extorted one thousand dollars from each of three major lawyers in municipal cases by saying he needed money to pay the medical bills of his mother as she lay dying of cancer. Instead, he pocketed the money for himself. This was in addition to what he was steadily receiving from perhaps ten lawyers in the nation's largest traffic court system, and then a two-thousand-dollar "Christmas bonus" from each of them.

Richard basked in the power he derived from his feudal rearrangement of the courts. One day when Lockwood was in the outer office, a black woman stormed into the older judge's office and complained that "there's a clerk in Room 12 who is prejudiced and a bigot."

LeFevour snarled, "And so am I. Now get the hell out!"

Yet Judge LeFevour had a gift for covering his greed, bigotry, and mean-spiritedness with an appearance of civic concern. The hoodwinked American Bar Association even presented him with an award for running the best traffic court in the country.

LeFevour, his wife Ginger, and their six sons lived in a red-shingled home in suburban Oak Park, where they often threw lavish parties. People found him charming, erudite, and witty. One of his stories was of a defendant who told a judge, "Your Honor, may the Lord strike me down if I had more than just two beers." Suddenly there was a power failure and the man shouted, "Five beers, Your Honor. Five beers!"

In contrast, Cousin Jimmy's career was stagnating. Jimmy often exuded alcohol at work and didn't always change clothes, even though he bought new cars and kept condominiums in Chicago and Florida. His wife left him and he was hospitalized seven times over fourteen years because of alcoholism. "Dogbreath" could thank his cousin for not having to live out the rest of his life in a squad car on the midnight shift, but he still resented being nothing more than Richard's messenger boy and picking up bribes for him as if he were cleaning out a stable. Silently, day after day, Jimmy was gathering all the actual and imagined injustices against him by his high-handed cousin. The day of reckoning was coming.

Judge Richard LeFevour may have been pleased that he loomed over Jimmy in more than just physical stature. But, for all this, Jimmy the bagman had a better grip on reality. The short, stocky man never pretended to be anything more than an insignificant, crooked cop. As with his father, the money he skimmed made up for his lack of esteem.

Clever as Richard LeFevour was, the judge alternated between two illusions. At times he seemed to believe his own respectable public image, and at other times he deluded himself into thinking he was untouchable.

Another of the presiding judge's bagmen was policeman Ira Blackwood, a one-time professional boxer who stayed in shape at age fifty. Lockwood found in Ira the same kind of endearing openness that I found in Jim Costello. Ira had relatives and friends in the Mafia but said he became a cop because the opportunities for money were better. As he explained, it was costing him fifteen thousand dollars a year just to send his children to private schools. One day he and Judge Lockwood left a Cubs game at Wrigley Field during the fifth inning because Blackwood wanted to stop by a bar and "pay the rent"—that is, deliver a bribe to a judge.

Judge Lockwood helped undercover agent David Victor Ries deliver five payoffs through Blackwood, but it was telling on the downstate judge. The already slender Lockwood lost twenty pounds and his hair started turning prematurely white. Like me, he had to do a lot more drinking than he wanted just to stay friends with the fixers. He also was concerned for his personal safety. Although he didn't think fixers or mobsters would harm his three-year-old daughter, Jessica, the child's presence heightened his concern about what would happen if someone retaliated. As Lockwood reports in *Operation Greylord: Brockton Lockwood's Story*, he dreamed of himself floating dead in the river.

Some of the cases the FBI arranged to come before Lockwood were hilarious. An agent posing as a drunk was being taken to the station when the officers got another call. They simply dumped him at a dark corner and drove off. But most of the cookie-cutter agents doing undercover work at the time didn't have the freewheeling nature needed to get arrested that squad member Ken Misner showed. Misner tried to drive wildly through the Loop in December. A fellow agent called the police to report an intoxicated driver, but no one felt like arresting him. So Misner kept going down State Street lanes reserved for buses and cabs. Only when he went the wrong way down one-way streets did a policeman finally pull him over. "The party's over," the officer said.

Misner jumped out in a pretended outburst and hopped onto the hood of the squad car. "You can't talk to me, you ignorant pig!" he slurred.

The backup agent watching from a distance was afraid Misner had gone too far, since Chicago police were known to crack heads. Instead, this officer grabbed Misner by the tie and said, "Okay, buddy, I gave you a break and wrote you for disorderly conduct. The ticket is written for December 24th in the afternoon. The judge won't show up, so they'll throw out the ticket. Now go home and sleep this off."

To make it look more as if Lockwood were making money "hand over fix," the Bureau moved him into a Gold Coast apartment over-looking Lake Michigan. Then his contact agent brought him a confis-cated but unclaimed television set for his sparse rented furnishings. The Bureau went so far as to supply him with a "girlfriend," attractive FBI agent Marie Dyson, who at times would also work with me in fabri-cated crimes.

The FBI even wired Lockwood's car in hopes of catching incrimi-nating conversations with fixers he sometimes drove around. But Lock-wood's position as a judge limited what he could do, and he was unable to get much information on anyone beyond Kangalos, Blackwood, and Judge LeFevour. Even so, the conversations he recorded contributed to our knowledge of all our other targets. They also helped us form a ring around lesser crooks who might be persuaded to "flip" and take the stand for the government.

In time Lockwood retired as a judge and set up a private practice, but Ries and I were still in place in separate courthouses, waking up every morning—and sometimes in the middle of the night—dreading what the next day would bring. No one was exactly saying so, but we were aware that from now on, every step we took would make the entire investigation that much more unstable.

14

BRANCHING OUT

Summer 1981

JUDGE JOHN DEVINE

One of the hardest aspects of my undercover work was timing. I had to find a spot in the Traffic Court Building where I could see witnesses, defendants, and lawyers coming and going without appearing to be watching, and then pretend to come across a target coincidentally. When I "bumped" into bagman Harold Conn, I was representing an undercover FBI agent who had posed as a drunken driver named James Cramer. He had made sure there would be no way of getting off lightly before a judge with integrity. During his arrest, he dropped his wallet, almost staggered over an expressway guardrail to grab it, and then refused to take a Breathalyzer test.

Conn told me I was lucky because a certain judge would be handling my case. "He's a nice young fellah," Conn said, "I'll speak to him." That meant he was offering to pass on a bribe. But the person who should have been handling the case didn't return after the lunch recess. Instead, Judge John "Dollars" Devine came over from another courtroom. I wasn't disappointed, since taking a second bribe after another drunken driving case the month before, involving an undercover agent going by the name of Benson, would qualify as racketeering.

Devine should have sentenced "Cramer" to a year in jail and revoked his license. But the fix was in, and "Dollars" just fined him one hundred dollars and placed him on court supervision. This meant I needed to confirm that Conn had informed him I needed a lenient ruling.

I found the judge having a cigarette in the hallway behind the courtroom. He didn't say a word when I thanked him, so I had to do something every mole dreads: asking blatantly stupid questions in hopes the response would be incriminating. I started by inquiring whether I should see Conn to express my gratitude.

"Yeah," the judge muttered and walked away from me, as if saying that he had already shown me how the system works.

A few minutes later I gave the bagman two hundred dollars for the judge and sixty for himself. "That was beautiful," I told Conn about the way Devine had swooped into the other judge's courtroom to set up the fix. Conn just shrugged me off. Things like that happened all the time in that building.

But, I wondered, when would I ever get to record Devine taking a bribe from my hand? The answer turned out to be in seventeen months! So, jumping ahead, the "James Cramer" case came up again in February 1983. This time my "client" was appearing for the termination of his court supervision, which he had intentionally violated by speeding. Since Devine was not around for a hearing, I had to tell two other judges offering to lift the supervision that there were special circumstances requiring that Devine hear the case personally.

So much time had elapsed that we could no longer use the original undercover agent because he had been appearing in federal court under his real name to testify against a policeman. A substitute agent brought in from Los Angeles perfectly matched the first "Cramer," from age and hair color down to his weight. Our source with the Illinois Secretary of State's Office then supplied us with a driver's license using a photo of the Los Angeles agent.

Not noticing the switch, Devine granted my request to vacate the supervision despite the speeding violation. Something in the judge's tone and expression told me *This is it*, the one time he was going to overlook his caution and deal with me directly.

Unable to follow Devine out of court because of a bailiff sitting on a rail, I went out a door used by the general public and hurried through the corridor to catch him before he could leave for lunch. I found Devine lighting a cigarette, as he often did to stave off his need for a drink.

Trying to sound casual, I said, "Well, judge, I did okay on this case. I made two fees on it. Listen, I can be fair with you, too. I'm willing to—"

"Whatever you want."

"Good," I said as my Nagra reels turned. "Is one [one hundred dollars] okay?"

"Yeah, sure."

With a one-hundred-dollar bill in my palm, we shook hands and he shoved the bribe into his pants pocket under his black robe.

"Thank you very much," I said, while thinking, *You greedy bastard.* I felt great.

Autumn 1981

While Ries and I were wearing wires in Traffic Court, the FBI had put a tap on phones in the warrant section of the building. The Bureau then began making a list of what eventually amounted to more than one hundred officers who would be subpoenaed for information about rigged cases. But the "Title III" (wiretapping) authorization didn't provide much we could use. Unknown to us, a phone company friend of bagman Ira Blackwood had alerted him about the tap. This might have given everything away, except that Traffic Court workers were so used to occasional investigations that they did not take it seriously.

The last thing we needed was a news leak. In early September, investigative TV reporter Peter Karl on his own began looking into corruption that was almost inevitable in a system that handled three-and-a-half-million parking tickets and eight hundred and fifty thousand moving violation citations a year. Almost immediately, Judge LeFevour called a meeting with his former deputy, John McCollum, now chief judge of Traffic Court; bagman Officer Ira Blackwood; and the city lawyer supervising Traffic Court prosecutors, *Carmine Lino, identified in later testimony as downtown politicians' facilitator in the building. "Flatten the building for sixty days," Judge LeFevour commanded. That meant shut the bribe factory down until this blew over. It worked.

Peter Karl's report showed court inefficiency and some suspicious transactions, but he could not pinpoint any criminal conduct. That is, until a physical therapist named Lauren Sacks called him to complain that she had paid two hundred and twenty dollars to police warrant officer Art McCauslin to have eleven parking tickets dismissed, yet she was still served with a warrant.

Usually motorists hid the bribe money in a magazine when handing it to McCauslin or his partner, Officer Robinson McClain, but this time McCauslin neglected to give Sacks any instructions. Sacks thought the arrangement of settling tickets by paying half the amount was legal, so she wrote out a check. Because McCauslin received the check as he was going on vacation, he cashed it at a bar and forgot to dismiss her tickets.

This sent Peter Karl digging deeper. For several days, Judge McCollum and the city attorney at Traffic Court discussed how to stop the TV reporter from getting too close. McCollum, a judge for ten years, was no mere underling. He had once yelled at an attorney, "I don't give a fuck about you, I don't give a fuck if you're in the middle. I want the fucking money, and you're going to give it to me!"

Karl was told the records were protected by privacy laws, but he knew better. He uncovered the paperwork showing how the Sacks check was cashed by Officer McCauslin rather than by the city. But paper records of all "non-suited" (dismissed) tickets under presiding Judge LeFevour had been carried out of the courthouse and destroyed. Although the television station hired a prestigious law firm to go after microfilmed copies in the county clerk's office, Richard LeFevour and the others weren't afraid. As Blackwood told Judge Lockwood about the firm chosen, "We get along good with those guys. They won't push too hard."

Karl and his two-man crew were able to get Officer McCauslin making damaging statements on camera, and he became so scared he was no longer sleeping. The FBI decided to take advantage of this and move in even though Greylord was still running. Federal agents, working with the police internal affairs division, persuaded McCauslin to wear a hidden microphone before talking to Judge LeFevour about his suspicions, making the officer the government's first target to switch sides in a deal with prosecutors.

But before long, bagman Jimmy LeFevour went to his cousin and said, "The rumor is that McCauslin is wired."

"Kill him," the judge said, according to later testimony.

"Not me," Jimmy replied.

"Get somebody to do it."

"You're crazy, I'm not going to do something like that," he told the judge. "We ought to shut down again."

"It's just a witch hunt," Judge LeFevour said. "It doesn't concern the club." He meant the hustlers' bribery club. Brilliant as he may have been, the judge couldn't resolve his dual thinking—that McCauslin should be stopped, and that the probe was unimportant.

The "Citizen Moles"

In addition to the day-in, day-out work Agent Ries and I were doing, the Justice Department in 1981 and 1982 was able to have several ordinary citizens gather information for Greylord, for one reason or another.

Wealthy lamp manufacturer Leo Zutler was persuaded to wear a recorder against Deputy Sheriff Alan Kaye, who had been demanding payments for favors in arranging the businessman's divorce. Kaye, who usually carried a gun, even threatened to burn Zutler's factory down unless he came up with the cash. While wearing a body mike, Zutler handed over payment in installments totaling ten thousand dollars.

Another single-target mole was attractive *Lucy Durkin, who at sixteen began a relationship in 1982 with the fifty-year-old Judge Frank Salerno. Salerno, it must be said, was a square-jawed, forceful-looking man who could pass for forty. Lucy met him while working as a cocktail waitress in a suburban strip joint. The judge soon used his influence to get a driver's license showing her age as twenty-one so she could work as a waitress and be his "bagman" at a downtown restaurant where he lunched daily.

Strangers sometimes gave her envelopes of cash for the judge. In telephone calls, some fixers used the code of "G for God" in referring to Salerno. Over the next three years, Lucy also passed on money to the judge's regular bagman, Victor Albanese. She hardly realized how criminal her acts were until the FBI showed her surveillance photos. In one snapshot, Lucy, Salerno, and Albanese are sitting at a restaurant table with a stack of one-hundred-dollar bills before them.

Some of the conversations the teenage waitress recorded for the FBI were embarrassingly personal, such as when the judge begged her to sleep with him. After all, he had showered thousands of dollars on her and gave her a fur coat every Christmas, even if he had bought it at a thieves' discount. But Lucy vowed not to have sex with him, and for a good reason—she was wearing a tape recorder.

Salerno eventually pleaded guilty to extortion and was sentenced to nine years in prison, and Albanese received eight years. As for Lucy, she is now living somewhere under another identity for her own safety.

Early Winter 1981

The rumor about my being a mole refused to go away even though I seldom showed up at the courts and supposedly had been in private practice for three months. I was eager to get back into action, but red tape blocked the way. There I was, with no office and no clients. At least some money was coming in. When I left the State's Attorney's Office, the FBI arranged to hire me as a "project development specialist." I've been told I was the only such person in the history of the Bureau.

During my period in limbo, Mark phoned me at home and said, "We haven't seen you around, where have you been? Have you been to Quantico?"

Was he testing me, or was it a joke? "What do you mean?" I asked.

"Silverman heard a rumor that you're working for the FBI, and he's paranoid."

"Hey, that's not true. I've been doing work for my uncle's business."

I reminded him that the policeman who had started that talk was only trying to be funny, and that I wished everyone would just lay it to rest. "Let's meet in person," I said, "and if you want we can discuss it some more." We then set up a meeting at a restaurant.

As a way of making it appear as if everything were normal, I brought Cathy with me, since Mark was bringing his fiancée, a cute brunette also named Cathy. Although she intended to work in the prosecutor's office and never wanted to become part of my undercover work, Cathy behaved that night as if she enjoyed Mark's company. I also had invited someone from my college days at the Rome campus of Loyola University, Peggy O'Hara, a nurse living in Los Angeles who happened to be in town. I hoped that having someone unconnected to the courts would reduce the shoptalk.

We should have been carefree, but both Mark and I were decidedly uncomfortable behind our facades. He was trying to appear honest, and I was trying to appear like someone who is dishonest but is attempting to appear straight.

To make sure I understood the undercurrent in his side of the conversation, Mark mentioned the hit film *Prince of the City*, from the book about New York City policeman Robert Leuci. Looking directly at me, and with our girlfriends beside us, he said, "Know what I think, Terry? I think that policeman who turned on his friends to become a stoolie was a rat. What do you think?"

How could I back out of this? Mark had known me when I was a guileless idealist, and I had to suggest that some trace of that lingered in me, such as I had found in some real fixers. "Sure, Mark," I said, "but don't you have to respect the guy for doing what he thought was right?"

"No, Terry, turning on your friends is never right." His eyes were cold.

Having made his point, Mark went on to other subjects as if nothing had happened.

I talked to my supervisors about how close I was coming to being found out. As Mark said, Bob Silverman was getting "paranoid," and Mark had practically accused me of being a mole.

Since I needed a law office as a business address, Far West Side suburban attorney Jim Reichardt agreed to list me as a partner, although the government did not explain why I needed a fake business address. At least I now had a dummy office to cover for my real work of organizing undercover agents to pose as crooks and victims so that I might fix cases. When I told Mark about my new office, he lent me two chairs.

The next step was finding a cover for what I would be doing. Reidy and others came up with the idea of establishing a company called, for reasons unknown, Independent Material Systems, Inc. The FBI rented a South Loop office and had incorporation papers list me as the corporate counsel. But the company existed only on a run of stationery and business cards, and no one bothered to figure out what kind of firm it was.

Perhaps this put Mark's mind a little more at ease. He invited me to his wedding the next month. During the sermon, the priest spoke about the promising future for the young couple. It was eerie knowing that I could tell what the future would likely hold for Mark: the end of his career, selling off everything to pay his fines, probably prison, and then—what? What happens to lawyers who have disgraced their profession? They just go off and disappear.

In December 1981 I was rigging a fake shoplifting case through bagman Harold Conn when I noticed Bob Silverman in the hallway. I had not seen him for months and felt I needed to renew our acquaintance. In a sudden decision, I was determined to bury that rumor about me.

"Hi, Bob, how are you?" I began.

"Fine. How are you feeling? All right, I hope."

"Good, real good."

"Glad to hear that, Terry." Silverman's mind seemed elsewhere, or maybe he really didn't want to talk to me. Did he suspect I was wired?

"If you got a moment," I said, "I want to tell you up front that what you might have heard isn't true—me being a mole for the FBI. Isn't that stupid?"

"I knew it wasn't true when I heard it," Silverman said, not convincingly. What choice did he have? It was too late for him and his mob connections to change. He had to believe that I was slime so that he could rest at night.

"I just wanted you to hear it from my own mouth," I said.

"I couldn't fuckin' believe it," he told me. "I had a long talk with Frankie Cardoni and decided it was absolutely impossible. I wouldn't be here talking to you if I thought different."

"Okay, Bob. I just wanted to get it straight. Have a good holiday."

"Same to you," he said as I turned away.

15

OUR CRIME ACADEMY

Winter 1981–1982

Jim Costello was watching his life fall apart. All our conversations that fall had included discussions about his daughter's boyfriend and his wife's drinking, as if Jim were a teetotaler. Jim wanted me to hang around with him so he could feel like a wise and kindly mentor again. We had gone to the track for thoroughbred racing in August and October, then to the enclosed stands for harness racing in mid-December. Costello fancied himself a gambler and didn't like seeing me in the two-dollar line. "You're a lawyer, for Christ's sake," he said, "go to the ten-dollar window. Here's something to get you started." Jim handed me a fifty-dollar bill.

I would study the racing form for information on the horses and jockeys, but Costello relied on divine inspiration. At the sound of "Here they come spilling out of the turn," he would jump in excitement, yet he never expected to do better than break even.

Between races Jim reeled off more corruption stories, such as the bribes Jimmy LeFevour delivered to Judge Allen Rosin, "the biggest kink [greediest judge] in the system." Rosin was an arrogant man given to depression and sometimes bizarre behavior. The Korean War veteran and former policeman once bolted from the bench, spread out his arms in his black robe, and proclaimed "I am God!" Then he looked at the shocked court reporter, asked "Did I say that?," and had the remark stricken from the record.

Costello also named half a dozen other judges on the take, and said bribes could be in almost any form. He explained that when Silverman was representing three prostitutes, he offered an ASA a date with one if he would throw out the case. The prosecutor said no, but the women were acquitted anyway. Maybe the judge was given a sample of their innocence.

Actually, bribes in the form of services rendered were more common than I had imagined early in my double role. A veteran officer claimed that once when the elevator doors opened in police headquarters, where "whore court" was located, he saw a woman performing a sex act on a judge. It was also said that judges sometimes demanded sex from the female junkies haled into the court bullpen to await a hearing.

Because Costello was forcing me to go to the ten-dollar window at the racetrack and I personally was only a two-dollar bettor, I believed the FBI should pay the eight dollars remaining. I had used this system on a couple of other outings and, in all, the Bureau lost about sixty dollars.

One evening I was really lucky, picking five out of the six races we stayed for. Since I was no longer handing over all my Greylord-related cash directly to my contact agent, I called the FBI the next day and deposited the winnings in a bank account. With these and some side bets I had made, I calculated that I had won a hundred and fifty dollars for myself and two hundred and thirty-seven dollars for the U.S. Treasury. A couple of days later, the assistant special agent in charge of the Chicago office told me, "What the hell did you tell anybody about it for, you could have kept all the winnings!"

Also in mid-December, Costello told Martha their marriage was through, which was no surprise. By waiting until his daughter turned eighteen before filing for divorce, he didn't have to pay child support. He packed all of Martha's clothes into his new Oldsmobile and drove her to a Sheraton Hotel in the suburbs, then he asked me to represent him in his divorce. He was all set to hand five hundred dollars to a courthouse bagman so he could keep the house and pay minimal alimony. When the bagman informed him that the judge assigned never took bribes, Costello exclaimed, "What the hell! The judge hears cases worth millions and he don't take advantage of it? That guy is stupid."

The case might have dragged on for years except for Costello's crudeness. To make sure he kept the house, he stormed into Martha's hotel room and shoved an agreement in her face. She put her name to it, in what he told me was an alcoholic stupor, in return for seven hundred dollars a month alimony for three years. Thinking over what he had done, he went back and gave a court secretary two dollars to change the figure to six hundred dollars.

At the time, I was conducting a sort of crime academy for FBI agents, which I had begun in my first couple of months as a defense attorney. After months of waiting, we had been denied permission to pass around bribes in real cases, since that might bring criticism of the Justice Department. So we decided to fabricate crimes, and at last I was having a little fun out of being undercover.

We had started out small because we didn't have much of a budget, and because breaking the law was still something new to all of us. At first some Chicago agents were involved, but we stopped this when one of them was recognized by a policeman walking out of the Auto Theft Court bullpen. Fortunately, the officer didn't realize the agent was now working undercover.

The risk of that happening again was just too great, so we had the Bureau send us agents from all over the country. This meant renting five apartments in the Chicago area to provide them with local addresses for receiving bond papers and notices for court appearances. We also had to be ready if the police went to the homes for any reason, but that never happened. The plushest apartment we used was in the Gold Coast. But the agents never actually lived in any of these residences, and the cast of characters kept changing because some of our men and women were needed in other cities.

The agents and I would meet at the offices of the fictional Independent Material Systems Company at 410 South Michigan Avenue, across from Grant Park, or in the apartment the FBI had leased for Judge Lockwood before he returned to southern Illinois. Originally we would have up to fifteen agents per meeting, making planning virtually impossible because they kept offering ideas or opinions. Even a simple set-up such as imagining two guys in a traffic dispute seemed to take forever to work out between the "Suppose . . ." and the "Okay, let's do it."

Everything went faster when we decided to reduce the number of agents at tactical sessions to four. Every Friday we would have a pop and beer informal meeting largely to boost the morale of the agents working undercover. Any plan for a contrived case was submitted for approval to one of the Assistant U.S. Attorneys working with us. In all, each crime we put together took about fifty man-hours to prepare. This included arranging identification, setting up phones in the apartments, and making sure the out-of-town agent who would be playing the criminal was familiar with his assumed identity, so the Chicago officers wouldn't be dubious.

As the supervisor of the entire project, Assistant U.S. Attorney Dan Reidy set ground rules for the agents to stay out of Cook County Jail. Not only were conditions there wretched, any FBI agent locked up would be in physical danger. For that reason we had to stage crimes so that the arrested agents would be able to make bond and avoid being sent to the jail. We also did not want the police arriving with guns drawn, and that meant no burglaries.

JUDGE P.J. MCCORMICK

The first of the nearly one hundred cases we concocted was designed to bring us before "P.J." McCormick, the self-glorifying judge who reportedly had threatened a motorist with a gun he later said was a cigar. I had been apprehensive about bribing him because I had prosecuted cases before him for four months before joining Greylord, and he knew the idealistic way I had been.

At a bench trial in misdemeanor court, many shysters would demand a jury trial for their guilty clients, just to remove them from honest judges. When the cases came up before McCormick, who sat in the misdemeanor jury courtroom for the entire city of Chicago, the lawyers would drop their demand for a jury trial and let P.J. decide the case. The beautiful system ran smoothly. Fixers routinely dropped money into his desk drawer, handed over cash in a Traffic Court hallway, and one once made a payoff in the steam room of the posh Illinois Athletic Club.

In one of our devised cases FBI agent Timothy Murphy, carrying identification giving his name as "Timothy Best," walked into a hardware store and stuffed tools into his pockets and under his belt. Agent Jack Thorpe, posing as a customer, reported this outrage to a security guard as "Best" tried to waddle out with a retractable measuring tape, wire cutters, long-nose pliers, and electric staple gun. The guard pounced on him outside and led him to the security office.

It took an hour before two officers arrived to bring "Mr. Best" to a police station in a dilapidated former Boys Club. Murphy managed to fall asleep in the lockup that evening but awoke half an hour later as a roach crawled across his face. The FBI headquarters in Quantico had trained agents for handling terrorists but not for spending a day behind bars. After seven hours in the cell, Murphy was released on a one-hundred-dollar cash bond. He then wrote a memo recommending that in the future all agents be sent only to sanitary, modern jails and that part of their standard equipment be a candy bar to relieve the hunger and chewing gum to ease the boredom.

I went to Judge P.J. McCormick in his chambers and pretended to be worried about him. "My client's giving me a good fee," I said, "but I don't have much of a case."

"I don't know," P.J. told me. I could almost see his mind working. "I'm thinking your man just put the tools in his pockets and forgot to pay for them."

The store guard never showed up in court, freeing the judge's hand. Even though the case had never been continued, McCormick pretended that this was the third time it had come before him. Faking impatience, P.J. dismissed the case and entered his private room without a hint that he wanted to be paid off. This left Murphy confused, and I myself didn't know what to make of it.

I entered McCormick's chambers and said, "Thank you very much, Judge."

"Okay, Terry."

"If there's anything I can ever do for you, let me know."

"Yes, you can," he said. "When I run for retention, I want you to take a one-hundred-dollar bill and buy stamps and postcards, and write to all your personal friends in the suburbs, telling them to vote for me. With your personal signature. A letter, that's all."

This wasn't anything that could be used as evidence against P.J. But as I talked it over with Costello a few days later, "Big Bird" sat there admiring what may have been the judge's shrewdness. "Know what he really said to you, Terry? He's telling you the first one is free, but the next one will cost you a hundred."

But there was to be no next time. Corrupt as McCormick was, I received the impression that he had heard the rumor about my being a mole and still believed it, and decided to stay clear of me. Although we did not capture him taking bribes on tape, the Internal Revenue Service was gathering evidence against him.

This was a new phase of the operation, which had been authorized when the interconnected evidence from various aspects of Greylord started showing that we were really onto something. Top IRS agent Dennis Czurylo worked closely with the FBI in tracing the sometimes tangled avenues of bribe money. It was only fitting that the expenditure tactic the federal government had developed to bring down the Capone gang in the 1930s was now being used half a century later in the same city to attack black-robed racketeers.

The IRS would analyze all expenditures a judge made and might discover that he was spending one hundred thousand dollars a year above his judicial income. At trial, the Assistant U.S. Attorney would point out that all such unexplained cash showed that the source had to be bribes.

Slowly the government learned how P.J. could avoid leaving a trace. He used his payoffs to purchase money orders at two Loop banks. Sometimes he would wait in separate lines to buy them from three different tellers to avoid suspicion over the amounts. Czurylo's people studied hundreds of these money orders or, as prosecutors would tell a jury in typical opening-argument rhetoric, "millions" of them. They learned that in three years P.J. spent nearly forty thousand dollars for which there was no legal source, and that he had bought one hundred and forty thousand dollars in relatively small money orders over two and a half years. The judge was eventually convicted and sentenced to six years in prison on tax fraud and extortion charges.

16

ALL HELL BREAKS LOOSE

January-March 1982

JUDGE JOHN MURPHY and THE TRUNZO BROTHERS

For some time we had felt secure enough to choose our targets rather than relying on contacts and circumstances. In early 1982 undercover agent David Victor Ries and I decided that it was time to begin moving in on Judge John Murphy, and that meant bagging his bagmen, the Trunzo brothers.

The portly judge, with thinning white hair and a ruddy face, lived at the exclusive Illinois Athletic Club downtown and loved the convenience of walking just a mile and a half to work in the Traffic Court Building, which has since been converted into commercial ventures. He became unhappy the year before, when Judge Richard LeFevour assigned him to Branch 29 in the mid-North Side Belmont Avenue police station. Each morning Murphy would grumpily look out over a court call of short-tempered people who had been involved tavern brawls or back-fence disputes. Legal skills were not required, because it was often impossible to determine who was at fault. Not only that, pickings were slim since most defendants were too poor to post bond.

Murphy's bagmen were policeman Ira Blackwood, the would-be mentor of Judge Lockwood, and identical-twin police officers Joe and James Trunzo. The two six-foot brothers were equally crooked and looked so much alike that even their gray toupees matched. Once after I left Murphy's courtroom I realized that I wasn't sure whether I had spoken to Joe or Jim. Not wanting to blow our case against them, I went back and asked the officer again about the time we should meet, giving me a chance to check his star number and learn he was Joe. In time

I noticed that Jim's paunch hung over his belt a trifle more than Joe's, so I didn't need to read their stars any more.

In late January 1982, Ries had been handling the case of two undercover agents who had staged a fight in Lincoln Park over a dropped wallet. This time my contact agent Bill Megary played the villain. At the same time, I was representing another undercover agent in a manufactured case involving a scuffle between supposed business partners. Meeting Mark in the hallway outside the courtrooms of Reynolds and Murphy, I offhandedly mentioned that I had just settled the arrest with Joe Trunzo.

"You should have used me instead, then you would know where the money went." Mark meant that he would be sure to pass the bribe on to the judge, for a share, rather than pocketing all of it.

As usual, he was right. The Trunzos seemed to enjoy working little scams among the fixers. I walked into Murphy's small chambers and found him reading a newspaper. "What can I do for you?" the relaxed judge asked as he motioned to a chair near his desk.

Nervous as always at the first meeting with a targeted judge, I said that I believed the Trunzos "talked to you about a battery case I'm handling."

"They didn't, but it doesn't make any difference."

"I sure could use a not-guilty. These guys owned a business, and three of them met to divide the assets. They got into an argument and my guy allegedly slammed the car door on the victim. It's nothing. The summons was filed two months later."

"Two months later?" That made Murphy's eyes light up. Now he had a peg to hang an acquittal on. "That means the victim filed against your guy out of spite. I'll throw the fucking case out the window."

"Okay. I'll go see Joe, then," I said, meaning that I would hand the bribe over to the slightly less heavy brother.

Murphy remarked that this would be fine, bringing himself into the bribery circle. Not only that, by talking to Joe Trunzo about the judge, and to the judge about Joe, I was establishing for our evidence that both men were involved in the fix.

Murphy tossed the case out as he said he would, but as yet no money had changed hands. I drove a few miles to Traffic Court and met Joe Trunzo on the second floor. He brought me to an empty stairwell and asked what was up.

"I talked to the judge and got an N.G. [not guilty], so I'd like to settle up with you."

Joe was silent at first but I could see he was upset because, as I had suspected, he had not called the judge at all. He had been hoping to keep all the money. "He don't wanna know nothing," Trunzo said. "He's a cool guy. He don't wanna know shit from shit. Don't bother him." In other words, don't fix a case directly, always go through a bagman.

"Okay, I screwed up, then." I always hated acting as if I were groveling before people I loathed. "I got another case Monday but my guy hasn't paid me yet, so I might just get a continuance. Hey, what do I owe you for Murphy?"

"You owe him a deuce [two hundred dollars]. Me, we'll see." He was still sizing me up.

I counted the cash on the stairs to make the bills rustle on the tape. "Twenty, forty, sixty, eighty; there's one. Okay, there's two [hundred] for Murphy. Now, is a hundred fair for you and Jim?" It was, in fact, more than the going rate.

"Good enough," Joe replied, almost salivating, "good enough."

Rather than waste an opportunity for branching out, I said casually, "Say, Joe, do you have any connections down at 11th and State?" That was police headquarters. "I got a case in front of Sodini."

"Fuckin' yes," Joe said, "he's my buddy. I was with him the other day. We were at a funeral together."

"Can you talk to him about me?"

"No problem."

Translation: tell Judge Ray Sodini that I bribe well.

I still had to firm up that bribe to Judge Murphy. So on Monday, three days after meeting with him, I visited his chambers about another case we had rigged and said I "kind of screwed up" in going to him directly rather than letting one of the Trunzo bagmen handle it. Murphy told me not to worry.

"Am I all set with you, then?" I asked.

"As far as I know. I haven't been back to Traffic Court in a while. I'm due over there Wednesday for something, so I'll probably see him."

As testimony would show, Officer Joe Trunzo caught up with the judge and slipped him the two hundred dollars in a handshake at a revolving door. Passersby apparently never noticed.

By now the FBI had authorized a lease on a brand new, white Pontiac 6000 so I could start looking more like a fixer. I felt a little sad at selling my old car, but the new comfort was worth it. Undercover agent Ries, who was already leasing a new Toronado to look crooked, was so envious he switched to a Pontiac Firebird with all the extras.

Things were going so well that I became a little too self-assured. Unconsciously I was assuming that everyone in the courts would discuss fixing cases even without an introduction by a bagman. So on a snowy morning in March, I appeared in Judge Arthur Ellis' chambers after Jim Trunzo assured me that he had made arrangements to rig the verdict. I told the judge my client was coming before him and mentioned our mutual friends, the identical cops.

Then the judge's private line rang, and the clerk called out that Joe Trunzo was on the line. The judge picked up the phone and said, "Yes, Joe. Right, Joe. Good to hear from you. Say hello to your twin."

When the judge hung up, I told him that "if an N.G. costs more, I'm willing to pay."

"What do you mean," Ellis erupted. "I ain't—don't go giving any-body any money up here! Are you nuts?"

"I'm a friend of Joe and Jim's," I said in a faltering tone while wish-ing I could crawl out of the chambers. "They said to maybe say hi to you this morning and see how you're doing."

"I don't take a quarter," the judge said. "When I was practicing law, that was something else. Up here, I'm as clean as can be. All these guys coming in and offering me money . . . Man, for what? You want me to go to prison? I'm telling you, Mr. Hake, 'cause I don't want you to get in bad with any other judges. If you want to buy those Trunzo guys supper for doing you a favor, fine, but don't go giving nobody money."

How could this be happening? Everything I knew from Ries and what I had been able to pick up was that this judge had at least three bagmen working for him. Was my information wrong—or was there some reason he could not trust me? At the end of his fifteen-minute tirade I thanked him and left his chambers both embarrassed and angry.

The seemingly outraged judge continued my case, and I drove to Traffic Court to cover myself with the Trunzos. I wanted them to hear my version of what happened first. But the judge, who had yelled about his honesty, had beat me to it by alerting Joe with a call as soon as I left his office. I know this because when I arrived, Joe told me that the judge was "fuckin' mad."

"Don't ever approach that judge, Hake. If someone spots you talkin' to him, it's all over. You don't know who's around."

The judge was never charged and has since died. As for whether what he had told me about his integrity was true, why didn't he report my flagrant attempt to bribe him? When authorities asked him about it later, he said it was because he didn't know my full name. What a lie. Years after Greylord was disclosed, the conversation I had in that judge's courtroom was entered into the evidence in the trial of former Traffic Court policeman Ira Blackwood. But for once, the tape was submitted by the defense rather than the prosecution. Blackwood's attorney wanted to prove that court workers who received bribes did not always pass the money on to judges. But the jury was unimpressed, and Blackwood was sentenced to seven years for racketeering, bribery, and extortion.

Spring 1982

The intricate Greylord tax investigations would have made our part seem simple, but we never knew what was going to happen. For example, while undercover agent Brett Fox was kept in a cell for twenty-six hours for a staged crime, another prisoner described to him how he had tried to kill a man. And an agent who spent a night in a lockup saw officers brutalize one of his two dozen cellmates for refusing to budge when the police van arrived to take him to court.

One of the federal agents I was representing forgot his fake address under questioning by a probation officer at a pre-trial interview conducted in an otherwise empty courtroom before Judge Maurice Pompey. Having a better memory, I was able to correct his mistake before the probation officer caught on. Something like that might have panicked me at the beginning, but now it was part of the adventure.

Expanding Greylord like this required a lot of money. In just the seven months from late 1981 to the next spring, the project cost the taxpayers more than one hundred thousand dollars, largely for apartments, bonds, leasing cars, and payoffs. When our wish for more funding came through, we were allowed to rent a warehouse in west suburban Addison as our permanent headquarters. But we needed the name of a dummy corporation for the lease.

Although the Bureau was always careful not to choose names that sounded too much like what an operation was designed for, one of our agents with a sense of humor called the bogus business Rico Enterprises. RICO also stands for the Racketeering Influenced and Corrupt Organizations Act, the 1970 law that is one of the most effective federal prosecution weapons. All that is needed for a RICO conviction is to show that two or more violations were committed in a pattern, and the sentence could include substantial fines, asset forfeiture, and up to twenty years in prison. By raising the stakes, RICO induced more attorneys to cooperate with the government than would have been possible in the fifties and sixties.

When the cautious Dan Reidy heard the name Rico Enterprises he became furious, but it was too late. As it turned out, no one made the connection because the building was in DuPage County and all the fixers and judges we were targeting worked in Cook County. We never figured out what Rico Enterprises was supposed to do, except that it somehow involved auto repossessing to explain why the lot was full of cars that we used in our undercover work.

The unremarkable building was lost in a labyrinth of single-story factories in an industrial complex nearly an hour from the Loop. At the front was a carpeted office with a small reception room. Behind that was a large empty area of beige walls about a hundred feet long and forty feet wide. The rear parking area had a large door for delivery trucks. This was where we kept autos we had bought for our phony car-theft cases. But most of our work was done in the small office, outfitted with several gray desks and generic furnishings.

Because events were happening quickly now, let me jump ahead again. When we had moved into the building in the fall, we relieved the sparseness by adopting a mascot, a toy penguin Judge Lockwood's little daughter had left behind. The nameless plaything was black and gray, only about two inches tall, and made of felt over hard rubber. We kept it in the freezer compartment of our refrigerator and brought it out for all our meetings as—one of the agents said—"a reminder to cool down."

But the meetings themselves were serious. Rigging crimes had to be calculated geographically. Chicago was then divided into twenty-five police districts. We arranged for the acts to be committed in the districts where the agents arrested would be brought before a targeted judge. In one case, a New York City agent tore a gold chain off the neck of one of our female agents near a Walgreen's at Howard Street and Western Avenue. As usual whenever a woman was playing a victim, the always-reliable FBI special agent Marie Dyson stayed nearby to step forward if there was any trouble. Marie was very good but she came from the Chicago office, so we did not use her in an active role in any of the bogus crimes.

The chain snatching was aimed at Judge John McCollum, who was now sitting in Felony Preliminary Hearing Court at the police station at Belmont and Western. Unfortunately the crime coincided with a pattern of similar thefts and our agent vaguely resembled the suspect. Detectives held him for thirty-six hours of repeated questioning. All that time we were nervous because we didn't want him taken to jail if one of the real victims mistakenly identified him.

FBI contact agent Bill Megary sent over undercover agent David Victor Ries from the Traffic Court part of Greylord as the man's lawyer, but even Ries couldn't get him out of the lockup. In time, the prisoner was charged with only one theft and released. The white-haired Judge McCollum took our money and seemed eager for more.

But no one will ever know how many other cases were fixed in that court. Two years after our rigged hearing, the FBI learned from a neighbor near McCollum's summer home in Wisconsin that after a federal grand jury had subpoenaed his financial records, his wife had dumped the contents of several bulging garbage bags into a fifty-five-gallon barrel and set them on fire. The FBI crime laboratory in Washington determined that ashes obtained by search warrant had been made from check paper. Under questioning, McCollum couldn't give a convincing account of why he had obliterated a trove of cancelled checks. FBI agents Jim Leu and Doug Lenhardt then began an intensive investigation of McCollom when served as chief judge of Traffic Court, which found numerous arts or bribery by him in DUI cases. He eventually pleaded guilty to bribery and tax violations, and was sentenced to eleven years in prison. This saved his wife from prison for destroying subpoenaed documents.

It was now time to go after Ray Sodini, perhaps the laziest judge in the system.

JUDGE RAY SODINI

Sodini, son of hard-working immigrants, presided over a courtroom of hobos, shoplifters, and street gamblers, and never took his responsibilities seriously. The previous year he had pulled off a stunt that remains a classic in Chicago jurisprudence. Awakening with a hangover, he knew he wouldn't get to court on time. So he called a policeman who was near retirement age, Cy Martin, and asked the officer to sit in for him.

Martin had no legal training and didn't even resemble the judge, but he enjoyed being in on a good joke.

The officer showed up at the judge's chambers, put on Sodini's robe, and found himself facing perhaps a hundred derelicts rounded up in the nightly sweep of the streets. "My object was to get them out," he would say later, "so when other people came in, there would be a little dignity in the courtroom. I think the bailiff swore them in all at the same time, and I kept hitting the gavel over and over to clear the courtroom as fast as possible." No one was punished for the switch.

On March 23, 1982, I met Officer Joe Trunzo at the employees' entrance of Traffic Court and talked about fixing a shoplifting case coming before Sodini. Joe left me to make a phone call. He came back and said it was done, and that I shouldn't talk to the judge or anyone else. After Sodini disposed of the case later that day, Joe led me to a stairway for the payoff.

"Okay, how much?" I asked.

"Two for the judge."

I handed over two of my one-hundred-dollar bills, a fixer's pocket change. Then I gave him two fifties for him to split with his brother, also involved in the fix. On top of that, I offered Joe twenty dollars more for himself. "Here," I said, "this is for being a super guy." I was hoping he would become my pipeline to more judges.

The Center Cannot Hold

The following day I returned to our "crime academy" as usual. Since the FBI agents and I needed to set up offenses that would bring undercover agents before certain judges, we plotted a robbery outside Water Tower Place, a spotless vertical mall with an atrium and a glass elevator sliding through several levels of upscale small shops. Since I was just one of several people involved in the planning, the agents didn't need me to carry it off when it occurred, and I decided to take a little time off.

We were feeling good about ourselves. No investigation in American history had obtained evidence against so many judges on the take, and it seemed that we would be able to charge virtually all of the corrupt ones we had learned about. But Greylord was about to come to an end sooner than any of us expected.

For my vacation I accompanied Cathy, now my fiancée, on her trip to the national mock trials finals in Houston. She was proud that her team of law students represented the entire Midwest.

At around noon on Thursday of that week, a black agent going by the name of Jesse Clugman hailed a cab across from Water Tower Place and an agent posing as a thief grabbed his bag. "Clugman" ran after the "thief," Mark Langer*, then tackled him in the crowd and they scuffled. A shopper kept whacking at the "thief" with her purse until two officers arrived and arrested him. One of the FBI agents posing as a passerby immediately slipped away and called the office to say the bogus robbery had gone as planned. But then all hell broke loose.

A routine police search at the scene turned up not only a driver's license with Langer's phony name, Mark McKee, but also his FBI badge and photo credentials, which were in his jacket pocket. "What's this?" asked the officer.

Instead of answering, Langer, who was white, made racial threats at "Clugman" while putting on a distracting show of strange faces and puckering his lips almost like a chimpanzee. The distraction worked, and the police didn't know what kind of madman they had on their hands. They conducted the two agents to a police station in separate squad cars.

Langer continued his wildman act until another undercover agent showed up with bond money, but police thought it was strange that "Clugman" had declined to press charges against his attacker. Police later called the agent's phony apartment and received no answer. They went through their thick book of Chicago phone numbers listed by address rather than by name and called people at the building. No one knew of a "Clugman" or any other black man living there.

There was never any love lost between the FBI and the Chicago police, and the officers were happy to see that one and possibly two FBI agents had been brought in for what appeared to be a botched undercover case. Acting on their own, individual officers apparently began making anonymous calls to newspapers and TV stations, and the FBI office responded by issuing statements designed to cloud the situation.

While this was going on in Chicago, Cathy and I drove to Galveston to visit the sandy beaches and fishing piers along the Gulf of Mexico. We were in a Baskin-Robbins ice cream shop when I read the Saturday edition of the *Houston Chronicle*. A brief story told of a Water Tower Place robbery in which both victim and offender turned out to be FBI agents. My heart felt as if it had stopped. *It's finished*, I thought, and handed the paper over to Cathy. "Look at this," I said.

"They can't call it off, can they?"

"I don't know what they're going to do," I answered.

I should have lamented that the bungled set-up would mean that perhaps dozens of rotten police officers, court clerks, lawyers, and judges might never be brought to justice, since our evidence against them was still preliminary. But, being human, my first worry was that I would have to turn in my new Pontiac 6000.

I went back to my motel and kept calling the FBI office in Chicago. Finally I reached Megary and asked what the plans were now.

"We're going to have to shut down for a while," he answered quietly.

"How could they do something like that, after all we've gone over with these guys, over and over!"

"It was the weather."

"What?" I thought I had misunderstood.

"It got cold just before our guy went out, so he took a heavier jacket. He forgot that's the one with his credentials. That's not going to happen again, Terry. I want your people to start keeping their revolvers and credentials locked in a safe before they go out. I'm also going to see that everyone gets searched for anything that can be traced to us, including government pencils. Don't worry, the cops still don't know anything about us. We'll redirect this thing somehow."

"Don't worry"—the words were as wasted as telling a jury to disregard what they had just heard.

I don't think any of us could sleep for some time. Then one of the Greylord supervisors decided to create a false news leak. Certain reporters who commonly received tips from federal sources were told that the agent arrested had been involved in an undercover probe of possible police corruption, a situation that was entirely plausible since a commander in the district had already been convicted of taking payoffs from bar owners. The ruse made what the press called an "Abscam-like operation" seem localized, diverting attention away from the courts.

Greylord gained steam again, but the organizers decided after the Water Tower Place fiasco that as soon as any undercover agent was sentenced to jail they would shut down the entire operation and seek indictments against everyone we had solid evidence against.

Summer 1982

We still had to stay cautious to see if the misinformation campaign had worked. But we were not idle, we just kept our eyes and ears open as we went on with our work. Only when no one behaved differently toward Ries and me by mid-summer did we feel it was safe to go ahead.

Cathy by now had graduated from law school, and we were planning an August wedding. I had already called Mark Ciavelli and brought up as if in passing that I couldn't invite him because we were having only a small reception. I knew I couldn't send an invitation to any of my friends from the FBI or the U.S. Attorney's Office, and the only one I really wanted to ask from the bribery underworld was Costello.

Cathy was always pleasant and understanding, but now she became insistent. "There's no way I'm going to have that man at my wedding."

"I sincerely like Jim," I said, "and he's going through a bad time."

"I don't care."

"He's expecting an invitation—it would be good for my cover."

"I don't want him to ruin my day, Terry. He's a *criminal*."

While I was wondering how to tell Costello, he brought the subject up on his own. As we were talking over the phone two weeks before the wedding, he said, "Well, I checked the mail today and it wasn't there."

"What wasn't?" I asked.

"My invitation to your wedding. You're gonna invite me, aren't you?" There was hurt in his voice.

"Jim, I'm sorry, but Cathy's mother is paying for it, and she's keeping it to the family only."

"Okay. What the hell, I'll send you a present."

In a way, I was glad he forgot to. The present would only have been a reminder of the friendships I had to break. Besides, it would only have gone in the FBI evidence vault.

We held the nuptials on a surprisingly cool day for a Chicago summer. Both Cathy and I came from large, close families and we couldn't force ourselves to cut the guest list shorter than one hundred and fifty. The ceremony was performed at Faith, Hope and Charity Church, the Winnetka parish where Cathy had been raised. She sweet-talked the priest into holding a small champagne pre-reception in the church garden, where our guests grouped for pictures.

After the ceremony everyone drove to a country club for dinner. I tried not to be self-conscious about dancing with Cathy although I felt the pressure of all those eyes on the back of my neck. Undercover work was easier.

For our honeymoon we drove to Toronto, Montreal, and Quebec, where we stayed at the historic Chateau Frontenac, then headed back through Maine. The land of rugged pines and clear streams had given me a sense of freedom. But once we returned to the urban sprawls, I could feel myself tensing up. I was never a machine manufactured to FBI specifications, and my brain and my body were threatening to shut down.

After a few days back in Chicago, I realized from a fresh viewpoint how unsettled our investigation had become. Two news reports of an investigation in as many years meant that anything could give us away. While we still could, we had to start going after a few corruptors within our reach.

October 1982

OFFICER JAMES LEFEVOUR and JUDGE MARTIN HOGAN

In Officer Jimmy LeFevour's capacity as chief bagman in the First Municipal District—Chicago—he kept himself busy delivering bribes to judges in the Gun, Auto Theft, Women's, and Gambling Courts. We put him at the top of our list of new targets. But "Dogbreath" wasn't as easy to fool as the Trunzo brothers, or as obvious as fellow bagman Harold Conn. Unless I had an introduction to him, he would never trust me. This set me on a long, roundabout route in which I had to work with past targets and bribe another judge just to reach him.

We started by plotting a car theft that would let us trace a bribe from my hand to Jimmy LeFevour and then to Judge Martin Hogan. This meant buying a new Oldsmobile Cutlass Cierra. Not only did we pull the ignition to make the auto appear hot-wired, we left pliers clamped in place to make it harder for Hogan to find an excuse for dismissing the case.

An undercover agent then called the police to say he had overhead someone in a pancake house at Diversey and Western attempting to sell a classy stolen auto parked outside. Police set up a surveillance at the busy North Side intersection until an undercover agent in street clothes climbed in the car and sped off. In a minute, the officers curbed him and asked for identification. The agent, posing as a Californian named Richard Duran, said he couldn't account for the car or the pliers hanging on the ignition. They put him under arrest, and I came in as his shady lawyer.

Then I found attorney Peter Kessler prowling the aisles looking for clients during a recess of sleazy Gambling Court in police headquarters.

The Cook County Courthouse at 2600 S. California. *Courtesy of Terrence Hake.*

Terrence Hake, while testifying. © *Chicago Sun-Times*.

James Costello, hallway hustler and Hake's entry point into the Chicago
courts' bribery and corruption. © *Chicago Sun-Times.*

Attorney Edward Genson (*right*) and Judge Wayne Olson (*left*), Narcotics Court Judge, who so widely accepted bribes that the FBI took the unprecedented step of bugging his chambers. © *Chicago Sun-Times.*

Harry Aleman (*left*), the mafia hit man whose acquittal was so egregious the federal government began investigating the Chicago courts. Aleman was eventually convicted in an unheard-of retrial—the first trial was proven to be fixed and therefore Aleman was not in jeopardy. © *Chicago Sun-Times*.

Assistant U.S. Attorney Scott Lassar.

Cousin to bagman James, Judge Richard LeFevour packed the courts under his supervision with corrupt judges so he could get a cut of their bribes. © *Chicago Sun-Times*.

Chicago FBI Chief Ed Hegarty (*left*) swears in Terrence Hake (*right*) as an FBI agent in the warehouse where the Greylord team gathered. The swearing in was held quickly and casually in case Hake needed to reveal himself as an FBI agent while undercover, as judges and lawyers became more and more nervous about the rumored government mole. *Courtesy of Terrence Hake.*

Bagman Harold Conn (*left*), deputy court clerk who passed bribes on to judges, sometimes publically. Conn's attorney Sheldon Sorosky is pictured on the right; Sorosky would go on to defend Illinois governor Rod Blagojevich in Blagojevich's 2010-2011 federal corruption trials. © *Chicago Sun-Times*.

Judge John "Dollars" Devine, who openly used bribery to run Auto Theft Court. © *Chicago Sun-Times*.

Judge Ray Sodini, famous for once having a policeman replace him on the bench while he was home with a hangover. © *Chicago Sun-Times*.

Judge Thomas Maloney, the first American judge ever convicted of fixing murder cases. © *Chicago Sun-Times*.

Charles Sklarsky today; Sklarsky was one of the
architects of Operation Greylord and the first person to
contact Terrence Hake about the investigation. He tried
Judge "Dollars" Devine and continues to practice law in
Chicago today. *Courtesy Charles Sklarsky.*

Daniel Reidy the lead Assistant United States Attorney on the Greylord Project. Later became First Assistant United State's Attorney. He was one of the prosecutors in the trial of Judge LeFevour, the most important of the Greylord Trials, along with U.S. Attorney Dan Webb and Assistant United State's Attoreny Candace Fabri.

Terrence Hake today; Hake has come full-circle in
his career and is again an Assistant State's Attorney in
Illinois. *Courtesy of Terrence Hake.*

"Can I ask you something?" I spoke quietly, in my shady tone. He waved me to an empty courtroom. "I got this auto theft case," I began, "and I don't know anybody else real well in the building. My client—let's face it, the case is a dead bang loser."

"Plea for probation," Peter said with a shrug.

"My client's a car thief, probation would kill him. The case is up before Hogan. I had another case with him I handled through the Trunzos. They screwed me around so much, I don't want that to happen again. So I was thinking—is Jimmy LeFevour more reliable?"

"Yeah," Kessler answered, "but he's a fucking hog."

Good, I thought, Peter's going to give me something on tape about Jimmy. I was wearing a new recorder, this one in stereo to pick up more sounds. But having a mike taped against each shoulder meant I was doubling my risk of discovery. Kessler startled me by saying, "I presume you're not wired."

"What a hell of a thing to say! You know me, Peter."

He reached out toward my shoulder. A year ago I might have panicked, but now I didn't flinch as his hand rested right on the tiny bulge over one of the wires.

"These days, no one knows," Peter told me with a shallow laugh. "Hogan's a very cautious man. If it's a bad case [in which there is no pretext for a dismissal], I can tell you right now, he's just not going to do it. If there was something for him to hang his hat on, then it's a different story. He'll do it for the people he trusts."

"I heard I've got to go to Jimmy LeFevour, but he doesn't know me."

"I'll tell him you're okay." That is, crooked.

"You know me, I don't want to put you to any trouble, Peter, it's just that I don't want to get screwed again."

"I know how it is, Terry. Look, we do the best for our clients. Unfortunately you and I didn't set the rules."

From any other fixer that would have been just self-justifying nonsense, but I knew that Kessler was sincerely telling me he hated being given the choice of paying a judge or failing to deliver as a defense attorney. As we learned later, he sometimes had sleepless nights over how he made his living.

After our talk, I left the boxy gray police building and pulled out of the parking lot. When I stopped for a red light, I noticed Judge Hogan's clerk standing on the curb. "Hello, Nick," I called out. "You know,

I really appreciate you always calling my cases right away." I reached out the window and slid five singles into his palm. The light turned green, and I took off. For all appearances, I was now scum on the way up.

So perhaps I really would look "dirty" to Jimmy LeFevour. When the day of our encounter came, October 14, I was jumpy even before leaving my apartment. This would be my deepest undercover penetration so far, for "Dogbreath" had a way of sniffing for trouble and was even more wary than fixer Bob Silverman or Judge "Dollars" Devine.

As I rode up the elevator to the police headquarters courtrooms, I still didn't know if Peter Kessler had spoken to Jimmy about me. A few minutes later I saw Peter in the hall and secretly turned on my recorder.

"Everything is cool," Kessler assured me. "Let me talk to Jimmy and tell him you're all right."

He left and came back to say, "This guy's expensive. To get you some real help, he wants a nickel. I told him five hundred bucks is a lot, but that's the going rate. Between you and I, he's the most dishonest person in the world."

"What should I do, Peter—do I talk [deliver the bribe] to him or talk to you?"

"Whatever you want, makes no difference to me."

"I think I better do it through him, all right?"

We found James LeFevour skulking near the tenth-floor stairwell. Peter led me over there and said, "Jim, this is a friend of mine, Terry Hake." Kessler then walked off as if washing his hands of us. He hated Jimmy and was glad not to be part of our deal.

"Dogbreath" did not smile or offer me his hand to shake. Instead he callously asked, "What've you got?"

My palms were perspiring, and Jimmy impatiently jiggled his pocket change as I outlined the auto theft case. He didn't care about the facts, all he wanted was the name of the judge and whether I was aware how much our conversation was going to cost me.

Pointing to the bond slip I was holding, he asked, "How much is that?"

"A thousand."

Jimmy explained that even if the case was thrown out because the witness failed to appear, it would still cost me "a nickel."

"That's okay."

"Find Kessler after it's over," he said and moved on to other business.

A short time later Jimmy LeFevour went into Hogan's chambers and followed the unwritten rules against mentioning a bribe when talking about one. "Dogbreath" merely commented that his cousin, presiding judge Richard LeFevour, had "an interest in this case."

"All right." That was all Hogan said. The case was fixed.

Judge Hogan was a trim man in his late thirties with the demeanor of an accountant, his field before switching to law. He had been appointed to the bench a year before I joined Greylord and quickly let it be known that he could be bought. Hogan lived in a dream world of spending, including a cabin cruiser, yet he let his credit card bills and parking fines go unpaid because he thought they were not worth worrying about.

Hogan was less cautious than P.J. McCormick, with his "millions" of money orders. He eventually would tell a jury that the twenty thousand dollars he had spent freely one year was a gift from a steel executive rather than bribes from lawyers, and that he had kept the cash in a drawer at home for two years.

While Jimmy was in the judge's chambers, I was asking Hogan's clerk, Nick, for the papers on the case. Then I slipped a folded five-dollar bill into the file jacket and handed the file back to make sure my case was called early. I also sent home the "complaining witness," a Las Vegas agent posing as the owner of the Olds. I had just learned casually that he originally was from the Chicago area, and I was afraid someone might recognize him.

As soon as the case was dismissed, I went to give Kessler the money as Jimmy LeFevour had instructed. But Peter didn't want to be in the middle again, and looked scared of having further dealings with the bagman. So I left him and found Jimmy sitting in Hogan's courtroom as other cases were being heard. He agreed to meet me in the hall.

Once we were in the corridor, Jimmy had me follow him to the washroom. The sticky floor tiles were littered with crumpled paper towels. The window had been painted shut, and the sink was cracked from some defendant's tantrum. Jimmy walked over to a stall where he wouldn't be seen by anyone coming in and wordlessly held out his hand.

"Sorry about the twenties," I said as I gave him two one-hundreds and fifteen twenties. Whenever I could, I used small bills to stall for time and create conversation for the recorder. Just handing him money without saying anything for the recorder would have meant nothing. I stiffened as the money left my hands.

"Have a nice day," Jimmy said in a monotone as he pocketed the cash and brushed past me as if I were contemptible. Well, that wasn't any less than what my role deserved.

Then a cold thrill of intuition went through me: perhaps we could use Jimmy's antagonism toward his cousin to bring down one of the most important judges in the huge Cook County court system. I hurriedly caught up with the bagman in the hallway and said, "Thanks, Jim."

"Any time."

"Are you available for anywhere in the First Municipal District?" This covered all the municipal courts in Chicago.

He nodded and walked on without a word. Too bad, because the nod was just silence on the tape.

Then I saw defense attorney Barry Carpenter watching me. Barry, husband of my friend Alice, was a scrawny six foot two or three. His receding black hair seemed to make his dark eyes more piercing, and I could tell he knew what had just gone down.

"Hey," Barry called out to me, "come here."

God, no, I thought. I had known early on that Barry was a hallway hustler, but out of respect for Alice I didn't want to learn anything more about him.

"I'll be right back," I said, "I got to get a bond slip." I could have returned to Hogan's court for the slip at any time, but this way I could pretend to myself that Barry wasn't trying to use me. Unfortunately Barry was still waiting for me when I came out of the courtroom.

"What were you doing there with Jimmy?" he asked with a knowing grin.

"I don't do all my cases this way," I answered as if ashamed.

"It doesn't matter. I don't tell Alice about anything *I* do. How much did you have to pay 'Dogbreath'?" Making a game of it, he guessed by holding up five fingers.

I nodded, but my mind was whirling. Do I tape Barry and start an investigation that would possibly destroy his marriage and my friendship with Alice? Or do I let him go as someone not worth bothering with now that we were going after both LeFevours? I switched on the recorder and began hating myself all over again. "Five is standard?" I asked. "I thought they were taking advantage of me because this is my first time."

"You could have come to me," Barry said.

"Oh, really?"

"You definitely could have come to me. If you do that, the judge gets all the money" that he is supposed to.

"Okay, Barry."

A few minutes earlier I had been jubilant at bribing Jimmy LeFevour, but now I left the police headquarters feeling polluted.

PART 3

THE RECKONING

17

THE LARGEST BRIBE

Winter 1982–1983

LUCIUS ROBINSON

From the beginning I had wanted to bring down Lucius Robinson, a bagman responsible for throwing out rape, child molesting, and murder cases I'd seen early in my career. But his street smarts would make him difficult to catch. While I was working undercover as a prosecutor in Judge Wayne Olson's court, Lucius had asked me why I wasn't moving forward in my assignments. He had picked up on something no one else had. He also conducted phone conversations with fixers in such a way that his words could never be used against him, something some of them never even thought about.

Robinson was the driver and bagman for Maurice Pompey, the judge who would find his bribes when he opened his briefcase at home. But all we could show so far was that his rulings nearly always went against assistant public defenders. This was because poor defendants and their public defenders were not paying bribes.

Here's an example. Even though state law permitted hearsay evidence at preliminary hearings, Pompey would not. This meant that when victims were still hospitalized, the state's case collapsed because it was not allowed to present what the person had told arresting officers.

As a fledgling prosecutor I had watched helplessly as the judge once threw out a charge of child molesting because the twelve-year-old victim couldn't pronounce "vagina," even though she gave a graphic description of her attack. Another time, Pompey set free a killer who was being represented by the judge's former campaign manager. Yet he could believe himself absolved from all consequences because Lucius Robinson was doing his dirty work.

Lucius kept all his contact numbers in a tin file-card container and handed out business cards featuring a snake coiled around a cane. This muscular former bodyguard for Muhammad Ali sauntered down the halls like an intimidating bully, knowing that well-educated defense attorneys in their tailored suits would be nothing without him.

Even if we couldn't gather sufficient evidence against Judge Pompey, we might put a scare into the system by recording the bagman. After all, we already had evidence against most of the people he worked with. For a while I considered taking my time because he was naturally suspicious, but then it hit me: if we were ever going to snare him, it would have to be now, before the fixers could talk over their doubts about me.

Lucius was probably the most aggressive bagman in the system, as fixer Bill Swano would later explain to authorities. Swano said he was just starting out when a LaSalle Street stockbroker paid him a large fee of four thousand dollars to get him off on a charge of sexually assaulting a young woman. Lucius went up to Swano and asked, "Do you want help on that date-rape case?"

"What do you mean?" Swano asked.

"You know—do you want to win this case? It's going to cost you two hundred dollars."

After Swano paid, Judge Pompey found no probable cause to hold the prosperous client for trial. Swano claimed that this single act of extortion is what drove him to becoming a fixer. He wound up a few years later bribing Judge Thomas Maloney to throw out a murder case, and the eventual disclosure would make national news.

In January 1983 I rapped on the rear door of Pompey's courtroom. Lucius opened it and went back to his desk with the rapid movements of a blunt businessman. I sat across from him and brought up my case of a young Hispanic man (an FBI agent) who had pushed down a beautiful young woman (a fellow undercover agent) and stole her purse.

"What are we talking about?" Robinson asked. "First, what do you want? You don't want no probation on this guy, right?"

"I'll take probation. Just no jail time."

"We had one that was similar the other day, and Pompey gave him a couple of weekends in jail to make everybody happy."

"Yeah," I said, even though a real fixer would likely not agree to that, "my guy could take a couple of weekends if he has to."

"Okay, so what are you talking about in dollars and cents?" His words always carried a threat. Robinson kept a gun with him at all times and loved being pushy, even extorting further money from the fixers in the form of contributions to Judge Pompey's retention campaigns.

"If I can get straight probation, I can go to a G [one thousand dollars]," I said, holding up my index finger. "My client would be real happy that I kept him out of jail, but that's as much as I can pay."

My tone suggested that I might be a sucker, but I was on a personal vendetta against Robinson because his corruption and arrogance had caused so much misery. Even though this was a routine case, I was determined to make this my biggest bribe so far, a payoff so large there could be no mistake about the covetousness of these people.

The next day I called Lucius about the purse-snatching robbery case and he said that some people he had spoken with thought a new law would bar probation for my client. I double-checked the statute and called back to say he was wrong. He agreed, glossed over his bluff, and suggested that I see him the following day. As I set the phone down, I wondered whether I had pushed too hard, considering how shrewd Lucius could be.

When I met Lucius in the courthouse on Wednesday, he invited me for coffee in his office. His friendly act always meant he was about to put on the bite. He explained that he had mistakenly thought my purse-snatching case had involved a gun or drugs. In other words, he wanted more money because he mistook me for a patsy.

As if trusting him, I pressed for straight probation.

"Put on your strongest case," Lucius told me, "and we'll just sit back and give him [Pompey] something to hang his hat on. He will give you what you want."

"He can give me what I want?" I asked.

"He *may* give you what you want."

"Great. So you have talked to him?"

"Yeah, yeah, I talked to him."

"Thoroughly?" I asked, overstepping the boundaries I had set for caution, in hopes of getting him to say something more definite on the tape. Of all my lying to fixers, bagmen, and judges, this was the one time I felt something might backfire.

"We don't need to talk no more," Lucius answered gruffly. He seemed to be searching for something in my face.

"You're a good man," I said, keeping myself from showing alarm, "I trust you."

"See you."

Now I had to follow through with the situation I had created or arouse concern. For some reason, I had a feeling that Lucius suspected me when he had asked for another meeting, so I arranged for backup. As I waited for Robinson by the snacking area vending machine in the courthouse, one of our all-purpose agents, Marie Dyson, moved about the hall as a spectator waiting out a court recess. Relaxed though she appeared, she was prepared to rush in and force the bagman's hands behind his back if he became physical or accused me of anything.

Robinson said hello and bought a cup of hot chocolate. I was glad he didn't seem suspicious. My surge of adrenaline from too little sleep had made me jumpy and irritable, but I had to appear trusting and grateful. I told Lucius that my client was picked out only because he was Latino, that he had not been caught with anything stolen, and that he did not match the description given by the victim.

"Just hang around and we'll work something out," Lucius said. "Things like this [bribes] go on every day."

"Are you included in the figure?"

"No. You have to include me in. Whatever you feel like."

I took a stab. "I'd like to give you three [three hundred dollars], if that's fair."

"Okay, you got no argument. None whatsoever."

When the case went to trial, I cross-examined the FBI agent posing as the victim, and she gave a great performance of someone unsure of what really happened. I destroyed her identification of my client and asked Pompey for a directed verdict of acquittal on the grounds that the prosecutor had not proved his case.

"I find the defendant not guilty," Pompey ruled.

We had pulled it off.

The judge then said that my client's fifteen-hundred-dollar bond would be given to me as my fee. Lucius stepped over and said I should hurry because he was going to close up the courtroom even though the prosecutor was still inside.

I put my papers in my briefcase and we walked into the main hallway. I put an eye against the crack between the doors to make sure the ASA wasn't listening. Without turning his head, Robinson asked,

"Got it in an envelope?" I reached inside my suit coat and came up with thirteen hundred dollars in cash, the largest bribe that would ever be made in Greylord. "No," I said for the tape recorder, "I just got it in my hand here."

Lucius snatched the money and said, "Here comes Paula," referring to the prosecutor.

Rain was bouncing off cars and the sidewalk as I left the courthouse, but I was feeling so good that I didn't even realize that I had left my raincoat inside. I drove a mile and stopped to call our warehouse headquarters, where Greylord architect Dan Reidy was having a strategy meeting with our team. When Reidy turned away from the phone to announce that Lucius had taken the bait, I could hear the agents cheering.

Now that we had hard evidence against Robinson, I was sure we were well on our way to netting Judge Pompey.

Playing Troubleshooter

Cathy's friends helped us move into our first home, an apartment in a Far North Side building that we later learned was owned by a veteran policeman related to a well-known defense attorney. So well known, in fact, that the chances were good he would be defending some of the crooked lawyers and judges we would be putting on trial.

The FBI was so concerned about this that it sent someone in to install extra locks on the front and back doors, just in case. Our landlord naturally asked why we did that, so I said Cathy was afraid of a break-in. He wanted an extra set of keys, but I kept telling him I forgot to bring them. He must have wondered how I could make a living as a lawyer with a memory like mine.

Although the Chicago office of the FBI was quick to act on my safety, the bureaucratic wheels of Washington were hardly moving. Nearly three years into Greylord, the agency became afraid we were being duped by all the lawyers and judges who had been taking money from us. In mid 1983, I had to interrupt our regular "crime session" in the Addison warehouse to show our agents the tape of a recent *60 Minutes* segment on the failed Operation Corkscrew, in which a man and woman confidence team in Cleveland had set the FBI up with thieves identifying themselves as disreputable judges to collect one hundred thousand dollars in taxpayers' money as payoffs. At least the show gave us all a good laugh before we went back to work as usual.

I kept waiting to become sworn in as a federal agent. The previous November I had been flown to Indianapolis for my FBI interview, then drove to the Milwaukee office for my physical. The Bureau notified me in March 1983 that I was cleared to be hired as a special agent. But no one in authority seemed to know what to do with me for the present, since there had never been a situation in which an applicant was already working undercover with no end in sight.

FBI agents Bill Megary and Bob Farmer were urging officials to make an exception to the requirement that new agents undergo four months of training, since I could not be spared for that long. Until approval came down, I would have to continue as an untrained, unprepared undercover operative in charge of specially chosen skilled agents. The arrangement made no sense, and yet it was working.

But unaware how soon the operation was about to unravel, I saw myself hopelessly caught in something that was grinding me down in body and spirit, and was losing my sense of self. It's hard to explain why. I was at the center of Greylord and yet was made to feel like an outsider, a pawn. I was not even allowed to have a life of my own. Cathy and I had wanted to buy a house, but the FBI didn't want me to fill out a mortgage application, since that would mean either lying or disclosing the Federal Bureau of Investigation as my employer.

After the *60 Minutes* show on Operation Corkscrew, FBI Director William Webster had members of the Bureau's undercover school in Quantico fly out to give all agents in Greylord an abbreviated course. Doctor Soskiss, a short psychiatrist from the specialized training team, told me I was holding up well, considering that moles in some other investigations were easing their stress by excessive drinking or promiscuous sex.

He advised me to seek professional counseling and flew away, leaving me with feelings of uncertainty and abandonment. In my growing cynicism, I thought that perhaps the word "mole" was appropriate. A mole is a creature that must keep digging and yet remains in the dark.

But the FBI came through on the house, as it eventually did with everything else. Cathy and I were directed to a downstate bank run by an ex-FBI agent. We filled out the forms truthfully and had to wait for several agonizing weeks before the application was approved. When we barely made the deadline to arrange financing, I felt rejuvenated and was looking forward to some real training. As it turned out, it would be a long wait.

Behind my back the Bureau was conducting other faked cases, unaware that this would be putting me in even greater jeopardy. It's just as well that I also didn't know that Silverman had already told Mark, concerning the rumor about me, "If I ever find out that he is the mole, I'll kill him."

While I was branching out into Costello's territory of the southwestern suburbs, an undercover FBI agent using the name John Miller was being held in the men's lockup at police headquarters for auto theft. A sheriff's deputy notified fixer Barry Carpenter of a potential client.

Barry spoke to "Miller" and a second agent, let's call him X, who bailed "Miller" out. Agent X had no knowledge of the fixer mentality. For one thing, everything they say is roundabout, although bagmen are sometimes direct. And fixers never discuss bribes on the phone. One of the reasons they trusted me was that when they called, I cautioned them with such phrases as "Let's not talk about it now" as if I were really trying to protect them.

Agent X phoned Carpenter and said something to the effect of "I want you to guarantee my friend will get off." Barry didn't have to think twice in turning away from him. The Bureau now knew it had blundered with that "guarantee" remark, so Megary asked me, in effect, to save everyone's ass. "You don't have to do it," he told me. But between the lines he was saying that unless this hole was patched up, Greylord might fall apart.

Each court case I became involved in had a potential trap at each end, and the idea was to ensnare the target without getting caught myself. But in this instance, the trick was to get an agent out before the trap snapped shut on him. I didn't discuss all the situations with Cathy, but sometimes I talked about them generally, more to sort out my own thinking than to let her know what was troubling me. In "Miller's" case, I decided to lose at a preliminary hearing so we could advance the case to the criminal trial courts and fix it with Lucius.

As I came into the courtroom with "Miller," I felt completely exposed and had no idea what would happen next. I could see that Barry Carpenter wanted to talk to me about something but didn't want to draw attention to himself, so he waited. That night he called my home and said, "Watch out about your guy."

"Why? He's paying me pretty good."

"The consensus is that it's some kind of set-up."

This meant the situation was even worse than I thought. Barry went on to explain that X had asked other hallway sharks at Auto Theft Court to take his case and again demanded a "guarantee." Even the judge suspected that "Miller" and X were federal agents. If I had known about this earlier, I would have dropped my attempt to get them off the hook, but it was too late now.

"Who knows what's going on with this guy," Barry went on. "We've been backing off. This guy may be nothing, but on the other hand he could be with the feds or he's a state's attorney investigator. That's why I'm warning you."

I had to dissociate myself from my client, fast. "Well, I didn't give any guarantee, so I'm okay," I told Carpenter. "Maybe he's just a mope, Barry. You know how there are always guys who talk big about being able to fix their case, but it's all talk."

Giving up my plan to fix the case, I just had "Miller" not show up in the trial courts and a warrant was issued for him. This allowed me to get on with my own work and shore up evidence against our major targets.

By now we were using some Chicago police officers in our contrived arrests in the city, and state troopers in the suburbs. But the Chicago Police Superintendent may not have kept our secret. We heard a rumor that he had informed a high-level police official about the Traffic Court aspect of Greylord, unaware that the official had a close association to the mob.

And so we may have finally reached further than any of us had ever dreamed possible, the potentially deadly shadowland where the Chicago crime syndicate had its hands on the police department and the courts. My increasing anxiety was like being surrounded by electrically charged air before a storm comes on and not knowing where the lightning will strike.

Summer 1983

As this was happening, there was a shakeup in the mob gambling operation in the Rush Street entertainment district just north of downtown. Two hoods were supposed to kill one of Bob Silverman's clients,

Ken Eto (pronounced ET-oh), known as "Tokyo Joe" because his parents were Japanese. The short, ordinary-looking man in his early sixties ran a number of mob-protected gambling operations and had gained trust as its liaison with black "policy" operators. But to keep Eto from talking about the mob to the police and federal agents after his gambling arrest, he was taken for a one-way drive and shot three times in the head. Possibly because of the angle, the bullets failed to cause any major damage.

In the hospital, Eto reluctantly told authorities he was willing to give evidence against the men who had turned on him. Reporters were led to believe he was gravely wounded, and Eto was hustled out a back door under government protection that very night. Since the mob could no longer reach him, they killed both would-be assassins for botching the hit and stuffed them in the trunk of a car. Although the events had no direct bearing on our investigation, they were a reminder of the kind of people we were dealing with.

We had made so many inroads by now that our targets were bound to be comparing notes. Why was I hanging around only with fixers, why did I keep talking about the money I was handing over, why were a number of my clients apparently middle class and educated rather than the usual drunks and addicts that beginning defense lawyers normally handle? There were also questions about undercover agent David Victor Ries in the municipal courts as well as some of the "citizen moles" the FBI had persuaded to help with specific investigations.

FBI agent Bob Farmer and other Greylord supervisors felt it was time to pull up stakes. But there was no relief and no sense of accomplishment because so much work still needed to be done. We decided to take a risk in trying to "flip" someone who might be persuaded to wear a wire for us. Since Ries had used policeman Ira Blackwood ten times as a bagman in Traffic Court, Assistant U.S. Attorney Dan Reidy felt he might want to save himself.

At five foot ten and weighing a hundred and ninety pounds, much of it muscle, the one-time boxer looked like someone who might stuff you into a meat grinder. Although his family came from the Missouri backwoods, Ira's father had been an enforcer for Al Capone and ended up in Alcatraz. In fact, Blackwood once bragged about being the only member of his family who never went to prison. To us this meant prison had a grim reality for him, and the fifty-three-year-old policeman had a pension at stake.

One morning in July, the always well-dressed Blackwood was walking to his garage when two FBI agents identified themselves and asked him to accompany them downtown. At a meeting in the Dirksen Federal Building, Dan Reidy told the officer that two people he thought were friends of his, Judge Lockwood and attorney Ries, were working undercover and had taped seventy-five criminal conversations with him.

Blackwood sat seething as Dan also informed him that forty-four hundred dollars he had taken to pass on to judges had come from the FBI. In a theatrical touch, a door then opened and Agent Ries stepped into the room. Ira cringed.

Dan Reidy played a sampling of their tapes so Blackwood could hear just what a jury would. The bagman's options were to plead guilty to a misdemeanor and keep his pension or take his chances in court and be convicted of racketeering. Not only would this mean prison, but everything he bought with those bribes could be confiscated by the government. Reidy gave him twenty-four hours to think it over.

If this had not been a tightly controlled situation, I think Blackwood might have bashed someone's face in. Instead he didn't say anything except, "I'm talkin' to my lawyer."

"Does that mean no?" Reidy asked.

"It means I'm talking to my lawyer."

"You understand, Mr. Blackwood, we must ask that you not discuss this conversation with anyone."

He walked out, leaving the entire FBI staff in anxious doubt. If he agreed to cooperate, everything would go as planned. If he didn't, nothing could stop him from telling every fixer in the city what we were doing, and it wouldn't be long before lawyers working out of the Criminal Courts Building and the courts in police headquarters began figuring out who the mole among them was.

Ira got back with the investigators at a downtown hotel, and a McDonald's lunch was sent for. The burly policeman had brought an attorney with him, and the only names he gave up were of people who had died or those, as he must have somehow known, we already had evidence against. Obviously he was protecting the rest.

"Is that all?" Reidy asked distrustfully.

"Yeah. Like I told you, those other guys might be bums but I never had much dealing with them."

"Forget it then," Reidy said. "It's all off, Ira. But I suggest that you get a new lawyer—one who really has your best interests at heart."

For two weeks I kept appearing in court on contrived cases without knowing whether Blackwood would join our side or expose us. I kept looking over my shoulder although I had been assured my name was never being mentioned.

In time, Ira's lawyer notified Dan Reidy that his client had declined the suggestion of cooperation and felt compelled to advise "certain persons" of his current situation. We feared the worst. But, surprisingly, Ira didn't play Paul Revere by shouting from one end of the system to the other that the federal government was coming. He apparently notified just the judges he had personally passed bribes to on behalf of Ries and let it go at that, and those judges were so busy trying to cover themselves that they failed to call a strategy conference with the others.

Such was the tenuous state at the time for everyone involved on both sides. State's Attorney Richard M. Daley, who had been informed about Greylord shortly after his election, went to a White Sox game with Judge Richard LeFevour and treated him like a buddy while knowing that the U.S. Attorney's Office was planning to throw him into prison.

Blackwood's refusal to cooperate worked against him. Eventually convicted of racketeering, bribery, and extortion, he lost his pension and was sentenced to seven years in prison. "My life has been wrecked, my wife is on the verge of a nervous breakdown," he told his sentencing judge. "Four of my five kids don't talk to me. This whole thing has been a nightmare."

Still hoping for cooperation from a Greylord target, the government approached Harold Conn, the bagman whose boldness in passing a bribe in public had aroused FBI conjecture of widespread corruption in the Traffic Court Building. But Dan Reidy didn't hit Conn with everything we had on him. To save me from disclosure and keep me out there fixing cases, the prosecutor told him only about David Victor Ries' evidence, and once again Ries was brought in as part of the show.

Conn was shocked but recovered quickly and said hello to the undercover agent with unexpected warmth. The dapper black man listened politely to Reidy's offer, then responded with a gentlemanly "No, thank you" and shook everyone's hand before leaving. Just from the way Conn had said "No," Reidy knew he would never reconsider, but no one knew if he would keep his mouth shut.

My greatest fear was that Lucius Robinson might get off with a minor sentence unless we could record a second bribe, to secure the racketeering conviction I had been hoping for. Feeling a sweat-dripping-down-my-back sense of urgency, I dropped by Judge Maurice Pompey's chambers in early August and asked Lucius if he would serve as my go-between in a suburban auto theft case.

"I'm only getting fifteen hundred on the deal," I said, "so I can give maybe five hundred. But, see, all I'm asking you right now is if it's possible, because my guy hasn't given me my full fee yet."

"It's possible that I know the man [the judge] well enough that I can say something to him."

"Great."

"But the judges are dropping hints that you guys got to start asking for more money [from your clients] on these kinds of cases [bribed decisions]. They feel like the price on everything else is going up. They're taking a chance on putting someone on the street for just five hundred."

This was the first time anyone had suggested to me that judges wanted fixers to keep up with inflation. That gave me two ways of playing the scene. I could just complain, or I could use their own greediness against them.

I mentioned that the price used to be one hundred dollars in Narcotics Court and said the way it kept going up was ridiculous. In a gesture so bold I could hardly believe I was making it, I reached into my briefcase and took out a list of thirty judges handling felony trials in Chicago. "Can you deal with any of these people?" I asked.

My heart once more was thumping. Lucius was sharper than the cordial Harold Conn—would he sense the snare? The bagman went slowly down the list, then took my pen and checked off the names of three judges we coincidentally had nothing on. One of them was that law-and-order gavel-banger Thomas Maloney. *Oh God*, came a pulsing in my brain, *I hope this operation holds together.*

18

THE WALL COLLAPSES

August 1983

Lucius Robinson's checklist made me feel almost mellow as I drove to a southwest suburban court where one of our FBI agents was about to appear before Judge Michael McNulty in a fabricated drunken driving case. I had promised to deliver five hundred dollars to bagman Jimmy LeFevour if the judge gave my client supervision. When I arrived, I asked the prosecutor if he would accept a guilty plea in return for court supervision to keep the defendant out of prison.

"McNulty doesn't give supervision," the prosecutor said. I knew that, but I just wanted it for the record and my FBI report.

The judge had the case called last, apparently so there would be fewer people around when he just fined my "client" two hundred dollars and put him under supervision, letting him keep his license. The prosecutor abruptly turned to me as if he had just heard a rattlesnake, so I gave him a fixer's haughty smile and strolled out.

Judge McNulty would later plead guilty to three tax counts and be sentenced to three years in prison.

August 5, 1983

Since the supervision ruling meant a payoff, I went the following morning to police headquarters and met Jimmy LeFevour in a vacant stairwell. A few hours later that Friday, August 5, Bill Megary told me by phone that investigative reporter Peter Karl—who earlier had come close to discovering our work—had just announced on the five o'clock news that an Abscam-style investigation was being conducted in Chicago-area courts. Karl called it "the largest undercover operation in the history of the Justice Department."

I was dumbfounded. For months I had longed to call an end to my undercover work, but now it seemed as if I had hardly begun. In an instant, my life had become a book with the second half ripped from the binding. I was upset with Karl for breaking the story. There were judges greedier than Olson we could have reached, along with fixers worse than Costello, Mark Ciavelli, and Peter Kessler. Now we would have to let them continue unlocking the jail cells.

Cathy and I had just laid out thousands of dollars to buy our suburban home, but now we might be moved to some other part of the country for our protection. I didn't even know how I was supposed to act now that the secret was out.

I had been invited to a downtown bachelor party that evening for a man who had been one of my bosses when I was an ASA. Common sense told me to stay away because of all the lawyers who would be there, but I thought I had to make an appearance to keep them from talking over suspicions about me.

There must have been fifty lawyers and a dozen judges along the bar at the Counselors Row Restaurant, a favorite haunt for political figures because it was near the LaSalle Street legal district, city hall, the local Democratic Party headquarters, and the federal building complex. The place kept an informal, coy atmosphere and one of its hamburgers was nicknamed "the Lawbreaker."

When I walked in, the news report had already caused a stir. The courts formed such a closed world that it meant every attorney and judge in the system personally had met the mole, whoever he might be. Speculation was so rampant that it almost eclipsed the entertainment for the night, three strippers.

One took everything off, then went into the audience, unzipped a partygoer's pants, and started playing with him in front of everyone. She then went over to the honoree of the evening and stuck her tongue down his throat. I joined in the hooting and laughter to keep from appearing suspect but kept glancing at my watch and wishing someone would shut off the television set before the news came on. If I changed the channel myself, it would have been a confession.

The strippers let it be known they were available for separate negotiation, and a police sergeant I knew took one to his car. The two others went off to dress, leaving us to our drinks. Everyone crowded in front of the bar TVs, and a score of raucous conversations erupted when the ten o'clock news came on. The gaiety drowned the first few words of the exclusive, then one by one the party guests fell silent and either became tense about himself or sad for the corrupt people he knew.

"Federal sources say it's bigger than Abscam," Peter Karl announced. "Thirty judges, attorneys, cops and court bailiffs are expected to be indicted by the time the investigation is completed."

You could hear a glass clink at the other end of the room. I inched closer to the television set suspended over the bar and couldn't help watching the open-mouthed reaction of guests who I knew were corrupt. A few others slowly backed away, aghast, as if to say: it's not me, it's not me! Then a photograph of Judge Pompey appeared even though we didn't have enough evidence to charge him. Apart from this one misguess, the report was startling for its depth.

I was prepared to walk out fast at the first mention of my name, before I could be mobbed by people demanding answers and maybe pounded with fists. Standing beside me was Harry Wilson, a former prosecutor. He was one of the few who had known of my role all along, and now he leaned over to say in his low voice, "I bet you're glad it's all over, huh?"

"Harry," I whispered back, "I'm still undercover!"

Wilson's face reddened and he started moving away as perspiration broke out around my collar. When I saw that no one was singling me out, I became almost giddy with relief. Before long it was fun to mingle with the party crowd and add a little misinformation here and there about the mystery government informant. If I heard a wild supposition about a lawyer who was in no way involved, I would saunter over to another group and repeat this so that the erroneous guess would pervade the courthouses for weeks.

An IRS agent even jokingly called August 5th "the day the world changed" because crooked judges suddenly went straight rather than be caught taking bribes or making major purchases with telltale cash. Yet a few of the Greylord targets still did not know about our investigation. Bagman Jimmy LeFevour learned of it when he opened the Saturday newspaper. As we discovered from testimony, he sat in shocked silence until receiving a call from Judge Richard LeFevour's eldest son asking him to phone his cousin at his Michigan summer home. Jimmy was scared, but the judge told him not to worry, that he now knew all about the investigation. Well, not exactly everything, as it turned out.

The next day, the *Chicago Tribune* reported that an unnamed lawyer who had become "sick and tired of corruption . . . put his career on the line" to go undercover. That was me, but I felt safe since the article didn't describe the lawyer as a former prosecutor. Even so, I was hoping my telephone would not ring.

When it did, Costello was on the other end. "Did you see the papers?"

"Yeah. What do you think?" I tried to sound enraged.

"Jesus Christ," Costello replied, "it's unbelievable. I'm not worried, though. I'm a low-volume guy. You know, I mind my own business. You just pick up enough to fucking eat. This stuff is after the big guys, they're not looking for Mickey Mouse hustlers who just hang around."

"What about Wayne?" I asked about Judge Olson.

"Hundreds of lawyers have dealt with him, they'll never figure it all out."

"Who's the mole?" I was testing him.

"I don't know—fuck it."

"It's not me," I said with a forced laugh. "I don't volunteer for anything."

"Okay, Terry."

"I heard it's some guy named Victor who has an office at 2 North LaSalle," I suggested. Why not throw the heat on David Victor Ries, alias David Victor? The FBI had pulled him out of the investigation by now because the press was on to him, although his name had not yet appeared in the papers.

"You think it's him?"

"That's what I heard."

"I'll ask around."

As I hung up, I felt that perhaps Costello had suspected me, after all. His tone had seemed like a halfhearted effort to sound innocent or at least not worth bothering about. It was as if under his loud voice, a whisper had been saying: go easy on me, won't you, Terry?

Early Monday, bagman Jimmy LeFevour drove to his cousin's home, and the influential judge met him still wearing pajamas and a bathrobe. As the two men went over the newspaper articles together, Jimmy mentioned that State's Attorney Daley said on television that he had known about the investigation for nearly three years.

"That little bastard," the judge roared. While dialing Daley's number, he said, "My sons helped in his campaign. I went to the God damned ballgame with him last Tuesday!"

When no one picked up the call, he slammed the receiver down and shouted, "That bastard!" He then told his cousin, "I won't be in this week. See what you can find out."

When the judge returned to his office seven days later, he pulled the framed photos of the smiling Daley family off the wall. One was of LeFevour swearing Daley in as State's Attorney.

During the week of LeFevour's absence, Brocton Lockwood held a news conference on his own to disclose that he had been a government mole for a time. His news conference actually worked to my advantage, since this reinforced the impression some people had that the investigation had focused on the Traffic Court Building.

There was still no more information about the unnamed attorney who had been working for the government. Since my best cover was nonchalance, I pretended to be as curious as everyone else. Then I went back to our "crime academy" warehouse in Addison for our last session and to plot our next moves with Dan Reidy, Bill Megary, Chuck Sklarsky, and the rest of the Greylord team.

For two years we had been kicking around ideas for what our final day would be like. In one fantasy, I would storm into the chambers of the judge who had thrown me out when I offered him a bribe, then slap two hundred dollars on his desk and say, "Let's leave the Trunzos out of this one, judge. I know you take the money, and you know it, so let's cut the nonsense!" But now that the day was here, we had nothing to do.

Maybe that was just as well. In me was the whimpering emptiness of a child who didn't get a Christmas gift. Then one of the agents answered the phone and handed me the receiver, saying, "It's Hegarty," the man in charge of the FBI office in Chicago. I seldom had contact with him, but I assumed he was calling to congratulate us and to say that my merry band of men and women should dissolve.

"Hello, Ed," I said. "This is Terry."

"I have some news you've been waiting for. I have been authorized to swear you in as an FBI agent."

This was what I had wanted ever since I was a child, and I didn't know what to say.

"We're going to keep it secret for now so you can stay undercover," Hegarty added. "You can do your training later."

The agents around us could not hear what the call was about, so I turned and said with almost adolescent enthusiasm, "I'm going to be one of you guys now!" I must have been beaming.

I would have been happy to drive an hour to the faraway tollway rest area where Hegarty wanted to meet me. But Reidy thought all the work I had put into the project deserved a little respect, so he took the receiver and persuaded Hegarty to swear me in at the warehouse. I excitedly called Cathy at her law firm, but she was busy and I couldn't reach her.

The festive mood in our warehouse was a little like a football team locker room after a championship victory. We celebrated by sending one of the agents out for beer and wine while I took a lot of kidding. "You'll never be one of us dressed like that," one of them said about my sport shirt and casual pants. "Hope you don't mind a pay cut," another called out. As a project development specialist for the FBI, I was receiving thirty-seven thousand dollars a year, and agents were starting at thirty-four thousand.

I was so pleased about my new career that I wanted to kick off my shoes and lean back to enjoy the moment. But then came a call from my supposed law partner, Jim Reichardt, saying that Mark Ciavelli wanted to get in touch with me. I knew why, and dreaded phoning him. I certainly didn't want to talk to Mark in front of all these agents. "Sorry, guys," I told the gang, "I don't want to tie up the line, so I'll call from the gas station. I hope to be back before Hegarty comes."

I picked up my briefcase with the tape recorder and drove with an agent to a Shell station a mile away. I attached the suction cup of the recorder to the phone and dialed. The agent stood in front of the receiver to block out the whoosh of traffic so we would get a clearer recording.

Mark picked up the phone and started talking about a client he was going to refer to me, but I could tell that this was just an excuse to talk to me. I interrupted by asking, "Did you see the Trib story about the mole?"

"Who is it?"

"Well, it's not me. We just bought a house, and the last thing I need is to throw it all away by stooling for the government."

"I thought about you when I read it, but then I figured it couldn't be." There was a deadness in Mark's voice. "I'll have the client give you a call."

He hung up and I drove back to the party in our warehouse, my joy now mixed with concern for the man who had once been my closest friend in the courts.

With the reality of the moment settling in, I started thinking that Megary and Bob Farmer must have urged my swearing-in because some of the lawyers and judges were probably becoming desperate. If they ever cornered me or started acting tough, I could now reveal myself as an FBI agent and they would think twice before turning violent.

"Hide the beer, Hegarty's coming!" one of the team members called out as a car pulled up, setting off a stampede to shove bottles into the refrigerator and hide wine glasses and half-empty cans in the cars we kept in the building for our contrived cases. When the head man arrived, there wasn't one hint of our celebration. We could have posed for a photograph of FBI stereotypes from the 1950s. So could Hegarty, a middle-aged man with a manner reflecting his small-town background. He greeted me and waited for one of the agents to fetch a camera. Raising my hand and taking the oath of office, I probably was the first FBI agent ever sworn in while dressed as if for a game of golf.

"Thank you, Mr. Hegarty," I said. At important moments, cleverness eludes you.

"You're welcome," he replied. "Good work."

Megary clapped me on the back as everyone else swarmed around to shake my hand. I felt not only like a bona fide federal investigator but as if I had just been ordained. "Hegarty's gone," someone hooted. That meant open the refrigerator and bring out the beer.

Later that week, top county and federal law enforcement officials held a news conference to disclose that our evidence would be presented to a special federal grand jury and that the first wave of indictments should be returned in about two months. The name "Greylord" was mentioned for the first time but not explained, leading reporters to assume the code word somehow referred to the British legal system rather than an American racehorse.

The announcement created what some called a "climate of fear" in the marble halls of the criminal courthouse. Attorneys refused to talk to one another. Some of them patted each other down for a recorder, and not as a gag. A friendly judge who was known for his honesty became so afraid lawyers would suspect him of being a stool pigeon that he began eating lunch in his chambers rather than mingle with them at the cafeteria or nearby restaurants. The FBI intentionally increased the tension by leaking false information suggesting that ten lawyers were expected to cooperate with the investigation under immunity from prosecution, contributing to the gallows humor throughout the courthouses that late summer.

Still in my undercover role, I joined Costello for coffee one day at the first-floor snack shop at the Criminal Courts Building. He whipped out his black beeper, shoved it at me as if it were a microphone, and asked, "Can you say a few words?" I pretended he was funny.

Costello then talked about how nervous Judge Olson had become. "His chambers could have been wired," Costello said. "Fuck it, we were just doing a few bonds."

"They'd never bug a chambers," I said. "One branch of the government can't intrude on another, we've got separation of powers."

"But so what," Jim said dismissively, "they'll never be able to tell who was talking there."

"Hey, you're right—they'd need a video camera."

Of course he didn't know that I had used a transmitter to notify agents when dirty lawyers were going into the chambers, or that I kept a log of each person going in so we could match a name with the incriminating words picked up by the microphone. And he could not have known how I had gone over those tapes repeatedly with the agents to identify each voice.

At the time of our conversation, some of the fixers were holding private meetings over the situation. They threw out a number of conjectures about who the "rat" might be but my name, we learned, never came up. If I had known how fully the fixers had believed my role, I would have had a lot more sleep in the last three years. Next they settled down to discuss how deep the probe could possibly be. Since no federal investigation had ever been as penetrating and extensive as Greylord had been, none of them even came close.

The crooked attorneys felt protected by two aspects unique to criminal trial work. One was that they could use rainmaking as their defense, saying that the bribes never reached the judges and that they were just tricking their clients into thinking the result had been paid for. The fixers also hoped that juries might believe they were victims of entrapment, that the bribes never would have been made if someone working for the FBI had not arranged everything. Greylord organizers had known of these problems from the start, and there was some nail-biting about whether all our unprecedented effort would hold up.

The only way to get around such defense tactics would be if one of the fixers—not just a bagman—turned against his friends to testify how bribery had been going on for decades. What chance was there of that happening? As one of the shysters put it, "If you stonewall the government, this thing is going to fizzle out."

Each fixer spent these apprehensive weeks according to his own personality: covering up, denying, or using alcohol or drugs.

I was talking to Costello in a courthouse lobby when Peter Kessler came by nervously and bluntly said, "Terry, I hear *you're* the mole." Looking back now, maybe he wanted me to help him, but I froze and kept quiet.

"Bullshit," Costello exploded for me, "I been hearing that for three years. Maybe you're right, Peter"—Jim's tone was mocking now— "maybe Terry *has* been working for the G and he got me to join him and now I'm recording every fucking word you're saying." No laugh was louder than Costello's when he was making people feel uncomfortable.

Later that day, I drew Peter aside to tell him how the rumor had started. Trying to sound as terrified as the fixers had become, I mentioned seeing Jimmy LeFevour's name in the papers as being under scrutiny. "Is everything shut down?" I asked.

Peter Kessler said with a nod, "I think there are some lawyers who are spilling their guts already." He probably was thinking of the fictitious ten.

"Who?" I asked.

"I don't know. God, I hate the U.S. Attorney's Office. They offer immunity to some people and tell the others to forget it." He had the desperate expression of someone whose foot is caught in the tracks and can hear a train coming.

"Maybe it's first come, first served," I suggested and let my hint go at that.

At the time I was appearing in court for all my remaining cases, but for a couple of weeks I dared not risk trying to pass another bribe. But if there was one last thing I wished I could do, it was to hand a second payoff to Lucius Robinson. That way we could charge him with racketeering and pressure him into giving up judges we didn't have enough on, including Pompey.

Autumn 1983

FBI agent Bill Megary advised me against packing my Nagra because the recorder was too bulky to be overlooked by Lucius Robinson's searching eyes, so I was equipped with a small radio transmitter instead. With two agents parked outside the criminal courthouse to record us on tape, I met him in Pompey's empty chambers about a cocaine possession case that might involve a lot of money.

"Too much heat," Lucius said with a jiggle of his head. "They're still following me around with the television cameras. Just present your case. That's all you can do, isn't it?"

And so, with great reluctance, I had to let him and Pompey go and accept that my undercover role was over.

"You can't stay out there forever," said one of the FBI agents from our crime school. We still had to shore up my side of the operation, and that meant getting someone to testify for the government. We talked over who might be the most vulnerable of all the disreputable people I had come to know so well. I sat back, tired, and said, "Costello." Why not? Jim's life was a mess, and leniency might help him put the pieces back together. Besides, no one respected him, so there would be no old boys' network to break through. And, in the back of my mind, I wanted to protect him for the hundreds of hours we had shared as friends.

But no one was enthused because Costello was only a hallway hustler. "Jimmy LeFevour's running scared, and Kessler would be easier," they said. Perhaps. But I felt no loyalty to them.

"No, *Costello*," I insisted. "We got him talking about everything from when he took bribes as a cop to cheating on last year's taxes. Besides, if we get him we can nail a lot of people."

"It's Costello, then," Dan Reidy said without enthusiasm. "We'll send a couple of agents over and bring him down here."

"I want to do the flip," I said.

"These things are tricky, Terry. You don't have the training."

"He won't open up to people he doesn't know. I know how he thinks. I can talk him into it, I know I can."

"Okay," Reidy said. "But remember he keeps a gun and sometimes gets violent. Pick a public place so you can have some backup."

I spent half a day driving around looking for a location before settling on the lounge of the Sheraton Hotel in suburban Oak Lawn, where Jim had dumped Martha when he started divorce proceedings. I called him that evening and said, "I want to talk to you about something, Jim. I spoke to a federal prosecutor about Greylord and your name came up."

I must have sounded like the voice of doom to him.

"What did you hear?" Costello asked.

"This one's too hot for the line, I'll tell you tomorrow."

"I'm just curious, you understand," he said. "I got nothing to worry about."

I mentioned the hotel and said, "So you'll be there?"

"Yeah, Terry," he said, "I'll be there."

I arrived alone but nearly half a dozen male and female agents were already in casual poses around the bar, along with Chuck Sklarsky, my friend from the U.S. Attorney's Office. If Jim raised his voice or moved back his arm to strike me, these agents would grab him in a blink. And if Costello stayed peaceful but balked at what I was about to tell him as a friend, I was to signal for Sklarsky to come over and speak with the authority of the Justice Department.

Jim arrived looking none too happy to be there. After we ordered drinks, I tried to make light conversation but he impatiently asked what was so "hot" we couldn't discuss it over the phone. I reached inside my suit jacket and set an envelope between us either like a threat or a way out, depending on how Costello regarded it.

"First, I have to tell you something," I said. "Jim, those rumors you'd always been hearing, they're true. I was working for the FBI since before I met you, and in August I was sworn in. I'm an FBI agent now." His face turned ashen. "You paid me bribes on nineteen occasions. I wore a tape recorder on all those conversations. In addition to bribes you gave me, I gave you one hundred dollars on one occasion in which you said you would give it to the judge who replaced Olson. You also committed tax violations. It's all on tape. What happens with those tapes is out of my hands."

If Jim had only said something, I would have known how to continue. But he just stared at me as if wishing I would take my words back.

"A couple of times you told me the government isn't after people like you, and you're right, we want people like Wayne Olson," I continued, now knowing that Dan Reidy had been right about my being the wrong person for this. "Judges like Olson put you and other lawyers into positions where you were forced to pay bribes or practically starve. We'll take what we can get, but we're after the judges."

He downed his martini and gave me a broken smile. "You got to be kidding. Aren't you?" I could almost sense his heart sinking.

"No, Jim, I'm not. See those men and women at the bar? They're FBI agents. Now I want you to read this letter."

I opened the envelope and handed him the folded page. The message was from U.S. Attorney Dan K. Webb, inviting Jim to his office for a talk. The paper shook in Jim's hands and his shoulders drooped. This was the first time I had watched someone realize his life was over, and I never want to see it again. I grabbed the letter back to avoid drawing attention.

Costello rose to his feet and told me, "I'm not going downtown. No fucking way." He turned his back to me and started out. As I went after him, he pivoted near the door and asked for the letter, which was still in my hand.

"I can't do that, Jim."

"Just give me the fucking letter."

"Come downtown."

"No."

He hurried to his black Oldsmobile 98—the car he had proudly said Olson "bought" for him by referring cases for an even split in bond money. With Sklarsky and the FBI agents trying to keep up with me, I sprinted across the parking lot in the bright September sunshine.

"Jim, listen to me," I said, "we aren't interested in going after people like you!"

"I don't believe in cooperating." He moved away from his car door and towered over me, this man capable of threatening people with a gun and smashing windshields with a baseball bat. "You are a sick young man," came that rough voice of his. He made a sudden motion but abruptly stopped himself. "I took you under my wing, Terry. I tried to show you how to be a lawyer in the real world. I had you in my home, introduced you to my family." He threw open the car door. "Someday you are going to regret what you have done."

Costello started the engine, but I couldn't give up. Over the years he had said he loved me like a brother, and now I found that the feeling was mutual.

"Are you going to talk to Webb?" I asked through the open car window. "Jim, it's really in your best interest."

"I don't know yet," he answered. "I'll drive around for a while and I'll think about it."

As he pulled away from the lot, I saw that I had blundered by thinking I could get him to cooperate. The only thing he had seen in our meeting was betrayal.

The Greylord team had struck out three times in trying to flip someone—bagman Ira Blackwood, bagman Harold Conn, and now fixer James Costello. We knew we could get some convictions from our three years of work, but not all the ones we had been hoping for.

In our brooding, we came up with a few ideas that sounded rather unlikely. Federal prosecutor Sheldon Zenner said he might be able to get through to Peter Kessler, whom he had met over a case a few months before and spoken with off and on. Some of Zenner's colleagues thought that would be a desperate move since Peter was like Jim Costello, paltry compared to what we had discovered about some others.

The rest of us thought it was worth a try because no one had a better idea. Zenner had realized that the forty-three-year-old defense attorney wasn't only concerned about prison and the loss of his career, he was going through a personal crisis over Greylord. Peter was living on nerve endings and looked haunted by a ghost he alone could see.

Peter had grown up in poverty, persecution, and horror in wartime Poland. He came to America at the age of nine and for the first time knew religious, political, and economic freedom. But he had betrayed his adoptive country and the ethics of his profession. Facing the possible destruction of his family, he began seeing himself as others might. As he would later say, "I had expected more of myself." He was, to our knowledge, the only fixer who still had a conscience.

With Zenner's advantage of not being directly involved in the investigation, he arranged a meeting with Peter and explained that pleading guilty and testifying against others would be a way to pull himself together. Kessler left without a hint about his thoughts, and we considered the meeting just one more failed attempt.

But in October Peter and his lawyer—former U.S. Attorney Tyrone Fahner—met over coffee at the Orrington Hotel in downtown Evanston. Since federal prosecutors were desperate for someone to come over to their side, Fahner suggested this deal: Kessler would give up his law license and plead guilty to only one count of mail fraud. In return, the government would recommend probation rather than prison.

And that was how the fixers' stone wall came tumbling down.

Kessler told us of personally delivering bribes to judges Martin Hogan and John "Dollars" Devine. In fact, Kessler said Devine once yelled at him, "Whatever cases you have in this courtroom come from me. These are not your cases. I don't have to appoint you to them. One-third of your legal fees are mine. These are the rules!" Although most of this had been suspected in a general way, it was astounding to hear it first-hand.

Once word was out that Peter was talking, dozens of minor attorneys suggested to U.S. Attorney Dan K. Webb's office that they might be interested in hearing a government offer. It started to look as if the fictitious ten cooperating targets might become a reality.

Still smarting from the disastrous Operation Corkscrew in Cleveland, the FBI put up photos of various judges on the wall of a back room in their downtown offices. Then for weeks agents asked potential trial witnesses, "Is this John Devine? Is this Wayne Olson? Is this . . .?" It was probably the only "photo lineup" ever conducted in which all the suspects were jurists.

Still making cash expenditure analyses, IRS agents Dennis Czurylo, Bill Thulen and Bill Doukas were no longer looking for big purchases. Even the smallest entries added something to the total. As Doukas said, "We get orgasmic over one hundred dollars." Even the absence of checks for such things as doctors' appointments helped put them on a fresh cash trail. The agents weren't kidding themselves. They considered themselves lucky if they could trace a nickel out of every bribe dollar, but they knew that juries would understand nickels more than points of law.

Eventually the IRS computerized information on one thousand companies and shops patronized by our targets. The same computer printed out label forms for subpoenas and dialed the phone numbers of the businesses for interviews.

Because we still hadn't heard back from Costello since he drove away from me at the hotel, Megary and Larry Dickerson drove to Jim's home one late afternoon in October. Costello assured them he was going to hire a lawyer and fight them. There was nothing more to be said, except one thing. "Mr. Costello," Megary commented as he was leaving, "it might be wise to dispel any thoughts you might have about harming Mr. Hake. If something should happen to him, the full weight of the FBI will come crashing down on you. Do you understand?"

Jim didn't say a word, but I am told that as he nodded there were tears in his eyes.

19

JUSTICE ON TRIAL

Autumn 1983

Since the identity of the much-discussed mole remained a secret except for the persons we chose to tell, I still occasionally showed up at the courthouses for cases we had rigged before Greylord became public. But my main task was to get our evidence ready for the grand jury. That included making transcripts of six weeks of tapes from Judge Olson's bugged chambers and all three hundred and sixty-eight conversations that I had secretly recorded.

That autumn I ran into bagman Jimmy LeFevour near the downtown Traffic Court Building. We only exchanged hellos because he was talking to someone else, but I sensed that he was looking me over to determine whether I might be the impostor. Little did I know that his cousin, Chief Judge Richard LeFevour, had recently sent him to my dummy law office in the suburbs to see if my name was really on the door. Jimmy reported back that my practice appeared legitimate, and so virtually every one of our precautions had proved necessary.

In late November all of Ries' court files and documents on my FBI "clients" were subpoenaed from the clerk of the circuit court's office. Ries had already been identified as an undercover agent, and those files linked my name with his. Newspapers were starting to figure everything out. A reporter phoned my bogus law office but my "partner," Jim Reichardt, refused to talk about me. Actually, there wasn't much he could say since we seldom saw one another.

December 1983

At this time I wanted the Bureau's electronics experts to remove background noises from our recordings. I was at O'Hare International

Airport heading for Washington, D.C., with a briefcase stuffed with tapes on Sunday, December 4, 1983, when I saw a *Tribune* headline about a former ASA who had been a government operative for more than three years. Since every fixer in Cook County must be figuring out who it was, that was the final moment of my undercover work. I felt relief and even a faint thrill at seeing people reading a story about me at the world's busiest airport and not knowing I was at their elbow.

I was still in Washington on Wednesday when my name was at last disclosed to reporters. Cathy answered the phone at our home and told news people only that I was out of town. My mother joked with them by saying that "mothers are always the last to know." That sent the reporters scrambling for anyone who knew what one embarrassingly called "the white knight." The papers even resorted to using a picture of me from a high school yearbook.

When I returned to Chicago the next day, two agents met me at O'Hare and drove me to Chicago FBI chief Ed Hegarty's office. Cathy met me there and we went to a hotel upon instructions from the FBI for our own protection, as if Silverman, Yonan, the Trunzos, Olson, and Devine wanted to use me for target practice.

The courts were in such turmoil that when Judge Maurice Pompey found a construction worker guilty of cocaine possession, the man filed a motion demanding to know "whether or not the court was to some degree influenced by the abusive and uncontrolled power of the press." That is, he was claiming Pompey might be intimidated into finding innocent defendants guilty just to avert suspicion that he took bribes. There had been unconfirmed rumors for years that such things went on.

The judge's response was totally unexpected. He paused to announce from the bench that he was retiring from his judicial career—all the while denying that his decision had anything to do with criticism that he had been excessively lenient in drug cases or that he was under possible federal investigation.

He threw in that he knew of two contracts to kill him in the twenty years he had been a judge and that four men he had sent to prison surrounded him on the street just a few weeks before, and he had to do some "fast talking" to escape them. For all to see, Pompey held up three casings of bullets he said had been fired at him in his career: one dug out of the back seat of his car, another that cracked a window of his home, and a third taken from the roof of the house.

Without mentioning race, the African-American judge also implied that the FBI was using Greylord to persecute him. His statement over, Pompey sentenced the construction worker to ten years in prison, stepped down, retired to his chambers, and slammed the door on clamoring reporters.

Wages of Corruption

The end of the undercover investigation allowed the IRS to call in some of our targets for meetings in the federal building about their spending beyond their salaries. If they were to be believed, people who were then dead had always lent them more money than people still living. Czurylo and Doukas spent months going through boxes of Judge Richard LeFevour's original records in the basement of an Oak Park bank. When the accountant federal agents were ready, they met with the judge in his chambers. Fifteen minutes later he ended the conversation and refused to answer any more questions without legal counsel.

Exactly one week from the day my name was revealed and Judge Pompey announced his resignation, Chicago police sergeant Roger Murphy was scheduled to appear before the first Greylord grand jury. Murphy was an avuncular sort of man in his mid-fifties who had always been helpful to rookie officers and attorneys, including me. He had been looking forward to retiring in a few months and moving to Galena, Illinois. And why not, since we had absolutely no evidence against him. All we wanted to learn was whether, as the court sergeant for judges including John Murphy—no relation to him—he had seen bribes coming from fixers. But, like Ira Blackwood, Sergeant Murphy was bound by the corruptors' honor system.

He spent the night with his lawyer at home. The attorney told him that if he refused to testify in the morning, he could be jailed for the entire grand jury session, perhaps a year and a half. When the attorney left, Murphy went out drinking. The lawyer was so bothered by the officer's hints of despair that he made a couple of calls to the police about whether there had been any suicides on the Northwest Side. The officers didn't know what he was talking about.

Sergeant Murphy awoke as usual the next morning and had a breakfast conversation with his daughter. Like many officers, he never showed his feelings, especially now in dishonor. His daughter asked if he was worried about an indictment, and he told her that one thing was for sure: he wasn't going to jail. Then he said he wanted to go outside for some fresh air.

Instead, Murphy walked into the vestibule of his condominium building. He placed the muzzle of his thirty-eight-caliber service revolver to his right temple and put a bullet through his brain. His daughter heard the shot and rushed downstairs only to find him sprawled on the cold floor.

Just a few hours later, Hegarty and U.S. Attorney Dan K. Webb stood before an American flag and announced in a room packed with reporters the first round of charges in the most sweeping undercover investigation in the history of American courts. The news was so big that the press conference preempted soap operas in Chicago. The indictments were returned against Judge Olson, Judge Murphy, Judge Devine, Jim Costello, Bob Silverman, former assistant city attorney Thomas Kangalos (who had fled to Greece), and three people snared by FBI agent lawyer Ries and Judge Lockwood in the Traffic Court Building. They were police officer Ira Blackwood, Deputy Sheriff Alan Kaye, and court clerk Harold Conn.

The authorities also announced that forty more people were under investigation. The reason for the delay in those charges was not discussed, but it was mainly because the IRS was still working on the financial evidence. Former first ASA William Kunkle, reached a short time afterward, called the investigation "the system cleansing itself."

So where was the "white knight" who had been at the center of all this? I was napping in the FBI medical office on a lower floor of the building. That was because I had accidentally scratched my left eye while reading in bed at the hotel where the FBI was hiding me until new locks and an alarm system could be installed in our home. I visited the emergency room at three a.m. and was put on prescription painkillers that knocked me out. This was the only harm to me resulting from my more than three years in domestic espionage.

Someone awakened me and said Webb wanted to see me in his office now that the reporters were gone. The private meeting was a little like a sedate victory celebration as I was congratulated by Webb, Dan Reidy, and State's Attorney Richard M. Daley, who in five years would be elected mayor. I came out still groggy but feeling really good. The downside would come later.

I hoped I would never again hear from my friend Mark Ciavelli. As a mole, I had changed the type of people I went around with but could never alter my feelings. I had done what I had to in gathering evidence against him, and I didn't want to know any more about him. In fact, only now, reading the court transcripts years after my undercover work, have I learned the full extent of his corruption.

The professionals involved knew that even a dead friendship would get in the way of my trying to "flip" Mark, and no one asked me to make the first step. In November, just before my name was disclosed, Ries and Megary drove alongside his BMW as he was heading for his home in the suburb of Park Ridge. Mark sensed that they were from the government and pulled over a block away.

Without easing into the subject, the men announced themselves as agents, told Mark he was the subject of an investigation, and handed him a letter requesting that he go immediately to the federal prosecutor's office. Mark's answer was just as brief—he wasn't going anywhere until he consulted his lawyer.

Over the next few days, an attorney negotiated an arrangement in which Mark would testify in as many trials as needed but no charges would be brought against him. With this agreement he joined the walking dead, those lawyers whose careers are finished because of corruption and, in their mid-thirties, saw the life they had imagined slip away from them. Mark stopped seeing some of his friends, and eventually his marriage ended as well. He became just another reluctant government witness, taking the stand occasionally and then disappearing.

Altogether, the Justice Department had thousands of pages of reports and tape transcripts on perhaps sixty lawyers, police officers, court clerks, and judges. Webb assigned to the case several assistants who had not been involved in Greylord until now. One of them was Scott Turow, who already had written a well-reviewed account of his law school experiences, *One-L*. He would be writing his blockbuster first novel, *Presumed Innocent*, on commuter trains to work on Greylord prosecutions.

On an early December night, federal prosecutor Sheldon Zenner and two FBI agents went to Barry Carpenter's expensive condominium overlooking Lake Michigan. Barry and his wife, my friend Alice, heard them out but had nothing to say.

Afterward, Zenner mentioned that Alice wanted to speak to me. I was hesitant to call her, but I felt that she would understand because she had been just as much against corruption as I was. Instead, she asked me, "Why did you do this?"

"You know why, Alice. Did you talk to Barry about what he did?"

"No, I haven't," she answered as I heard Barry speaking to her in the background.

"I don't think we should talk like this over the phone," I said. "How about if we get together this evening? I'll have to have someone with us, you understand."

"Yes, I understand. I'll call you back in fifteen minutes."

Fifteen minutes later my answering machine picked up a call, but the person didn't give a name or leave a message. Maybe it was Alice. This fine, reputable prosecutor with a promising career soon resigned from the State's Attorney's Office, and I never heard from her again.

I might as well have become a leper. The fixer reaction toward me was expected, but even honest attorneys turned on me as a traitor, a violator of professional sanctity. People I hardly knew became rude to me, and to this day, I'm told, lawyers who have never met me hate what I did.

We had no control over which trial came first. Chance fell on Traffic Court bagman Harold Conn, who had been seen passing a bribe in public. Our evidence showed that he had accepted sixteen hundred and forty dollars to fix cases, including two hundred dollars intended for Judge John Laurie in a Christmastime shoplifting case involving a store in Water Tower Place.

In effect, there would be two trials going on at the same time—of Conn, and of the entire Operation Greylord. The jury would have to decide whether we were guilty of entrapping him or violating regulations against presenting manufactured evidence. An acquittal in this first trial would jeopardize all the other prosecutions.

I managed to work in part of my Quantico training before testimony began. I was at class or on the firing range from eight-thirty a.m. to five p.m. every day, then spent hours going over copies of the Conn tapes again before going to sleep. We already had transcripts for the jury but wanted them to be as close to perfect as possible.

After two weeks in Virginia, I returned to Chicago for the trial preparations. I spent a full weekend listening to the tapes again with prosecutors, going over questions they might ask me on the stand, and answering questions that might come up in cross-examination. But because of the enormity of our investigation, there was no way I could ever feel ready.

March 1984

During opening arguments in March 1984, defense attorney Sheldon Sorosky suggested that Harold Conn was only rainmaking with Agent David Victor Ries and me, pocketing the money without the judge knowing anything about it. "He just saw two young, naive attorneys with a lot of cash . . . and he figured, 'Oh, my God! This is like taking candy from a baby' . . . [because] these lawyers were talking about cases that almost any lawyer would win." Sorosky conceded that in taking the money his client wasn't as bright as he thought he was. But the issue, he stressed, was whether Conn affected interstate commerce, a requirement for charges under the RICO anti-racketeering law, and further, "was the taking of this money induced under the color of official right?"

Then the prosecution called me to the stand. This was my first time testifying in a federal trial, and the courtroom looked nearly twice as large once I took the oath and sat down. In all, I had given the bagman seven hundred and forty dollars in three bribes. I told the jurors how I delivered one of them to Conn and then how Judge Laurie, to whom most of the money supposedly went, advised me to point out that the security guard involved in the arrest had neglected to bring the stolen items to court, which under the law was perfectly all right. I said that after the judge threw the case out, Conn told me that "Laurie done his job."

Sorosky tried to suggest that in my undercover role I had been attempting to rack up as many judges as possible to please my superiors. Maybe thinking that because of my boyish face I would be rattled, he hammered at what constituted proper conduct in undercover work. He entered into the record the Illinois canon of ethics, including that a lawyer "shall not knowingly make a false statement of law or fact" and shall not "participate in the creation or preservation of evidence when he knows or when it is obvious that the evidence is false."

Then he asked me, "If a lawyer did what you did and he wasn't an undercover agent, he would certainly be guilty of the crime of subornation of perjury, right?"

U.S. District Court Judge John Nordberg sustained an objection and told the jury to disregard the question. But Sorosky merely rephrased what he had in mind and added, "Anywhere in the criminal code does it say that if you are doing a federal investigation that you are excepted from violating the criminal law?"

"No," I answered.

"I have nothing further from Mr. Hake," he said with a contemptuous flourish.

Under re-direct questioning, I assured the jury that Chief Criminal Court Judge Fitzgerald had been aware of my undercover work. When Sorosky took over for re-cross examination, he tried to make the jurors think that any kind of falsehood from a public servant was unethical and illegal.

"When I acted in my role in this case and told something untrue," I said, "I told them because I was a law enforcement officer and I didn't consider that a lie. A lie is something you do for personal benefit."

Rather than turn the case over to the jury as soon as the closing arguments were over, Judge Nordberg wanted a day to make sure each item in his instructions was legally permissible. "This is one of the first cases of its kind in the federal system," he told the jurors. "We're sailing in uncharted waters."

On the final day—while I was back at FBI training in Virginia—Nordberg refused to dismiss charges against Conn on his claim that Ries and I had introduced false testimony in our contrived cases. The judge said that "while the vast number of judges and court personnel are hardworking and underpaid, there are a few bad apples in the barrel. . . . It may be that the only effective way to root out corruption is a sting operation like the one used in this case."

Megary called me in Quantico to say that after less than four hours of deliberations, the jurors came back with verdicts of guilty on both racketeering and extortion. Instead of celebrating by myself, I had to study late for a test on organized crime. A month later, Conn was sentenced to six years in prison and fined two thousand dollars.

For a while the U.S. Attorney's Office was as exhilarated as a sports team that feels invincible. But prosecutors were taking an even harder look at the next case coming up, Judge John Murphy's. They felt iffy about the outcome. We would be up against the natural reluctance of a jury to convict a sitting judge, especially one who looked as judicial and grandfatherly as the plump, white-haired Murphy. We needed a clincher but couldn't find one—until it walked through the door.

Jimmy LeFevour, the newly retired policeman who was called "Dog-breath" behind his back, entered the U.S. Attorney's Office with his lawyer and said, "I'll cooperate."

It turned out that after serving as chief bagman in the municipal courts, Jimmy had been so shaken by Conn's conviction that he decided to jump the sinking ship. He was a fifty-three-year-old recovering alcoholic facing a long sentence, and perhaps in the back of his mind he wanted to get back at his domineering cousin.

We negotiated with Jimmy's lawyers and agreed that he would plead guilty only to misdemeanor tax charges. The pleas brought him two and a half years in prison but allowed him to keep his pension. In return, Jimmy gave us enough information to work out something with one of the "miracle workers" at Traffic Court, attorney Joseph McDermott. In time, McDermott pleaded guilty to tax violations and racketeering bribery for fixing cases with twenty-four judges. So much for just "a few bad apples." In return, McDermott was fined thirty thousand dollars and ordered to serve one year in prison, a leniency granted because he was in his seventies.

But crooked judges remained our primary concern. U.S. Attorney Dan K. Webb decided that he would personally spearhead Murphy's prosecution. If I still seemed like a Boy Scout, as many people said, then Webb looked like a Cub Scout. His incredibly youthful face and enthu-siasm made it easy to underestimate his intensity and cunning.

He pulled me out of my FBI training in Quantico to prepare me for my testimony. That was fine with me, because my academic exercises could not compare to experiences I was getting first-hand. Not knowing when the next trial would begin, I went back to finish my FBI training, which was almost over. But I could not stick around to take the oath with my classmates because I was being called to testify sooner than expected. Before I left Quantico, there was a small graduation party for me with Ed Hegarty, who just happened to be in Quantico, and the head of FBI training, Jim McKenzie, later to be put in charge of the Chicago office. Flying back, I felt that I was now the person I had longed to be ever since I was a boy, but something was missing even though I was unaware of it.

During Judge Murphy's trial, we played more than two dozen tapes. There was a loudspeaker for the spectators, but each juror was given a stereo headset. On one of the tapes I recorded in his chambers, the jury heard him saying he would take the case and "throw the fucker out the window."

Taking the stand again, I told of giving a total of twelve hundred and twenty dollars to the bagmen Trunzo brothers for cases before Murphy. Joseph Trunzo, who was cooperating with us after his indictment, was sworn in as a witness and said he had passed one of those bribes to Murphy in a handshake. Four ASAs testified that they always lost cases in front of Murphy when they were up against his favored defense attorneys. That included the time a defendant admitted under oath that she had been drunk at the wheel but the judge found her not guilty, anyway.

Jimmy LeFevour's first appearance as a government witness caused a stir when he said Murphy had fixed one hundred drunken driving cases as a favor to the presiding judge of the municipal courts, Judge Richard LeFevour. Jimmy added that his cousin received a total of ten thousand dollars for clearing the records of the dangerous drivers.

Mark Ciavelli testified that he gave Murphy seven hundred dollars in three bribes, beginning with three hundred dollars in an envelope after Murphy suppressed evidence in a case. "It was an arbitrary figure that I had picked out," Mark said of the sum. "I didn't want to give him too little to insult him." The next time Mark bribed Murphy in his chambers, he said, he felt he no longer needed to put the two hundred dollars in an envelope to thank him for referrals as the bar association attorney that day.

Murphy's lawyer, Matthias Lydon, rapidly asked Mark about when he learned I was working for the government and whether the U.S. Attorney's Office had agreed not to prosecute him for passing along a one-hundred-dollar bribe from me. Then Lydon badgered, "Has anyone suggested that you might have an income tax problem of any sort?"

"Through conversation with my own attorney, I know that I suffer a small possibility of an income tax problem for the years 1980 and 1981," Mark replied rigidly, as if his usual energy were running out.

"Your agreement with the government is that you won't be prosecuted criminally, right?"

"Yes, that is correct."

Lydon left it for the jury to decide whether Mark might have been lying to save himself.

When Murphy took the stand in a conservative blue suit, his perpetually gruff ways were replaced by meekness. Asked about Trunzo's testimony about a bribe, the judge answered, "Absolutely false; it never happened.... I never fixed a case for any human being, alive or dead." The sixty-eight-year-old jurist also insisted that if Jimmy LeFevour had ever told him he could get money from a fixer, "I'd have thrown him out of the building." Then he smiled and studied the jurors.

But the mask came off under cross-examination. Murphy turned red and pounded his fist on the witness chair while denying all our damning evidence. If the jurors had been leaning in his favor before, they probably were now sure that such an explosive man might be capable of all the charges against him.

On June 14, 1984, John Murphy became the first sitting judge in Illinois to be convicted of a crime associated with his duties. The fourteen hours of deliberations had concluded with verdicts of guilty on charges of mail fraud, extortion, and racketeering. In sentencing Murphy to ten years in prison, U.S. District Court Judge Charles Kocoras called him an "infidel to justice."

Everyone involved in the prosecution held a little party in a bar across from the Loop Federal Plaza. FBI agent David Grossman who was the lead investigator on the Murphy case, even brought along the toy penguin that had presided at all our meetings in the crime academy. Grossman put the penguin on the counter and someone bought it a beer. We were happy and thought all our targets were going to prison. But we were wrong.

20

ON THE STAND

January 1984

That January Mark Ciavelli sent word to Dan Reidy that he wanted to meet me privately at the downtown Midland Hotel, near Federal Plaza. We said hello and acted like buddies, but awkward silences fell between our sentences. At first Mark assured me that he knew why I went undercover, but a few minutes later he asked, "Why did you do it? You got what you wanted on the judges. Why didn't you just let me go?"

It was difficult replying, with his searching for some ulterior motive that just wasn't there. "You tried to bribe me, Mark," I said. "What was I supposed to do? You kept pushing and pushing."

"You should have just said, 'Hey, I don't want to talk about that' and changed the subject."

"No, Mark," I said, "I couldn't. I took an oath. You just misjudged me. I can't help that."

"I'll never know why you did me in, Terry. Weren't we friends?"

"In my mind, we still are."

"Yeah, Terry. The hell we are."

It was too late. It had been too late for too long. There was heaviness in me but I wasn't upset, and I didn't feel guilty.

This was our last conversation, though I glimpsed him in Chuck Sklarsky's office while he was being prepared for his testimony in the Judge Devine trial. While delivering a transcript to another room, I waved enthusiastically and he waved back in a gesture that seemed to say he never wanted to talk to me again. I saw him a final time as we were walking in opposite directions in the Loop some years later. I went to acknowledge him, but he turned away and kept walking.

Our investigations were having repercussions that none of us could have imagined. I've heard of a doctor who could tell from his concentration camp experience when people were going to die soon even if they seemed healthy. It had something to do with the spirit leaving first. That might explain why so many of our targeted attorneys and judges died of natural causes within two years of the initial disclosures.

First was seventy-six-year-old attorney Paul Ross, who was facing indictment on charges of taking a bribe to fix a case before Judge Hogan in Auto Theft Court and conspiring to bribe a judge in a divorce case. After Ross suffered a heart attack at home, friends said he had been deeply distressed over the investigation.

This was followed by the deaths of a court clerk we had evidence against and of the judge who had thrown me out of his chambers when I offered him a direct bribe. Two other judges on the take died before we could bring charges against them, including one Costello claimed would trade his grandmother for a bribe.

Any one or two of these deaths might have occurred without Greylord, but doesn't five within two years seem like more than coincidence? Such a rate among court people had not happened before the investigation, and it has not happened since then.

Even robust Judge Wayne Olson suffered a heart attack one day after going to his lawyer's office and hearing some of the government transcripts from the bugging in his chambers. But Olson was a fighter. He survived and decided, with his enemy Jim Costello, to challenge the legality of the bugging until every legal avenue was exhausted.

The only one of our targets known to have been seriously ill, Judge Alan Lane, continued hearing cases. However, in the midst of a rape trial in October 1982 he had asked three sheriff's deputies to accompany him to the bench for his protection. Everyone in the courtroom knew something important was about to happen. Lane sat down and announced that he was withdrawing from the proceedings because of a state investigation into a possible one-thousand-dollar bribe from attorney Arthur Zimmerman.

Lane, only in his late thirties, had no idea the FBI knew a lot about him as well. A woman he had been dating, Marlene Friedman, had briefly been a citizen mole for us. In addition, there was the case where Lane sent Roth to the Cook County Jail to extort Henry Sutherland for overturning his rape conviction. But the U.S. Attorney's Office decided not to seek an indictment because Lane was dying of cancer, though we at the FBI thought that this should be no bar to an indictment.

Lane was taken off the bench by a vote of the circuit court judges and lived under open suspicion until he entered a hospital in March 1985 and died that same day. The following month, Zimmerman was acquitted of state charges in the 1982 rape case. But eventually he pleaded guilty in federal court to two tax counts arising from Greylord and was sentenced to three years in prison.

Some of our targets began drinking more heavily, and at least one tried to lose himself in cocaine. How much the lawyers drank, I can't say. But a news report said that a month or so before Jimmy LeFevour went over to us, he was staving off his panic with twenty-four cans of beer and two quarts of whiskey a day for two weeks. As he recovered in a hospital, he realized that his life depended on going straight.

Mark's partner, Frank Cardoni, sought medical help from the stress and then arranged to plead guilty on two counts of mail fraud. His mild ninety-day term was later revoked, so he got off with probation and a one-thousand-dollar fine.

With all these deaths, convictions, and plea deals, you can understand our confidence that there would be no stopping the Greylord sweep. We should have remembered that in trials, nothing is ever certain.

The next judge to be tried was John Laurie. His attorney was the formidable Patrick Tuite (pronounced TO-it), an imposing man who held the respect of state and federal prosecutors even though his list of clients read like a crime commission's watch list. Tuite had a knack for sensing which strategy would work best and then using his juror challenges to pack a panel of men and women likely to consider the evidence that way. Next he would present a defense that might not seem rational to an outsider but made perfect sense to those jurors.

In hearings before the trial began, Tuite contended that several of our tape transcripts did not reflect what actually was being said. He sent over his own versions, but these sheets were really inaccurate, and they even omitted Laurie's coarse language.

Deciding to leave no room for doubt, I went to the FBI's electronic surveillance room and took out the original tape of my conversation in Laurie's noisy chambers in a court at police headquarters. Until now I had been using my memory and a faint duplicate tape. There was so much background noise on the original that I had to scrutinize practically every word. I discovered that Laurie had not really said "We'll see" when I asked for a not-guilty. He had told me "Sure."

Sure! I couldn't believe it. I had put my name to "We'll see" on the government transcript, and that's how I had testified at the Conn trial. Since this was something I absolutely wanted the jury to hear clearly, I flew back to FBI headquarters and had the experts enhance this recording along with tapes that would be used in several upcoming cases. I was eager to get back to Chicago.

Newspapers had been playing up the prosecution as a sure thing even though Tuite's presence in the courtroom on the twenty-third floor of the Dirksen Federal Building gave the proceedings a make-or-break atmosphere. Respected Judge Prentiss Marshall contended out of the presence of the jury that of all the trials in his long career, this one could most be characterized as being tried by the news media. Marshall ordered both sides not to use the word "Greylord" in front of the jurors, to avoid influencing the outcome.

In opening arguments, prosecutor Scott Lassar said fixers put their bribes in Laurie's desk, in a coat hanging in his chambers, and in his palm. In his usual one-note drone, Lassar added that Peter Kessler, who by then had pleaded guilty to mail fraud, gave Laurie two thousand dollars in kickbacks for referrals. Having learned from the Murphy trial, Lassar assured the jury that in my undercover work I had portrayed myself as a corrupt attorney "legally under the law." He also explained Judge Richard LeFevour's practice of replacing honest judges with corrupt ones, and said that this was why Laurie took over for a judge who had barred hustlers from his court.

When the electric Tuite took over, he said that if you go to a ballgame expecting a fix, you will think that each strike, each error, and each hit is rigged. He emphasized the relative youth of the thirty-eight-year-old

Laurie and said the new judge did not want to be disciplined as Judge David Cerda had been in 1975 for barring hallway hustlers on his own authority. Tuite neglected to bring up that it was only after Cerda's reprimand that regulations outlawed hustling.

Tuite also described Jimmy LeFevour as a drunk for twenty years who could no longer tell reality from fiction. Jimmy, he said, "must have a melon for a brain by now with all the alcohol it has absorbed." He added that Jimmy shook down the lawyers to set up the hustlers' bribery club "and that not one dime went to Judge Laurie." The phrase "not one dime" came again and again, no doubt to make sure jurors kept thinking about it. As for why bagman Jimmy LeFevour would testify against Laurie, Tuite said the answer was simple: the former officer wanted to save his thirteen-hundred-dollar-a-month police pension.

Touching on my role, he told the jurors that "Hake uniquely and very disturbingly believes that you can commit perjury if you are doing it for the government." He claimed that the tape they would be hearing would show what could happen when a "voodoo expert" in Washington got his hands on an ordinary conversation.

When I took the stand, I testified that Laurie had agreed to see me after getting a call and told me "I talked to Harold," meaning Conn. My tape let the jury go back in time to when Laurie advised me how to handle a case, even telling me to "scream" when the prosecutor asked to have a charge reinstated.

"And then we can get an NG [not guilty]?" I had asked.

That was when, I am certain, Laurie gave me a "Sure."

As brought out in testimony over the next couple of days, Laurie went back in court and found my undercover FBI "client" innocent of shoplifting, completely ignoring testimony that he had been arrested with a candle snuffer and a pair of salt and pepper shakers in his pockets. Instead, Judge Laurie said the arresting guard was unreliable because he had testified that all the exits at Water Tower Place had heavy doors. What? Laurie claimed that he, himself, had recently been there and did not believe that this was true. Even if the doors were made of matchsticks or diamonds, or there were no doors at all, the issue was immaterial. It was just a tactic to obscure the facts.

The prosecution testimony also concerned a later illegal gun case the FBI and I had concocted. So I decided to talk to Laurie about the gun case when he was alone in a hallway, when judges are more amenable to

defense attorneys. Our conversation continued on the way to the elevator and then into his chambers.

"I want to show my appreciation for my case coming up on Thursday,"
I had said.

"Just do a good job and don't worry about it," Laurie told me.

But contradicting the FBI account I had written just hours after the
conversation, Laurie insisted he lectured me about how I should not be
engaged in bribery and then threw me out of his chambers. He testified
he never reported my bribe attempt because he did not want to ruin my
career. I had no proof he was lying because the tape recorder had failed
to record our conversation. I conceded that when I returned to Laurie's
chambers a third time to get more evidence against him, he really did
throw me out.

Unfortunately, Lassar could not ask me to speculate on what might
have been behind Laurie's turnabout. I would have said that in the inter-
vening time the judge might have heard the longstanding rumor about
my being a mole, and that both the *Chicago Tribune* and the *Sun-Times*
were carrying rumors of an investigation.

Throughout my direct examination, I was dreading cross-examination.
Tuite always presented himself as a pleasant gentleman to the jury but
could be nasty on attack. Hardened police officers who had done nothing
wrong were known to bead with perspiration under his questions.

Tuite had often seen me around the Criminal Courts Building, and for
months he would have had a chance to talk to Greylord targets such as
Bob Silverman to learn the best way to turn inside out everything I did.
Whether Tuite actually did this, I don't know, but he seemed determined
to portray me as someone crazed with ambition. He started out by having
me admit that I lied in my work for the government. "Well," he said, "do
you think that as you testify now, you are doing it for the government?"

"I'm doing it for the people of the United States, I believe."

"So that if you tell an untruth, in your mind it's not wrong, even
here on the witness stand?"

"Here, under oath, it's wrong," I answered. "Yes, it is."

Although we had been cautioned never to mention the name of
Greylord in the trial, minutes later I made a slip while explaining our
precautions and said I had discussed such issues "before I ever entered
into the Greylord project."

Judge Marshall sternly interjected, "This is the trial of John Laurie; this is not a 'Greylord case.'" I could almost hear a whip crack over my head.

Tuite lost no time sniping at my credibility. After referring to the oath I had taken on the stand, he asked whether indeed I had once told Bob Silverman that "there is a rumor going around I'm working for the FBI, but honest to God I'm not."

"I told him that, yes. Should I have told him I *was* working for the FBI?"

"Well, you didn't have to tell him anything. . . . Your motive was that it was not criminal, isn't that right?"

"We were doing it for a good 'motive.'"

"But motive isn't an element of a crime. You should know that, don't you?" he asked, no doubt hoping the jury would not realize how nonsensical his argument was.

"Mr. Tuite, the case laws—"

"I'm talking about testifying falsely in court under oath," he interjected. The last thing he wanted was for me to set the jury straight. At an objection from Lassar, Judge Marshall gaveled and ordered Tuite to let me complete my answer.

"The case laws interpreted that, at least in the federal courts, it is permissible for these men [undercover agents] to go out and break the laws of our country to get criminals off the street," I said.

"So now you agree that you were breaking the law?" Tuite asked.

"We weren't 'breaking the law.'"

I then went into the long-ago Mort Friedman case, which had laid the groundwork for Greylord by having Chicago police officers lie in court to help establish payoffs by defense attorneys. "There was no other way to ferret out bribery," I pointed out. "It's a very difficult crime to prove."

And so the cross-examination continued, with Tuite trying to turn each of my replies into something it wasn't. *Oh, come on now*, I thought as the tiresome and distorted questions kept coming at me. To hear him, you would think judges gave just "constructive criticism" for defense lawyers on how to win acquittals, and that I had set Laurie up so I could use FBI money to buy a ten-dollar-and-ninety-five-cent paperback law book and fill my car tank with gasoline.

From out of nowhere, Tuite threw in a line of questioning intended to have me say that it would be all right if a judge decided on a verdict for free as a personal favor. It didn't work. But I conceded that FBI agents and I rigged cases in such a way that there would be something for a judge to base a "not guilty" verdict on. When Tuite asked if I ever heard of rainmaking, I sarcastically replied, "I've heard of that, and ESP and everything."

If Tuite and I were speaking like this in a private conversation, I could have laughed and told him he was being absurd. But because of restrictions on trial procedures, I had to hold back what would have been my human responses even while realizing how my abbreviated answers must sound to jurors who were being asked to take Tuite's word for how courts work.

Later in the cross-examination, I was paraphrasing a prosecutor's speech in a case and did not include an exact word the ASA had used, "fine." Tuite pounced on this and asked, "Is this another part of your lying on behalf of the Government because you think it's good?"

Although the judge ordered the remark stricken from the record, I calmly replied, "I'm not lying, Mr. Tuite."

The defense attorney got around to Traffic Court bagman Harold Conn, who had been convicted of accepting a bribe intended for Laurie. He asked whether Conn at the time had been "pulling a scam on Judge Laurie."

"No," I said, "because Judge Laurie responded to that. He said 'No problem'—twice."

"That doesn't mean he received any money, does it?"

"To me it did."

After more questioning that seemed to go nowhere, I was finally excused. I was glad Tuite had not been able to upset me, and I had no doubt the jurors saw through him.

Once the prosecution rested, Tuite called his strongest witness—Judge Laurie himself. He took the oath looking like a minor movie actor, with a slightly rugged face and his light brown hair combed nimbly to give him a spontaneous appearance. During direct questioning, he answered softly and never acted like the chair-pounding Judge Murphy. When it came time for cross-examination, Laurie mildly denied everything attorney Peter Kessler and bagmen James Trunzo and Jimmy LeFevour had told the jury about giving him money.

Prosecutor Scott Lassar stepped up and asked incredulously whether Jimmy LeFevour ever told him that his cousin, Judge Richard LeFevour, wanted him to split kickbacks from "club members" for their bond referrals.

"No, he didn't," Laurie said, and explained that Jimmy LeFevour had merely asked him to give more business to Kessler and certain other attorneys to make up for having assigned so many cases to lawyers sent by the Chicago Bar Association.

"Now, didn't it seem very strange to you that Jimmy LeFevour was asking you to help these four attorneys?" Lassar asked.

"It seemed strange, yes."

"And did you think that maybe they were bribing him so that he would help them? . . . Didn't you suspect that there was something funny going on here, judge?"

"If you are going to ask me to speculate, yes, I suspected there was something 'funny.'"

"What you suspected is that there was some type of bribery scheme here?"

"I didn't suspect any bribery scheme, no," Laurie replied. He added that when he found an envelope with two hundred dollars from attorney Lee Barnett on his desk, he reprimanded the attorney (who would later plead guilty to bribery) but did not report him to the disciplinary board because "I had no specific evidence as to what his intent was."

"Just came right out of the blue, two hundred dollars in an envelope?"

"That's correct."

And so it went, with Laurie presenting himself as a decent man who never listened to rumors about bagmen and was always willing to hear what attorneys had to say—just a victim of his own credulity.

In closing arguments, co-prosecutor Vincent Connolly compared Laurie and me as lawyers in our thirties, but then started contrasting us by claiming the judge virtually put a "for sale" sign on his bench. "Where Terry Hake saw wrong and tried to correct it, John Laurie saw money and was glad to take it. Where Terry Hake submerged himself into this cesspool in order to do something about it, John Laurie jumped in and helped himself."

During the defense's "closing," Tuite went to a portable blackboard he had set up next to Judge Marshall and, without explaining why, wrote INNOCENT in big letters and GUILTY just as large below that.

Turning to the jurors, he said the government had arranged "deals with scum" to make a case against a good and honorable man. Then he focused on the discrepancy between the original tape and the version I had enhanced, giving jurors an issue they could think about aside from Judge Laurie's guilt or innocence.

"Oh, he says here, 'I wouldn't lie,'" Tuite insisted as he pointed to the empty witness chair. "It's scary. We sort of joke about it. I suppose somebody ought to bring Hake along to bars on Rush Street, and when some guy says to a young lady 'Will you go out with me?' and she says 'We'll see,' Hake would say that's 'Sure.' He would be a great asset. To Hake, a lie is not a lie. Perjury is not perjury. And 'We'll see' is 'Sure.'"

"We hear about these things happening behind the Iron Curtain," he went on. "What was done here to change those words like that, it's frightening. It's an affront to the whole system. And if you can't believe that, you can't really believe anything Hake tells you, because he will tell you anything."

"Maybe they say he's a hero," Tuite commented, "and I'm not saying that what he had in mind was not heroic; he got his lance, and he pulled that visor down his face and he went out there charging, and he didn't care whom he trampled—and he didn't care if with that lance he would stab the truth a few times, or run over the oath a few times to save a fair maiden or to win the crusade. And that's what's wrong. Sometimes a zealot like Terry Hake will not care about the truth."

He went on to compare our activities with the Watergate break-in when, as he said with a biting inflection, "a group of people in Washington, D.C., . . . thought for the good of the country you could break into offices, break into doctors' offices, steal documents, perjure [yourself], obstruct justice, destroy evidence—as long as you are doing it for the 'good of the country.'"

There it was, a complete misrepresentation not only of all my efforts but of the sacrifices of people like Judge Brocton Lockwood, who had resigned from the bench after being disgusted by the corruption that had surrounded him in Chicago.

"Maybe as Judge Laurie sits there now, he says 'I should have gotten involved' in ridding the halls of fixers," Tuite told the jurors. "He didn't. That's not a crime. Sometimes it's an act of compassion as well." Now the large, smiling attorney erased certain letters from the word INNOCENT on the blackboard, above GUILTY.

"Give everybody the benefit of the doubt," he implored. "Don't ruin their lives."

The letters remaining on the blackboard read NO T GUILTY.

Our case was so strong we expected a quick verdict. But the jury spent day after day going over the evidence and playing the tapes. The strain was crushing for Laurie's sixty-two-year-old father, the owner of a pizza restaurant. All during the trial, his face had seemed bleached.

By the third day of deliberations, we suspected that Laurie might be acquitted on some of the lesser charges but convicted of racketeering, extortion, and mail fraud. How could any jury ignore first-hand accounts of bribery from Jimmy LeFevour and Peter Kessler and hearing a tape of the judge coaching me about presenting a case to him for acquittal?

On the fourth day, after a total of more than twenty-two hours of deliberations, the foreman notified the bailiff that the verdicts had been reached. At the time, I was at the FBI office in the same building interviewing a policeman about Auto Theft Court corruption, in preparation for another trial. Judge Marshall summoned attorneys for both sides and waited for them to come through the doors. Judge Laurie returned to the defense table looking drawn. He must have feared the worst for months. Only now, when his real feelings could not affect the verdict, did he allow the struggle to show.

The jurors stood with stone faces as the judge read off that the defendant had been found not guilty on all fourteen counts. Tuite triumphantly crossed the courtroom and shook Lassar's hand, but the prosecutor only glared at him. The rejuvenated Judge Laurie walked silently out of the courthouse with his beaming girlfriend. U.S. Attorney Webb hid his reaction in a courthouse corridor and said into half a dozen microphones shoved at him, "Now that the jury has ruled, I wish Judge Laurie and his family the best of luck as he resumes his career."

When I heard of the acquittal in the FBI offices I felt as if someone had punched me in the stomach. I took a phone call from Cathy at my desk. She said just "I love you," and I started to cry. After setting the receiver down, I went into the evidence room and locked the door to be alone. I felt personally rejected. Five men and seven women had as much as called me a fraud. And why? Because I had to tape a conversation in a noisy chambers. Because the on/off switch of my recorder wasn't working one day. Because of a dispute over "we'll see" and "sure." Because of a clever and relentless defense attorney. I could imagine all defense attorneys across the city, whether crooked or honest, applauding the rapidly spreading news. The verdict gave about twenty Greylord defendants awaiting trial their first reason for hope. As one lawyer said, "A rising tide helps all ships."

When someone called Laurie's father to tell him the verdict, the man gasped, "Thank God!" Later that day he suffered a heart attack while driving. He died in a hospital a week later.

During that week I had been having neck and back problems so I took two days off and went to see a doctor. I explained that I hadn't twisted anything and didn't know what the matter was. "Could be stress," the doctor said. I didn't tell him what kind of stress I was under. If I had thought about it, I would have realized that I was entering a depression. I didn't know yet that this was a common aftermath among undercover agents. All sorts of feelings you have to keep back come flooding through you all mixed up. I was losing interest in outside activities as if they were from someone else's life, and I found it so hard to concentrate that people had to repeat things for them to register in my mind. I was trying to survive in a world that had fallen out of its orbit. I thought the doctor hated me, and my neighbors hated me, that they were all yelling behind my back, "Liar, liar!"

21

REBOUND

Summer 1984

All the federal agents I met that summer were so supportive that they helped me get over my ill feelings from the Laurie trial, but I remained a little on edge because my first child was overdue. Every time a Bureau office phone rang, I thought it might be Cathy telling me to rush to the hospital.

Since I was an FBI agent now, I couldn't devote all my time to Greylord, and so I went on my first raid. I joined hundreds of agents from the Bureau and the IRS for a briefing downtown, then we fanned out to various strip joints where a lot more than stripping was going on. I suppose helping to make mass arrests was important, but it wasn't what I preferred to do.

Cathy had left private practice to work in the State's Attorney's Office. She enjoyed the challenge and excitement of handling prosecutions in the northern suburbs, and she had gone on maternity leave only because the August heat was swelling her ankles.

Finally Christine arrived—blonde, blue-eyed, and the first girl born into the Hake family in sixty years. Still feeling dejected from the Laurie acquittal, I looked at the baby in my arms and thought, *Don't let the world get you down, Christine. Always do the right thing.*

After Laurie's acquittal, court bailiff Alan Kaye came to trial. I never had dealings with Kaye and was not involved in discussions on whether the evidence was strong enough against him. Testimony showed that he alone of our list of targets was just a loud-mouthed rainmaker. No one ever accused Kaye of being an upright citizen—his own attorney called him "reprehensible"—but witnesses made it clear that none of the money he took ever reached a judge. It came as no surprise when

U.S. District Judge Milton Shadur found him innocent of the specific charges but suggested that Kaye "need not go unpunished." Less than a year later, he was sentenced to five years in prison on state charges of extorting money from lawyers in the same cases.

But that came too late to help prosecutors in what reporters considered a period of disgrace for Operation Greylord. A few days after Kaye's acquittal, a *Chicago Tribune* editorial cautioned that we should be extremely selective in future prosecutions and "nail each one down tight instead of gambling on a big score."

Indeed, a third acquittal would make Greylord look like a ridiculous waste of time and taxpayers' money, so we took additional measures preparing the case against Judge John "Dollars" Devine. I was asked to transcribe every word spoken on my tapes against him, even if it concerned the weather. This way, the jurors would be able to study the conversations more easily.

Devine had recently been voted out of office by the Cook County court system's full circuit court judges largely because of Greylord disclosures. The alcoholic jurist also was rejected by his ex-wife, his son, and nearly all his relatives. Devine tried to open a law practice but couldn't attract clients because of the "heat," so he managed a small bar, selling beer a few blocks from the Traffic Court where he had once sold justice.

Because of his combination of avarice and contempt for the lawyers who bought his decisions, "Dollars" was considered the slimiest of our targets. What he needed was the very best defense, someone who might be able to throw the jury's attention completely away from the evidence and his abrasive personality.

The former judge hired Edward Genson (pronounced JEN-son), known for his merciless cross-examinations. "Terry," one of the lawyers in the prosecution office told me, "if you don't watch out, he'll tear you to shreds." Watch out for what, I wondered—after all, I hadn't done anything wrong.

Dan Reidy himself and Assistant U.S. Attorney Candace Fabri, put me through a grueling mock cross-examination in Reidy's office to get me ready for whatever questions Genson might throw at me. But, as I was to learn, it wasn't nearly enough.

The trial was heard in front of U.S. District Judge Susan Getzendanner, the first woman on the federal bench in northern Illinois. Getzendanner was tall and attractive with long blonde hair, and had been first in her class at Loyola law school. She read spy novels for relaxation and would relieve proceedings with light remarks about the meandering questions of attorneys and their knee-jerk objections.

The high-priced defense attorney appearing before her was a moderately plump man of average height with curly red hair and light skin. Genson's medical problems had him walking with a cane but, strangely, the limp seemed more pronounced in front of the jurors. His strategy in the Devine trial was not to attack the weakest link in the chain of evidence but what the prosecution considered its strongest one, me.

In corridor chit-chat before the trial began, Genson apologized to me for what he was about to put me through. Of course he didn't want me to hate him personally, but I also think he wanted to psych me out by making me tighten up. I already liked him in a distant way but made sure none of the jurors saw us having a friendly conversation. Let them believe he was a monster. I could play games, too.

One of the first prosecution witnesses was Peter Kessler, the unexpected wild card in Greylord. He told of bribing Devine in his chambers, and explained that lawyers at Auto Theft Court in police headquarters commonly carried around several hundred dollars for court workers on the take. He added that in one year, bond referrals from Devine made up eighty-five percent of his income from auto thieves. These cash bond referrals totaled twenty-six thousand dollars, minus one-third for the judge. As for why he had started handing over a cut, Peter said, "There is no doubt in my mind that I was being shaken down by Judge Devine."

Under Genson's questioning, Kessler admitted violating oaths "on numerous occasions" as a fixer.

"Sir," Genson bit in, "so long as you testify consistent to what the government's belief is, you won't be indicted for perjury. Isn't that right?"

"No, that's not right at all."

"That house you had in Highland Park, it's up for sale for, what, for half a million dollars?"

"No."

"How much?"

"What does that have to do with anything?"

"It has to do with what you would have lost in August of 1983 [when news of Greylord broke out] if you had to go to jail, sir."

"We could live in an apartment.... My family was my main concern."

Genson tried to press the point but the prosecution objected. Even so, he had Peter admit that Devine stopped him from hustling outside Auto Theft Court. The questioning never made clear that this was done to make him more dependent on referrals from the crooked judge. Kessler also admitted that Devine was an abrupt, stubborn, and hot-tempered man in a courtroom, a strange line of questioning until you heard what came next.

Pressuring Peter on bribes he was handing to other judges, Genson said, "Sir, you had a gold mine down on the eighth floor [of police head-quarters]. . . . Of all the judges that you named [as being on the take], sir, you got Devine who extorted you, right?"

"That's correct."

"Because you didn't like him, right?"

"Not because I don't like him."

Genson noted that Devine was indicted on forty-nine counts, in-cluding "for each and every one" of the bond referral checks the gov-ernment contended Peter had split with him, yet Peter was indicted for just one of those transactions. Genson quickly moved on to the practice of hallway hustling and suggested that such lawyers won acquittals not from bribes but by knowing the "idiosyncrasies" of the judges.

Closing in for the kill, Genson tried to use our witness against us by referring to the period after Kessler came over to our side but when I was still representing undercover FBI agents. "There was nothing wrong with Hake putting on this man to tell a lie under oath, is that right, sir, as an experienced lawyer in the criminal court system?" Genson asked sarcastically.

"There definitely is a lot wrong with that."

"But he told you he was going to do it," Genson continued. "He told you it wasn't the truth, and you said to him, 'The truth doesn't matter.'"

"Because I told him, based on what the system is like, the truth doesn't matter . . . as far as the outcome of the case is concerned."

"Sir, if the truth doesn't matter, telling a man to lie under oath in a courtroom, sir, is certainly less important to you than your family and your ability to get out of jail by telling a story, isn't that right?"

"I never told him to have anybody lie in court under oath. . . . The truth is very important today, the truth is very important yesterday, the truth is always important, Mr. Genson."

When the defense attorney had no further questions, Chuck Sklarsky called Mark Ciavelli to the stand.

Mark told of bribing Devine personally and seeing him put the money in his pocket. Mark also said he had never taken a bribe as a prosecutor, but he began handing money out soon after he became a defense attorney and had cases before Devine. Genson's assistant, Alan Blumenthal, asked, "Is it fair to say to you that when you left the State's Attorney's Office, you knew you were going into a corrupt practice?"

After a hesitation, Mark sadly answered, "I guess I will say yes to that."

He admitted bribing prosecutors, police officers, and deputy sheriffs but not necessarily for specific cases. He made clear that he would do that so they would be receptive to him in the future.

Such practices were new to the jurors, but it was a pattern we all had seen repeatedly in the courts: the judge mistreats a young prosecutor or defense attorney to set himself up for cash, and in time the lawyer learns to pass money around to corrupt everyone else, even before any services are needed. Then many of those corrupted lawyers become judges, and the carousel of greed continues uninterrupted and everybody has a good time. Until the reckoning.

Payoffs and kickbacks were so pervasive that Mark said that it wasn't until "the heat came on" with an article about hallway hustlers in 1981 that he fully realized the illegality of what he had been doing. "I looked at myself in the mirror one day and said, 'Hey, I have to get out of this activity,' and I took steps to get out of the activity. I knew it was morally wrong."

Mark couldn't force himself to use the word "bribery" or admit that the government had pressured him to flip.

The balding defense attorney asked Mark what he had thought about me while I was still an assistant prosecutor and he was a defense attorney. "Hake was a kind of boyish-looking young man, is that correct?"

"Boyish, yes, yes."

"You perceived him as being somewhat naive?" Blumenthal asked.

"I did."

"You know now that he wasn't naive, don't you, sir?"

"I know now that he is an FBI agent," Mark said.

"Your good friend Terry Hake, that slept over at your house, he was recording you, wasn't he?"

"That he was."

"And he was reporting on paper [in FBI reports] everything that happened, isn't that correct?"

"Yes, he was. Yes, sir."

Blumenthal asked whether he had suspected I was working for the government when the Greylord disclosures were made. Mark had never been at a loss for words, but now Genson's assistant and the jurors were staring at him, waiting for an answer.

"I suspected that he was the agent [mole] and I probably knew in my heart that he was the agent, and I tried to deny the fact that he was an agent, hoping that that would—he was not the agent. . . . I tried to live on with my life thinking that: Hope to God that the thing would go away and that I would not have these problems and he would not be an agent and everything would turn up [all right]."

Mark admitted that some of our recorded conversations concerned his wedding plans and buying gifts for his bridal party. None of this had anything to do with Judge Devine, but the defense wanted the jury to picture me as cold-hearted even before I took the stand.

Court rules had kept me from sitting in on Mark's testimony, and I know it now only from transcripts. Yet as I sat in the witness room, I could imagine what sort of questions would be facing me. A bailiff opened the door, and then I walked out and took the oath.

I told the jurors how Devine advised me to see his bagman, Harold Conn, when I tried to make a direct bribe. Next I explained how a year and a half later the judge personally accepted a one-hundred-dollar payoff from me in a corridor of the Traffic Court Building. The prosecution played a tape in which I asked, over background conversations and the sounds of shuffling feet, "Is one okay?" and Devine answered "Yeah, sure."

After Chuck Sklarsky as one of the prosecutors questioned me for two days, Genson took over for what would be my three days on the hot seat. He began by asking whether I knew when I taped a conversation that it would be played before my supervisors, a judge, and a jury. "You were in effect on stage at that point, weren't you, sir?"

"I don't think I was 'on stage.'"

"Well, sir, you were making those recordings for the purpose of memorializing what you hoped to be an illegal transaction on that day?"

"Not for what I hoped to be illegal transactions."

Regarding the time I gave Conn a bribe to pass on, Genson asked, "Did you go back to Judge Devine and say, 'Did you get the hundred and fifty dollars I gave you?'"

"No, I didn't feel it was necessary."

Genson went on to ask about favors I did by dropping charges against a few narcotics defendants early in Greylord. "And the dope peddler, he would go free, right?"

"That wasn't my purpose."

"But he would, just as a side issue."

"Yes, he would go free. Yes."

"You did . . . on numerous occasions instruct agents to lie under oath at various of these FBI-created cases, is that correct, sir?"

"Yes, I did," I said. But I quickly explained that this did not constitute subordination of perjury because it was part of my undercover role.

As he had me describe summer working conditions at Devine's stuffy Auto Theft Court, I admitted telling a lawyer that the judge was "scum."

"So we didn't have the most impartial of FBI agents going in on July 6, 1981, to Traffic Court with Mr. Benson [the name used by an undercover agent], did we?"

Having made his point, Genson said to an objection from Sklarsky, "I'll withdraw the question. It's easier than arguing."

Instead he went into my friendship with Mark. As he spoke, I separated a little from myself and could almost see how Genson wanted to portray me. This helped me couch my answers, but I could feel the energy I needed flow out of me.

"He confided in you?" Genson asked.

"Yes, he did."

"Even though you had the FBI money when you went into practice, you took some of his office furnishings?" Genson's eyes twinkled with mischief.

"He lent me two chairs."

"Did you ever give them back?"

"No, I haven't given them back yet."

Taking another tack, he asked, "Didn't you encourage him to go bribe Judge Olson?"

"I don't think [I did] outright, but I suggested it, yes." Since I could reply only to what had been asked, I could not explain that it was Mark who said I should introduce him to Judge Olson so they could work out an arrangement on a PCP case.

"Basically what you did say to him was . . . that he should bribe Judge Olson, didn't you, sir? . . . Didn't you say, 'What are you going to do if his eyes are going to bulge?'"

"Yes."

"Then you suggested that maybe you shouldn't introduce him, he should go through Costello."

"Yes."

"But he says he doesn't want to do that, and you said, 'Well, he's back there now, do you want me to introduce you to him' or anything like that? Do you remember that?"

"Yes."

"In your conversation, you make no attempt to discourage your good friend, the one who talks to you about his wedding and baby, from bribing or attempting to bribe the judge, did you, sir?"

"No, I did not."

"And would that have influenced or hurt your role as a law enforcement officer of the FBI if you had told your friend, 'Look, just stop all this and start practicing law the right way'? You wouldn't have had to uncover your identity by doing that, would you, sir?"

"No. But it would have been wrong for me to let it go by my eyes, too, Mr. Genson, as a law enforcement officer."

Judge Getzendanner apparently noticed from my slowing responses that I was wearing down and called for a fifteen-minute recess. We all could have used some water and a chance to walk around. When we returned to our places, Genson picked up a new thread by portraying Judge Devine as an innocent man in a corrupt world.

Referring to the "catch phrases" that fixers used, such as "see you later" as meaning I'll pay you a bribe, he asked, "Doesn't that assume that the person you're talking to knows the code?"

"Yes."

"Did you end a conversation with Ciavelli saying, 'Talk to you later'; Hake saying, 'See you later'?"

"Yes."

"Did you mean you were going to pay him any money?"

"No, I don't think so."

Genson apparently was disappointed that I wasn't unnerved when he had practically accused me of stabbing Mark in the back. He kept asking rambling questions as if trying to find a foothold until Judge Getzendanner recessed the trial for the day.

I felt as little relieved as a boxer sitting on his stool between rounds, knowing that he has to go back and get slugged some more. I couldn't enjoy looking at the changing fall colors as I drove home or even spending the evening with my family.

When I took the stand the next morning, I was fresher but so was Genson. He played tapes of conversations over again and hammered away at minor points until all of us were uneasy.

Admonished for his hostile tone, Genson promised the judge that henceforth he would "unantagonize" his voice. But he became abruptly accusatory when it came to the second time I tried to bribe Devine. "The fact of the matter is, at that time you were an agent trying to make a case, is that right?" he asked.

"That's correct."

"You were trying to inculpate Judge Devine in a crime, is that right?"

"That's correct."

"Did Judge Devine say, 'Go give Harold [Conn] some money?'"

"No, he did not."

"*You* brought up Harold, is that right?"

"That's correct."

"In that two years" when I was a project development specialist rather than an FBI agent "you had not put any money into any judge's hand. Is that correct?"

"No, I did not."

He tried to imply that I was setting the judge up to justify all the work we had been doing. But the questioning was punctuated by Sklarsky's repeated objections over Genson's repetitive and argumentative approach. The badgering returned so often that the judge sometimes acted as a referee between Genson and Sklarsky that day and the next.

Toward the end of my third day of grilling, Genson made an unusual request, that I stand before the jury as another of our tapes was played. He asked me to recreate how I had handed Devine the one hundred dollars.

"He kind of held his hand out," I said. "I went like this"—showing him the fixer's way of passing money from palm to palm so that anyone walking by would think nothing of it.

"You didn't offer it to him?" Genson asked with feigned surprise. I felt like saying, Well, I didn't exactly force the money into Devine's fist.

Imitating my motions, Genson asked, "So you held it up like this?"

"No, I didn't. I said, 'Is one enough?' or 'Is one okay?'"

"Sir, sir," the attorney said with practiced irritation, "I'm asking you a question. Was the person able to see the money in your hand the way you held it?"

"I don't know if he could or not."

"Devine didn't reach out with his right hand, did he?"

"No, he didn't."

"You can sit down," Genson said sharply.

"No," I said to complete my sentence, "he used his left hand."

With threadbare patience, Judge Getzendanner told Genson that she would like him to conclude the cross-examination soon. She must have known that the questioning had been protracted to wear me down.

"Well, I'll conclude it," he said curtly and spun around to me as I returned to the witness chair. "Now, sir, if you didn't know whether a man was guilty or innocent, you wouldn't lie or finagle or conjure up evidence to get that man convicted, would you?"

"No, I wouldn't do that."

"But if you did believe, based on your views about a man, that someone was illegal or immoral—corrupt, whatever you would call it— would you get up in a court and conjure up evidence or get up in a court and lie?"

"No, I would not."

That should have been the end of it, but Genson wanted to finish with a flourish. "Sir," he said, "you lied here today about having given Judge Devine a hundred dollars."

"No."

"Well, sir, I submit that you did." He turned away and added, "I have no further questions."

I assumed the worst was over and eased up when Chuck Sklarsky started his re-direct questioning. He had me clarify that all my actions were being supervised, and had me relate how I knew that my friend Mark had become corrupt. And so I told the jurors something he had said to me, that "in order to be successful in the court system, you have to pay the judges to get what you want. To protect your client's interest, you have to pay the judges."

Part of me was back in that painful time when I tried to warn Mark. I had told him it would be better not to buy the judges, no matter what they did. But he said to me, "It doesn't work that way." As I had learned, there would be more honest attorneys in this world if there were more honest judges.

Sklarsky continued asking about my personal reactions, trying to show the jurors the human cost of my work. I admitted that after the conversation with Mark "I went home and cried to my mother." Not only had I discovered that I had lost my closest friend at the State's Attorney's Office to corruption, I had been forced out of the illusion of basic human goodness that had sheltered me all my life.

"Do you want a recess?" the judge asked. I was unable to answer her, for I found myself crying and couldn't believe I was behaving this way in front of everyone. I just couldn't collect my feelings once the first few words tumbled out. I held up my hands in a time-out signal. "Let's take five minutes," Getzendanner said.

I had steeled myself for the cross-examination but let myself be open during the re-direct. That was when the deepness of my emotions caught me by surprise, and I headed for the witness room. Sklarsky was waiting for me. He gave me a manly hug and started crying, too. "I'm sorry I got you involved in all this," he said. "We asked too much."

"It's all right, Chuck." I was already feeling better. "I don't regret it." Any of it.

An assistant prosecutor resting up in the room said that there should be a special place in hell for lawyers who defend evil judges. Just that little joke lifted my spirits. A law school professor friend of mine, Randy Barnett, came in wanting to know what had happened to me on the stand. Barnett was attending the trial as a spectator but had gone to the washroom while I was still testifying, and when he returned the trial was in recess and a former public defender was complimenting Genson for his attack on me.

I couldn't explain without crying again, not with someone else near us, so I took Barnett to the empty hallway and told him what I could. But some things you can't explain. All the education you go through from kindergarten through law school doesn't prepare you for the human heart. There aren't any white knights. Just ordinary people. They get beaten, then they have to pick themselves up and go through it all over again.

When the trial resumed Genson seemed pleased with himself and was ready to attack me again. During re-cross examination, he tried to suggest that the jury had seen a staged performance. "*I* asked you many questions about him," he said about Mark, "and you didn't cry then, did you, sir?"

"No."

He asked whether, apart from the conversation that Sklarsky had me describe, I ever said anything to Mark about handling cases on their merits alone.

"No, I didn't."

"And this was your good friend, isn't that right, sir?"

"Yes."

"And you continued to use him as a source of introductions to other people who you thought might help you in your investigation . . . and continued to be involved with him and talk to him about the fixing of judges, isn't that right, sir?"

"Yes, I did."

"And this was the same good friend you cried about just a few minutes ago, wasn't it, sir?"

"Yes, it is."

Having milked the situation as much as he dared without turning jurors against him, Genson tried to minimize everything I did by saying my appearances before Devine were for just two drunken driving cases, and judges might be expected to temper justice with mercy.

"Mr. Genson, you were talking about judges' findings in general, which could have been a rape or a murder," I replied. "The judge has a sworn obligation to find that person guilty."

"And because you had a sworn obligation as an FBI agent-to-be, project development specialist, you felt it was more important to use Mark Ciavelli as a source than to treat him as a friend and dissuade him from what he was doing, is that right?" Genson was staying away from the fact that it was Mark who had initiated nearly all our conversations about bribes. In fact, I had never wanted to see him again after he let me know he was corrupt.

"Objection," said Sklarsky.

"You may answer," the judge ruled.

"Is that right?" Genson badgered. "Yes or no, *if you can* answer."

"That's not right, no," I said. By now I was too used up to give the question an answer it deserved.

"I have no further questions," Genson told the judge.

I stepped down from the witness chair and left through a side door feeling as if I had just survived a hurricane. I was not so much glad it was over as I was sad and tired, and wondering how to get on with my life.

Getzendanner recessed the trial for the day. When reporters later asked her about my breakdown on the stand, she replied that any man would cry after so many hours of harassment in which he was presented as "a completely insensitive person."

While she spoke, I went to the FBI offices downstairs. Everyone was nice to me but I felt stupid for losing control. I can see better now why it happened. The stress of undercover work builds up in the fissures of your personality, and you never know when the pressure will erupt. Genson's questions were not devastating—after all, I was not hiding anything and I was not ashamed of what I had done—but they had dragged to the surface all the things I had been trying to keep myself from thinking over. Now that my emotions had been released I couldn't hide them any longer.

The "closings" were divided into three parts, with the prosecution and the defense alternating. Assistant prosecutor Sheldon Zenner began by telling the jurors that "you have heard about corruption of such magnitude that it has never been seen before in a courtroom."

Getzendanner sustained a defense objection.

"The clerks were taking money, the sheriff's deputies were taking money, lawyers were paying money to the judge," Zenner continued. "You heard testimony from Mark Ciavelli about police officers taking money. You heard testimony from so many different people about the pockets of corruption, enormous corruption. And if you ever saw a need for an undercover project, you saw it here."

The judge called a break before the defense delivered its closing statement.

During the long cross-examination, Genson had been unable to suggest I was heartless. Now he needed another concept the jurors might think over. Somehow it came to him: that I had been so idealistic I was blind to the consequences of my zeal.

"Corruption doesn't belong anywhere in our system," he started off. "But the problem is, when you're fighting for a good cause it doesn't mean that you can forget the truth in a court of law." Then he said, "Terry Hake is misguided and the rest of them are slime. . . . The man lived a lie for three years. His primary goal was to get a judge. And I submit to you, that's what he did. And that he lied to get that judge."

The lawyer walked stiff-legged to the jury box and back to the defense table, where former judge Devine sat as if he didn't care. There might have been a reason he looked drunk—a rumor going around was that he had been downing a few during the recess.

"The end does not always justify the means," Genson said. "I'm asking you, ladies and gentlemen, don't make their wish come true. Don't make the Ciavellis and the Hakes and the Trunzos and the Kesslers, don't make their wish come true. Find him not guilty. Do John Devine justice, find him not guilty."

Silly as it may sound, was Genson hoping they would be thinking of "divine justice"?

In the final part of the prosecution's closings, Sklarsky said Devine's court had smelled of corruption. "You don't want to walk into a courtroom anywhere in the United States wondering, 'Do I have to go in that back room and lay some money on the judge in order to get fair treatment?' There was a cash station going on there, and it wasn't justice going on there [at police headquarters], and it wasn't going on in Traffic Court. If you don't believe it, listen to those tapes. Because when a judge takes money in connection with his official duties, we're all in sad shape, it goes to the very heart of our democracy. You cannot have a crime involving corruption that is any worse."

The jurors deliberated for four days, and we were practically biting our nails. As with the Laurie case, we were worried that, from the time they were taking, they would find Devine innocent of something. But how many charges—all of them? Then we might as well pack up and forget about all the trials still lined up. We had presented our strongest witnesses and one of our most damning tapes.

In the twentieth hour, the jury filed in. Devine, looking distinguished with his large glasses and trapezoid mustache, had hope on his face as one of his lawyers held an arm out for him at the defense table. Then the verdicts were announced. On two counts of extortion—not guilty. But on the twenty-five other counts of extortion, the single count of racketeering, and all twenty-one counts of mail fraud, guilty, guilty, guilty, guilty. . . .

I am told Devine held back tears from his glassy eyes as he rose and walked out of the courthouse with his arm around attorney Blumenthal for support. I wasn't there to see it because this was Columbus Day and I didn't have to be at work. And so I was home playing with my baby when my office called about the verdicts, and I felt like leaping around the room.

U.S. Attorney Dan Webb faced the inevitable microphones outside the courtroom and called the convictions "a resounding verdict on the entire Greylord project." Justice had been put on trial, and won.

The guilty verdicts were like cannon shots fired through the defense fortifications for all the men awaiting trial. For weeks afterward there were informal conferences in restaurants, bars, and law offices about what they should do next. A number of fixers decided to change their pleas to guilty rather than take their chances with a jury.

In December 1984, Devine returned to court for his sentence. His lawyers told Getzendanner about the downward helix of his life. "Judge Devine suffers from guilt; he suffers from shame and embarrassment," Defense Attorney Jeffrey Steinback told the judge. "His intellect and body literally have been decimated by alcohol. He lives a chronically lonely life. . . . He drinks himself to sleep every night. He is stripped of his robes and he has no prospect for a real future."

Devine removed his glasses and rubbed his eyes with crumpled tissue.

Judge Getzendanner looked down from the bench and told the defendant, "I'm not going to make any speeches, but your crime was despicable." She then handed down a term of fifteen years in prison, the longest sentence that had ever been imposed on a public official in Illinois.

Devine took his case to the U.S. Court of Appeals, but by then the justices had ruled in the Judge Murphy case:

> Bribery, like a wholesale transaction in drugs, is a secret act. . . .
> Because the crime leaves no complaining witness, active participation
> by the [undercover] agents may be necessary to establish an effective
> case. The agents' acts merely *appear* criminal; they are not, because
> they are performed without the state of mind necessary to support a
> conviction. The agents who made up and testified about the Greylord
> "cases" did so without criminal intent.

The FBI and prosecutors had acted honorably, the ruling stated, and Devine was convicted of "conduct so despicable we will not engage in a battle of adjectives in an attempt to describe it." The ruling added that "Greylord harmed only the corrupt."

The decision not only determined the fate of future Greylord defendants, it gave the Justice Department a green light for similar investigations anywhere in America.

Devine began serving his sentence at the federal prison in Oxford, Wisconsin, in July 1985 but doctors discovered he had terminal cancer. He lapsed into a coma and died in April 1987 at a federal prison hospital in Springfield, Missouri. I felt sorry for him because he was so smart, he had such potential, and he threw it all away.

22

FINAL JUSTICE

May 1984–August 1991

As the Greylord steamroller continued, the judge who took over the First Municipal District from Richard LeFevour, Donald O'Connell, immediately banned all hallway hustling and ordered that lawyers stop holding informal discussions with judges in corridors and cloakrooms. Chief Circuit Court Judge Harry Comerford imposed a badly needed system of assigning cases to judges by lottery, and a commission was set up to look into ways of improving the judiciary and reducing the political influence. But as we had learned, fixers can get around any new procedures.

The gentlemanly Bob Silverman did not want to go through the indignity of a trial. He pleaded guilty to racketeering, bribery, and mail fraud, but refused to cooperate with the government. He was sentenced to seven and a half years in prison and fined three thousand dollars.

From people who had flipped and witnesses called so far, most of the crooked judges knew whether they were marked. One of the men finding himself living in a troubled limbo was fifty-six-year-old former judge Allen Rosin, a decorated Marine from the Korean War. He was the one who once bolted from his chair, spread out his black-robed arms, and declared, "I am God!" U.S. Attorney Anton Valukas contended that the judge would buy and sell children's futures in child-custody cases. A group of outraged litigants banded together in a group called "Victims of Al," and Rosin lost his bid for retention in November.

Rosin did not want his daughters and elderly mother to be subpoenaed. In June 1987, the night before he was to be indicted for taking bribes in Divorce Court, the trim and good-looking judge walked into a health club on Chicago's Near North Side. He took with him things with deep personal meaning: his Marine Corps medals, a Father's Day card, and photos of his two adult daughters. Rosin laid these memories on the floor of a tanning booth and shot himself in the head with a snub-nosed revolver. A headline the next day read: FINAL VERDICT—SUICIDE.

Next on the government's list was our main target, Judge Richard LeFevour. The incredibly boyish-looking Dan Webb, who had entered private practice after the first Greylord trials, took over as a special Assistant U.S. Attorney just to make sure LeFevour did not slip away. Webb admitted that this would be "the big one" because of the judge's political influence. Reidy and Candace Fabri were also part of the prosecution team.

It was no secret that LeFevour—like Judges John Devine and Allen Rosin—owed his position to friends in the Democratic Party, and now those friends were being called upon for one last favor. Legal expenses were projected at one hundred and twenty thousand dollars, and an anonymous committee of lawyers and politicians felt that LeFevour would need no less than the attorney who had been successful with Judge Laurie, Patrick Tuite. His strategy was to conceal LeFevour's arrogance and encourage the jury to pity him.

LeFevour was only fifty-three, but by now he looked like he was pulled from a grave. The Greylord depression was upon him and he was suffering from a liver ailment. Instead of presenting himself as an upstanding citizen, as many defendants do, each morning Richard came to his trial with scuffed shoes and unruly gray hair lying like thatch across his rutted forehead. It was as if he were saying how dare we persecute such an unfortunate, ordinary man.

This was the first major case to come before U.S. District Judge Charles Norgle since being sworn into the federal bench six months before. The trial was such a showcase that among the spectators crowding into the benches for every session were members of the Courtwatchers Club, about thirty retired men and women who found trials more interesting than daytime television. They would issue newsletters analyzing defense and prosecution strategy in major cases.

I wasn't allowed to sit in at the trial because of the possibility that I could be called as a witness, so I kept up with developments from what people in the U.S. Attorney's Office told me and running newspaper accounts. Little by little, testimony showed that LeFevour had been able to set up a secret organization of corruption within a reformed Traffic

Court that at the time was being cited as a model for the rest of the country. He had looted the justice system like Long John Silver, installing pirates as crew members on a ship bound for Treasure Island.

Circuit Court Judge Brian Crowe testified that he was reassigned as soon as LeFevour discovered he was honest. Former policeman Robinson McLain—who had been sentenced to fifteen months on his plea of guilty to tax cheating—told of delivering forty to fifty bribes to LeFevour for dismissing the parking tickets of others. The judge, he added, called the payoffs "just a ripple in the pond." A parking ticket supervisor told jurors that after a 1981 television disclosure of wide-scale bribery in the building, computer printouts of thousands of tickets initialed by the judge as being "non-suited" (dismissed) disappeared.

LeFevour's cousin, Jimmy "Dogbreath" LeFevour, testified that he had delivered hundreds of payments of one hundred dollars each to his cousin and other judges. Jimmy then explained the workings of the hustler's bribery club, five lawyers who gave Judge LeFevour two thousand dollars a month. Jimmy also told of his cousin's terrible temper. He claimed that when he had mentioned rumors that bagman Arthur McCauslin was wired, the judge said, "Kill him."

So that the jury might understand the magnitude of the bribery, IRS agent Bill Thulen testified that over five years, Richard LeFevour spent or deposited nearly one hundred and forty-four thousand dollars for which the government could find no source.

Tuite did his best, but the evidence was overwhelming. On Saturday, July 14, 1985, the man who was once one of the most esteemed and powerful judges in the huge Cook County court system sat with a bloodless face as the jury returned from four and a half hours of deliberations. He was convicted on all fifty-nine counts of racketeering, mail fraud, and tax violations. A month later, Judge Norgle sentenced him to serve twelve years in prison.

Judge LeFevour was the twenty-first person to be convicted or plead guilty as a result of Greylord. Later, Mark Ciavelli and his partner, Frank Cardoni, testified at the trial of retired Judge John Reynolds that they had kicked back a portion of their bond referrals to him. Reynolds' lawyer mentioned me in arguments as having been a human microphone, arguing that I taped everyone in the world but Judge Reynolds and therefore Reynolds must be innocent. (We had wanted to bug Reynolds' chambers but he was transferred too soon.) The jury didn't buy the absurd contention, and Reynolds was sentenced to ten years in prison. Later he also received a two-year term for perjury.

Among the others convicted or pleading guilty were high-living Judge Reginald Holzer, sentenced to thirteen years; Judge John McCollum, eleven years; former Judge Roger Seaman, four years; and former Judge Michael McNulty, three years.

LeFevour was sent to the same prison in Wisconsin as Devine. Although the U.S. Appellate Court ruled against his fight for a new trial, Richard's health improved markedly in confinement to a facility set up like a dormitory. The inmates lived in three-man cubicles, not cells, and took their meals in a cafeteria line. There were so many judges and lawyers serving out their sentences in the facility that they named their softball team "the Bagmen."

In October 1985, the U.S. Attorney's Office turned over to the state's Attorney Registration and Disciplinary Commission thousands of pages of Greylord testimony and documents for possible action against lawyers who evidently were involved in bribery but were not named on criminal charges. As a result, the Illinois Supreme Court issued sanctions against a record one hundred and thirty-two lawyers in single year.

As another result of Greylord, the Illinois Supreme Court broadened the financial disclosures judges must make and ordered that the documents be readily available to the public.

With such reforms underway, both attorney James Costello and former judge Wayne Olson came up for sentencing in March 1986 following their failed effort to have the bugging of Olson's chambers declared unconstitutional. Wayne and Jim were the people I had been closest to in my undercover work and, corrupt as they were, I still had fond memories of them. These men, with their lives interlocked by money, often hated one another and yet in some ways were similar. They were loud and coarse but had teddy-bear moments, both liked to drink, and both had gone through their careers with blinders on about the consequences.

Assistant prosecutor Chuck Sklarsky told the sentencing judge how Olson had corrupted young attorneys and quoted him as saying on our tapes, "I love people that take dough. You know exactly where they stand."

"Time and again we find that if there's a judge who has a relationship with a hustler like Mr. Costello, clearly sharing money with him, it's like open season in the courtroom," Sklarsky said. "The bailiff, the clerk, the policeman, the court sergeant who sits there [say] 'Where is mine?'"

Olson's attorney, Jeffrey Steinback, blamed the system. He said that in the political process of becoming a judge, "even the most stalwart can become warped." Costello's lawyer told the judge that his client was a broken man and didn't even have a final friend to stand in support for him.

Before passing sentence, Judge Stanley Roszkowski asked if the defendants wished to make any remarks. Costello said little except that he was grateful his new wife, Susan, had stood by him. But Olson, the man who had reminded everyone of Rodney Dangerfield, looked crushed standing before the bench. He told of the "eight hundred sleepless nights" since his indictment and said of his judicial position, "I didn't know how much I loved it until I lost it."

Olson then offered one last thought: "If any other lawyer wants to go through what I've gone through in the last two and a half years, then there's nothing that you can do here today that's going to change it because he's got to be nuts."

Calling the defendants separately to the bench, Roszkowski sentenced Olson to twelve years in prison and fined him thirty-five thousand dollars. Costello received a term of eight years. *Jim, Jim,* I thought when I heard the sentence, *you should have listened to us.*

The following month I was called to the stand in the trial of Raymond Sodini, the easy-going judge who once had police sergeant Cy Martin sit in for him on the bench while he recovered from a hangover. This case was put together by a new group of Greylord FBI Agents, David Benscoter, Phil Page, Malcolm Bales, and Dan Lee, all of whom worked endless hours to put together the case on Sodini and 21 codefendents. This was the biggest Greylord indictment. As we would learn later, the frantic Sodini persuaded a man who had lent him money in the 1970s to sign papers indicating the loan was made in 1982, which would cover some bribes the judge took that year.

Being tried with Sodini were defense attorneys Lee Barnett, Neal Birnbaum, Vincent Davino, Harry Jaffe, and Barry Carpenter, and again I was called to the stand and faced tricky defense attorney Patrick Tuite. He smiled as he resurrected my changing the Laurie transcript from "we'll see" to "sure."

Tired of being hauled over his by-now lukewarm coals, I assured him that I had been "trying to make my testimony as accurate as possible." Another round of questioning went nowhere, and I was excused.

But Tuite's strategy to keep Laurie's acquittal in the minds of the Sodini jurors made the entire defense case collapse. During the cross-examination of admitted bagman Patrick Ryan, a former sheriff's deputy, Tuite asked if he recalled that Judge Laurie had been acquitted. Since Tuite had just violated a pre-trial rule of Judge James Holderman against mentioning the outcome of any previous Greylord trial, the U.S. Attorney's Office leaped at the opportunity and received permission to call Laurie as a witness.

A jolt must have gone through the team of lawyers at the defense table. Since Laurie had testified in his own trial that Barnett had tried to bribe him, he would have to do the same if called now. The defense asked for a recess because of the new development, and the court was adjourned for the day.

Outside of court, Barnett's attorney Alan Blumenthal yelled at Tuite for "scuttling my defense!" Deciding to minimize the damage, Blumenthal notified prosecutors that his client was willing to change his plea to guilty.

This turnabout emboldened Valukas and Assistant U.S. Attorney James Schweitzer to persuade some of the other co-defendants to plead guilty for reduced sentences rather than keep up a charade of innocence. And so, after weeks of trial, spectators from reporters to courtwatch hobbyists were startled when Birnbaum, Davino, and Judge Sodini separately admitted their guilt.

The trial continued and Barry Carpenter, the lanky husband of my friend Alice Carpenter, was convicted in the fourteen-week trial along with Harry Jaffe and another fixer who had bribed Judge Sodini, Robert Daniels. Carpenter was sentenced to serve four years. The elderly Jaffe was sentenced to a year in prison but died before he could begin serving his time. Daniels was sentenced to six years for tax evasion and bribery.

Barnett received six months and bagman Ryan was placed on sixty days' work release. Judge Sodini was sentenced to eight and a half years in prison.

Now that my involvement in the Greylord prosecutions was winding down, the FBI notified me in 1987 that because of a policy then in effect, I should report to the Philadelphia office.

This was shattering. More than disappointed, I was angry. If transplanted, all of my contacts and knowledge of Chicago through its underside would be lost. On the other hand, I could see where I was too well known in the city to be useful in some assignments.

When I requested Seattle, a nice city with a lower cost of living and where Cathy had a friend, I was told that headquarters had decided Philadelphia would be better for me. This was despite the fact that if I was to be transferred, according to policy, it was to be to a medium sized city, such as Seattle. It was almost as if I were being punished. Others involved in Greylord were given what they had requested.

In Seattle we could have lived on my salary alone. But in Philadelphia Cathy would have to take a bar examination for a position with the prosecutor's office and wait her turn. And I would be just another FBI agent tracking down forgers and hijackers. That would have been fine a few years ago. But my undercover life had brought me such highs and lows that I didn't think I could settle down so soon to life in the mainstream.

Yet I realized that nothing I had done entitled me to special treatment. So we put our nice house up for sale and prepared to move. But some part of me knew I still needed a period of emotional recovery, and that I was not yet strong enough to start another kind of life elsewhere. Having given up my friends, I did not want to give up my sense of self.

When I had agreed to go undercover—for what I assumed would be a few months rather than the three and a half years—I had expected to make a great difference in the court system. I had no idea that lawyers who I thought were honest would turn on me, and that at times it would seem as if the legal system had more of an effect on me than I did on the corruption. Now even the FBI seemed to be deserting me.

Having trouble sleeping again, I called the FBI psychiatrist who had helped me while I was working undercover. He told me to seek outside help. This led to a long talk with a private psychiatrist, Jacob Moskovic, in which I mentioned the other periods when I had felt down because of the corruption and the frustrations of my clandestine work.

Dr. Moskovic told me I was suffering from clinical depression and explained that anyone could get it, like a cold. He mentioned that I should have been receiving psychological help throughout my double life and was amazed that I had not been. The essential cause might not even have been my work as a mole, but guilt over my betrayals. He said I would need a brief period of rest and treatment.

Even during the two and a half weeks I was hospitalized, I still didn't realize how much the proposed uprooting was affecting me. I was seeding grass at the house Cathy and I were about to sell when I set the bag down and told myself that I did not have to take this.

We talked it over, but there wasn't much to say. Only my leftover dreams wanted me to remain an FBI agent even if it meant moving; my body and mind told me to stay where I was. Sadly, I drove downtown that week and handed in my resignation, effective January 31, 1988. That meant I would still be with the Bureau for other Greylord trials.

When fixer Bruce Roth was prosecuted in August 1987, I faced attorney Patrick Tuite for the fifth time. He was one of the patron saints of defendants facing long prison terms if convicted. Being Tuite, he naturally had a fresh trick. To use me to his advantage, he put my name down on his list of defense witnesses.

I wasn't asked much on the stand, just about the few weak spots in the government's case, such as every prosecution is bound to have. The federal case was so strong that the well-groomed, money-oriented Roth was convicted and given a ten-year sentence for racketeering, bribery, and conspiracy.

Lee Barnett, Peter Kessler, and I returned as government witnesses in the trial of former judge Martin Hogan. At his sentencing, Hogan said he was guilty not of greed but of stupidity. Claiming he had been corrupted by Judge LeFevour, the trim former Marine said, "I did not know the depths of his personality would lead me to hell." Not exactly hell, but to a ten-year prison term.

A month after Hogan's trial, I was back on the stand in the trial of Judge Daniel Glecier. I never had much contact with the white-haired jurist. But the prosecution's star witness against him was Jim Costello—whose term was recently reduced to six years in a Texas federal prison because of his decision to cooperate.

While I was in the witness room waiting to be called, I peeked into the courtroom to see Jim sitting in the witness chair. He looked like his old, defiant self. His bushy brown hair was showing a little gray but was as beyond a comb as ever, and he was in a prison uniform instead an expensive Capper and Capper business suit.

Costello rattled off cases in which he had bribed Glecier. Then under cross-examination, he admitted selling his badge as a policeman and told the jury that once when he and I were drinking together, he toasted: "Here's to money."

A witness against one of Glecier's co-defendants was former judge Roger Seaman, the first judge ever to be called as a government witness in northern Illinois. Seaman said he had refused to take bribes when he worked as a prosecutor and in the city law office. But soon after he was elected to the bench, a judge now dead told him that the "regular attorneys" would show their appreciation if he gave them defendants who came in without a lawyer. Now Seaman was serving four years for his mistakes. When questioned about why he had taken bribes, he answered, "Greed, ego; I wanted to be accepted by the lawyers."

Judge Glecier was convicted and sentenced to six years in prison. He also was fined sixty thousand dollars.

Next on trial was Judge "P.J." McCormick who, despite his silver hair, still looked like a football player. One reason he had not been tried earlier was that the IRS team had to be meticulous in tracing his paper trail through hundreds of money orders purchased with bribe cash. A prosecutor said that every time McCormick opened his desk drawer, there should have been a cash register bell ringing. After a jury convicted him of income tax evasion, P.J. secretly pleaded guilty to extortion. In 1989, McCormick was ordered to serve six years in prison.

The year before, sheriff's deputy Lucius Robinson had pleaded guilty to accepting a thirteen-hundred-dollar bribe from me and was sentenced to three years. That would seem to be the end of it. But in late 1991, the bagman who had once been Muhammad Ali's bodyguard was put on trial again on charges of lying to a special grand jury to protect five judges and nine lawyers who were never charged. Lucius claimed in the grand jury I was the only one who ever gave him bribes and that he had never handed the money over to Judge Maurice Pompey.

Since we never had enough evidence to charge the other jurists we were sure Lucius had passed money to, they were identified in court as Judges A, B, C, D, and E. I described for Judge Norgle in the bench trial—conducted without a jury—how I gave the money to Robinson and he checked off the names of three Judges that he told me were crooked. I left the stand with a mixture of sorrow for the system and relief that I had got my revenge on the man who early in my career helped set rapists free.

Judge Norgle found Robinson guilty of two counts of perjury. The judge held that the taped conversations and evidence showed that he indeed had bribed all five of the judges who were identified only by code, including Pompey and Thomas Maloney.

Pompey had retired, and the government could not prosecute him because the statute of limitations had run out. But the former judge's name would come up in court again, along with a case that prosecutors never let die.

March 1993

A light snow was swirling on the day in March 1993 when opening arguments began in the trial of retired judge Thomas Maloney, the only jurist in America ever charged with taking bribes in murder cases. Like Pompey, Maloney had been one of the sternest and most respected judges in the system. For thirteen years the rectangular-faced, curly-haired judge sat under a portrait of U.S. Chief Justice John Marshall and presided over a court with strict rules against whispering and gum-chewing. Only one other judge in the Criminal Courts Building may have sent more defendants to death row.

But there was another side to Maloney. His political sponsor had been a powerful alderman, and he had friends among the snide, cynical political set, the sort of people in power who take the rest of us for suckers. Maloney's hard line against defendants who could not bribe him only increased his price for those who could.

Like Judge Pompey, Maloney used Lucius Robinson as his personal bagman. Maloney had won a boxing scholarship to college, and Lucius had been a bodyguard for Muhammad Ali, so this connection made him as close to a friend as anyone Maloney had in the courts. But the friendship ended when Lucius decided to cut a deal with prosecutors.

Under the broad outlines of the RICO Act, all of Maloney's crimes on the bench were fair game. Young Assistant U.S. Attorney Diane MacArthur rose from her chair and told the jury that Maloney "conspired to change the course of justice, turning a courtroom into a pit of corruption and greed."

Greylord had laid the foundation for the trial, but this went beyond our work. Expanding the methods used to gather information on previous judges, the FBI in Operation Gambat, probing into bribery in the downtown First Ward, installed a spy camera in the law office of lawyer/businessman/bagman and now mole Robert Cooley. They learned that an influential alderman other than Maloney's political sponsor had acted as a go-between in some of the bribes to him. Three months before Maloney's trial, that alderman was convicted of racketeering, conspiracy, and extortion. But the jury acquitted him of fixing a trial before Maloney, because the tape was not clear enough.

In Maloney's trial, I testified about how I had changed from a trusting assistant prosecutor into a government mole, and how later, as a defense attorney with a mock practice, I delivered bribes to Robinson. He followed me to the stand. Breaking his years of silence and denials, he told of passing bribes to judges.

"How many times did you carry bribes to your boss, Judge Pompey?" asked Assistant U.S. Attorney Scott Mendeloff.

"Hundreds," Robinson said.

"Whose choice was it for the lawyers to pay you for the judges, yours or the judges'?"

"The judges," he replied.

Robinson also told of passing him twenty-three hundred dollars from attorney William Swano in the upscale McCormick Inn near downtown, and said that Maloney once called him into the judges' private elevator at the back of the court building so he could start his day with the exhilaration of a three-hundred-dollar bribe.

Next taking the stand was Swano, who had been a 1960s idealist and once felt the government could reform society. His harsh awakening came when Robinson demanded money to assure an acquittal in a date-rape case. Swano went on to represent some members of the notorious drug and robbery gang called the El Rukns. But now he was nearly bankrupt and facing prison as a co-conspirator. The U.S. Attorney's Office offered him one way out: tell all he knew about Judge Maloney in return for a lighter sentence on racketeering charges.

Swano testified that he had lost only one case before the judge, that of an innocent man charged with armed robbery. The judge found the hapless man guilty and sent him to prison just to teach Swano a lesson—move to another city, get out of law, or start paying up.

After a while, Swano even made a game of the secret arrangement. After furtively delivering a five-thousand-dollar bribe to Maloney's bagman to have a murderer convicted of only involuntary manslaughter, he bet the prosecutor five dollars how the judge would decide. When the verdict was handed down, the prosecutor was amazed at Swano's grasp of the vagaries of justice.

But one of the El Rukns cases was more complicated than most of the others. Two gang "generals" were arrested for murdering a rival drug dealer and his wife. The gang thought there was no way to fix a case before law-and-order Judge Maloney, but Swano knew better. He put ten thousand dollars in a file folder for one of Maloney's other bagman, attorney Robert McGee, at a restaurant on the first day of the trial. Since people who crossed the El Rukns had a high mortality rate, Swano wanted to make sure the judge understood what he was to do. During the trial, Swano reminded Maloney in a low voice, "We've got an agreement on this. You've got to live up to your end of the bargain."

But as the El Rukns trial wore on, Maloney started having second thoughts. There was a lot of publicity on this case. The back of the gang had been broken by an FBI raid on its South Side headquarters, some of the leaders were starting to listen to prosecutors, and Maloney thought the FBI was following him, which it was. An acquittal now would be the same as shouting "Bribe!" So McGee called Swano at home and said the judge had decided to return the money.

Swano arrived late the next morning and apparently missed the bagman. When he happened to see Maloney, the judge told him that "a lawyer left a file folder for you and said you should come and get it from the sheriff's deputy." But Swano and the deputy couldn't find it. They knocked on the door of the judge's chambers and he told them to come in. "Here it is," Maloney said, and handed over the file. Inside was the ten thousand dollars. Then the judge sentenced the two El Rukns to death, but later problems in their case meant they served time in prison instead.

Ex-bagman Robert Cooley told the jury that the price for fixing a case in front of Maloney was sometimes even higher. One defendant before Maloney was a hit man for the Ghost Shadows, a violent New York-based Asian gang. The evidence was pretty strong that he had committed a murder during a gambling war in Chicago's Chinatown. Cooley said the total bribe amounted to one hundred thousand dollars, including fees for go-betweens.

Maloney had thought he was invincible because of his years of laundering payoffs through money orders. But the precaution worked no better for him than it had for Judge P.J. McCormick. On April 16, 1993, after deliberating over three days, the jury convicted Maloney on every count of racketeering, conspiracy, and obstructing justice. He was the eighteenth current or former judge we had exposed as a thief of justice, in addition to more than fifty attorneys, policemen, and court clerks. The excitement over his sentence overshadowed a six-year term given to bagman McGee.

Maloney's sentencing in July 1994, allowed prosecutors to spread out his sordid life, even crimes for which there was no evidence to charge him. Admitted counterfeiter and killer Michael Bertucci testified that he and other crooks years before would hire Maloney as their lawyer because he knew how to rig a verdict. Bertucci added that in the early 1970s he saw Maloney pass money to Judge Pompey in a courthouse washroom just before Pompey dismissed an attempted-theft charge.

Bertucci even said the mob had Maloney appointed to the bench over his protests that the job "didn't pay as well" as being a criminal attorney. The mob wasn't concerned about making him happy, it needed someone on the bench to free its robbers, thieves, and enforcers. He was far from the first or last judge to take orders from the outfit.

The shocker for the general public came when former bagman Robert Cooley testified that as an attorney, Maloney had set in motion the 1977 acquittal of reputed mob hitman Harry Aleman in the killing of Teamsters union steward William Logan. Although many years had passed, this outrage was still very real to everyone involved in Greylord because it had compelled federal prosecutors to launch our unprecedented secret investigation of the whole system.

With this testimony, Maloney emerged as the most dangerous judge ever charged as a result of Greylord. But when asked if he had any statement to make before sentencing, he delivered a two-hour oration starring himself as an innocent victim of evil men whom the U.S. Attorney's Office had set upon him. When he was finished, Maloney was sentenced to nearly sixteen years in prison and fined two hundred thousand dollars. Because he was sixty-nine years old, his lawyers said the term would, in effect, be a life sentence. He served twelve years and died in a nursing home after being the last Greylord defendant to be released from prison in 2008.

Our investigation and major prosecutions were finally over, fourteen years after the undercover work had begun, but there was still important unfinished business. Although we had to let some of our intended targets get away, we knew that we had succeeded in reaching the heart of corruption with disclosures about the acquittal of Harry Aleman for the murder of William Logan.

Each Greylord trial had in effect been a stepping stone to the mobster, who was then living a life of leisure and occasionally painting in his cubicle at the federal prison resort in Oxford, Wisconsin, where he was serving time on an extortion case. For reasons clear only to him and his lawyers, Aleman had pleaded guilty and was looking forward to being freed in the year 2000.

Could he be prosecuted again for the Logan murder despite constitutional provisions against being tried for the same crime twice? After all, double jeopardy was one of the grievances that had led to the American Revolution.

Officials announced their intention to bring Aleman to justice again with an indictment based on fresh evidence that First Ward hoodlums had used Cooley as a bagman for two cash payments to trial judge Frank Wilson. The defense community mockingly called the bold tactic headline grabbing. But on October 13, 1994, a circuit court judge made legal history by approving the re-indictment. Members of Logan's family embraced one another in court. One of Logan's sisters, Betty Romo, called the decision "a big step toward final justice."

Mob-connected defense attorneys must have nervously assured their clients that the ruling would be overthrown, as a number of other attempts had been over the years. But ultimately the Illinois Supreme Court ruled that double jeopardy clause of the constitution did not apply in the Aleman case because he had committed a fraud upon the trial court by paying the bribe. That meant Aleman had never been in jeopardy of being convicted.

From what we had learned, Judge Wilson never wanted to acquit Aleman and ruin his career. But the crime syndicate needed Aleman to continue killing, and it relentlessly put unknown pressure on Wilson until he gave in. There is an unsubstantiated rumor that the mobsters succeeded only when they threatened to kill his son.

Judge Wilson—described by no less than Judge Maloney as "drunk, reckless, degenerate"—retired from the bench shortly afterward and was obscurely living in Sun City, Arizona. One day in 1989, Cooley made what must have seemed like a social call to Wilson's home. During their seemingly casual discussion, the visitor steered the conversation to the Aleman case. Wilson did not know that the mob lawyer was wearing a wire, just as I had in the criminal courthouse.

About eight weeks after the meeting, police officers and FBI agents talked to Wilson in person about the supposed bribe. Then they played Cooley's tape for him and he heard exactly what a jury would hear. Two months later, Wilson shot himself to death in his back yard—the third suicide stemming from Greylord disclosures.

23

FULL CIRCLE

January-September 1997

In January 1997, as outfit hit man Harry Aleman was awaiting his unprecedented retrial, former Judge Richard LeFevour died of natural causes, dishonored from Greylord disclosures of how he had systematized bribery throughout the municipal courts. He had left prison after six years, and his last job was as an insurance claims adjuster. At his family's request, there was no death notice.

LeFevour's influence went far beyond the four hundred thousand dollars in bribes he had taken from drunken drivers and parking violators over fourteen years. His career was bitter proof that when politics place a criminal at the top, corruption becomes a way of life for the whole system.

Yet the highest prize of the Greylord years would be Aleman, and the Chicago style of doing things was about to be tried along with him. This time, no one was coming to Aleman's aid with veiled threats to the judge and envelopes stuffed with cash. Times had changed.

Aleman showed an arctic haughtiness when his retrial began in late September 1997. His I'm-tougher-than-the-world pose gave no indication whether he was in suspense about the outcome, but I doubt that he was. As witnesses described that long-ago night of the Logan murder, jurors kept darting their eyes to the defendant, probably to imagine whether Aleman could have done it. Aleman ignored them and slouched at the defense table like a bored schoolboy.

Once more taking the stand, Robert Cooley said the fix had originated with two behind-the-scenes political bosses of the First Ward, John D'Arco and Patrick Marcy, both deceased. D'Arco formerly was an alderman, and Marcy was a Democratic Party puppet master. Their ward controlled the Loop and Little Italy on the Near West Side. Through the early 1980s, those two men kept the secrets and called the shots as First Ward police officers, politicians, and crime syndicate figures formed an impenetrable network of cross-interests.

Judge Wilson had not been known to be corrupt, and that worked to the defendant's advantage. If a judge with a bad reputation were to set Aleman free, there would be an outcry. Cooley testified that he told D'Arco and Marcy that as a personal friend of his Judge Wilson might be talked into taking the money.

At first Cooley assured Wilson that the evidence was weak—the killing was committed at eleven o'clock at night—and that agreeing to an acquittal would be a personal favor. But as Wilson heard the incriminating evidence day after day, he began to realize the political consequences of what he had agreed to do. Whether he ever had any moral concerns died with him.

I wish I could have been at the trial, but I recently had been hired as an investigator for the U.S. Department of Justice's Inspector General's Office, and that meant I was often out of town. Even so, I kept up with the daily unfolding. I learned that Cooley wept on the stand as he detailed that the judge took the ten thousand dollars in installments. "He was a broken man," Cooley said in describing the final payment, made in a restaurant washroom just hours after Aleman's acquittal. "He told me, 'You've destroyed me, you've killed me' and walked out."

In later testimony Bobby Lowe, the neighbor who had seen the murder of William Logan while walking his dog twenty-five years before, was called to the stand and asked if he could still recognize the killer in court. Walking toward the defense table, the bearded auto mechanic pointed at Aleman and said, "This man, right here." He went to identify Aleman five times more in testimony. When asked if he was sure, he replied, "I'll never forget that face!"

The man who admitted driving the getaway car, Louis Almeida, testified—just as he had before Judge Wilson—that the killing had been set up weeks in advance, when Aleman wrote out for him Logan's address, license plate number, and the time the man usually left for work. With a flourish, Aleman jotted down "Death to Billy," the mob wheelman told the jurors.

To offset such vivid testimony, the defense tried an unusual tactic and called the respected retired chief judge of the Criminal Court Building,

Richard Fitzgerald, commonly called "Fitz." He testified that he knew of no improprieties in the Aleman trial before Wilson.

When the final arguments concluded, Aleman was brought back to his maximum security cell in the downtown federal jail, where he was temporarily being kept as part of his unrelated twelve-year sentence for extortion.

Jury deliberation began on the pleasant fall evening of September 13, 1997. Four hours later the jurors came out with a verdict of guilty. Aleman rested his expressionless face on his raised forearm, but his family wept and Logan's relatives appeared emotionally exhausted. Their long wait was over, and justice had come full circle for all of us.

There was no celebration. Assistant State's Attorney Scott Cassidy told reporters, "This will close the books on an ugly era in Cook County." A too-large judicial system that had broken down well before any of us had been born had been stitched back together for now, and we could go on with our lives.

There was little excitement when Aleman was sentenced to serve one hundred to three hundred years in prison, where he died of natural causes in 2010.

When I was sworn in as an attorney amid the ruins of a riot-scarred West Side neighborhood on a cold, wet, and windy Halloween evening, there had seemed no way to reach judges who were protected by their robes, their political party, their bagmen, and the lawyers' code of silence. When Mort Friedman made an attempt, he was ostracized and threatened with contempt of court and loss of his law license. Now we had brought down crooks ranging from hallway hustlers like Costello to some of the best-known judges in the country's largest court system.

Serving as a reminder of what happens to fixers and crooked judges when they are caught, no one trapped by the Greylord net emerged with a life intact. After ex-judge Glecier served his term, he worked for Catholic Charities Institute of Addiction. Following Costello's testimony in the Glecier trial, he returned to prison to complete his sentence.

He gave every indication that when he came out he would be a better man. The last I heard of him, he and his second wife were living quietly somewhere in Colorado.

Returning from prison, former Judge P.J. McCormick was employed as a route salesman for a dairy company. An award-winning feature in the *Chicago Lawyer* magazine described how Mark and several other lawyers wound up selling real estate. Bruce Roth went into construction work but said, "I hope to get my license back some day, I think of it all the time."

Bob Silverman—admired by so many in the courthouse, and the role model for all young fixers—could not get a job after prison and was living on social security. If there is a moral to all this, it's that if you are crooked, the first person you destroy is yourself.

There is no way of telling how our investigation affected the families of our targets. But we know that the son of bagman Ira Blackwood refused to speak to him after Ira was convicted and sentenced to seven years. Peter Kessler's mother, who had survived the Holocaust, died soon after he pleaded guilty to bribing Judge Devine. Fixer Neal Birnbaum's father died soon after his son's indictment, and Neal blamed us for his death.

This was the most extensive undercover campaign in American history, but that was only because we were making up for the failure of our law schools and attorney disciplinary boards to deal with realities. Removing the malignancy should not start with recruiting moles. It needs to begin with realizing the special stresses and drives of attorneys engaged in criminal law. It comes as no surprise that several studies have shown that lawyers have the highest depression rate in the country.

Judges should be allowed to be judges and not politicians, who run for election on a party ticket and whose campaigns are run by the attorneys who appear before them. And monitoring agencies should act more quickly on reports of court improprieties.

Shortly before the Maloney conviction, I appeared before an Illinois Supreme Court commission on the Cook County court system. No one was fooling himself that Greylord had turned Chicago honest. I said that of the three hundred and twenty-five judges in the system, insiders such as bagman Harold Conn and others identified eighty-five as being corrupt, but there had to be more. I was then asked by a central illinois appellate justice what percentage of the judges in Cook County of thought were corrupt. I testified that perhaps fifty percent of judges at the time were on the take. Maybe not continually, as Olson had been, but they grabbed cash whenever the amount and the circumstances were right. A judge panelist whispered to someone that she had heard the number was only forty percent. Only!

A lot of this book has been about the downside of our work, but it had some rewards. The Loyola University Chicago School of Law honored me for contributions to the community. The Chicago Council of Lawyers gave former judge Lockwood and me awards, and well-known defense attorney David Schippers, who had represented a lawyer convicted of bribing Judge Sodini, sent me a letter of praise for my contributions to the profession. Former U.S. Attorney Webb, a leader in the Cook County Republican Party, even asked me to run for State's Attorney. But I felt incumbent Democrat Richard M. Daley was doing a good job and chose not to accept.

One year after Aleman's sentencing, Scott Lassar—the tall, slender, and determined prosecutor who had seen Greylord's creation—was sworn in as U.S. Attorney for Northern Illinois. He told reporters he must have won the appointment by "dumb luck," typical Lassar humor.

Operation Greylord may have been just the start of a new era in monitoring the judiciary. In Chicago alone, its methods were expanded for staggering sweeps against bribery in several city departments as well as ghost payrolling and insider trading. But the struggle should never let up. Let us not say, as nineteenth-century English poet Josiah Holland did, that "Wrong rules the land, and waiting Justice sleeps."

Epilogue

I ultimately testified at the trials of 23 Greylord defendants from 1984 through 1993. In 2008, I testified before an Illinois Supreme Court Commission when attorney Bruce Roth, who had received 10 years in prison, petitioned to reinstate his law license. The Illinois Supreme Court denied Roth's petition in 2009. In fact, not one Greylord defendant convicted of a bribery-related act has ever received his law license back.

My first job after leaving the FBI was as the Inspector General of the Regional Transportation Authority in Chicago. After five years, I decided to return to federal service and eventually became an agent with the U.S. Department of Justice Inspector General's Office, the next best thing to being an FBI agent. We conducted criminal and administrative investigations relating to various agencies of the Justice Department. I retired in 2008 and went to work for the Cook County Sheriff's Office, where I eventually headed the internal affairs department.

But I longed to work in the courts again. Would the Cook County State's Attorney's Office want to hire a 63-year-old assistant prosecutor? Was the job I left to go undercover still open? When First Assistant State's Attorney Dan Kirk and Chief Deputy Walt Hehner interviewed me in 2014, they praised what my role in Greylord did for the for the State's Attorney's Office and the criminal justice system in Cook County. After considering their recommendation, State's Attorney Anita Alvarez hired me.

So after over 32 years I am living the dream I had just out of law school. Currently, I am working in the Felony Review Unit, deciding whether to charge defendants with felonies or not.

Dan Reidy told me when I agreed to work undercover that I would never be able to practice law again in Cook County. He wasn't wrong, but conditions have changed considerably. Many judges now on the bench went to law school or entered practice during the Greylord trials. They and their fellow attorneys absorbed the ethical lessons the

Greylord team had fought so hard for. Bill Haddad, who served as an assistant prosecutor, a defense lawyer, and then a judge, told me that Greylord made an immediate difference in the courtrooms where Judges Murphy and Reynold used to sit. Many other criminal defense attorneys have thanked me and told me that the system has changed completely for the good. One lawyer recently told me that all criminal defense attorneys are now on a level playing field rather than competing against fixers, and judges are no longer extorting bribes.

Cathy retired from the State's Attorney's Office in 2013, after serving for over 28 years. Her last jury trial was my daughter Christine's first. A mother and a daughter had never prosecuted a case together in Cook County, and they won a conviction in a felony theft case. Christine is still an assistant state's attorney. Perhaps someday we can be father and daughter prosecutors before a jury. My daughter Elizabeth in the catering business, and my son Thomas is a high school lacrosse coach.

To this day, I speak to law enforcement personnel, law students, and attorneys about the ethical lessons learned from Greylord. During the past year I have appeared at law schools such as Harvard, Boston College, Loyola University in Chicago, the University of Chicago, the University of Arizona, the University of St. Thomas, and Northwestern. I've also given continuing legal education seminars to the Los Angeles County District Attorney's Office and the Illinois Prosecutors Bar Association. I am an adjunct member of the faculty at the Inspector General Academy at the Federal law Enforcement Training Center in Glynco, Georgia, where I have taught programs about undercover work and public corruption.

This is the post-Greylord status of the major judges and lawyers who were investigated. (Source, in part, *Chicago Lawyer Magazine*.)

Name	Sentence	After Prison or Trial
Judge John Devine	15 years	Died in 1987 of cancer in prison in Springfield, MO
Judge John Laurie	Acquitted	Cook County Judge (Retired)

Name	Sentence	After Prison or Trial
Judge Richard LeFevour	12 years	Insurance claims consultant, died in 1997
Judge Martin Hogan	10 years	Worked for the Safer Foundation, which places former prisoners in jobs
Judge P.J. McCormick	6 years	Dairy route salesman
Judge John Murphy	10 years	Retired
Judge Wayne Olson	12 years	Prison job: law librarian at the federal prison in Lexington, KY. Died in 1994 at age 63
Judge John Reynolds	12 years	Administrator at an orphanage
Judge Raymond Sodini	8 years	College criminal justice professor; died in 1993
Judge Thomas Maloney	16 years	The last Greylord defendant to be released from prison, at age 79
Judge Maurice Pompey	Not charged	Retired to Arizona
Mark Ciavelli	Immunity	Successful in real estate sales
Frank Cardoni	Probation	Moved out of Illinois
Harold Conn	6 years	Gofer for an attorney. Conn said that prison was no worse than being in the army
James Costello	6 years	Living in Colorado
James LeFevour	2 years	Living in Florida
Bruce Roth	10 years	Worked construction
Peter Kessler	Probation	Successful businessman
Cyrus Yonan	1 year	Moved to Florida

The Investigative and Prosecuting Attorneys

Michael Ficaro, Scott Lassar, Dan Reidy, Charles Sklarsky, Sheldon Zenner, Thomas Sullivan, Dan Webb, and Anton Valukas are all partners at major law firms. In fact, Sklarsky, Sullivan, and Valukas practice at the same firm. Candace Fabri is a Cook County judge. Morton Friedman retired as general counsel of a State of Illinois agency. Bob Cooley is living in secret in another state. Assistant U.S. Attorney Thomas M. Durkin who, along with FBI Agent Steve Bowen, guided Gambat, the Cooley offshoot of Greylord, is now a federal judge in Chicago.

The Investigators

Lamar Jordan	Retired from the FBI and living in Texas
Bob Farmer	Retired from the FBI and living in Washington State
Bill Megary	Retired as Special Agent in Charge of Newark and living in Virginia
David Grossman	Retired as Assistant Special Agent in Charge of Chicago and living in Chicago
David Victor Ries	Retired as Special Agent in Charge of Knoxville, TN and living in Virginia
Malcolm Bales	Left the FBI for the U.S. Attorney's Office in the Eastern District of Texas, where he is now the U.S. Attorney
David Benscoter	After leading the team of agents on the Judge Sodini indictment, which had 22 defendants, he left the FBI and retired as an IRS Criminal Agent in Spokane

Acknowledgments

I want to thank all of the Assistant State's Attorneys who cooperated in the corruption probe. Some of them bravely testified against Greylord judges when the legal community did not look favorably upon that. The ones whom I recall are Barry Gross, Thomas Burnham, Harry Wilson, Larry Finder, Kathleen Nathan, Jonathan Regunberg, Marilyn Koch, Randy Barnett, Joel from the shoplifting court and Bruce Paynter. Former FBI Supervisor Mike Dyer was very supportive of me during the trials and guided my career after I left the FBI. Former FBI Assistant Director William Beane was instrumental in me receiving the Lou Peters Award, the most distinguished award given by the Former FBI Agents Association, together with the FBI. I thank my former office partner, James Reichardt, who not only gave me an office while I was undercover, but has provided me with friendship and support over the years. Former Dean Nina Appel of Loyola Law School was the person who turned the tide in the legal community as far as the community's acceptance of Greylord. Nina understood the importance of the Greylord legal ethics issues for students and lawyers and I still speak to her classes. More recently, Professor Henry Shea of the University of St. Thomas and the University of Arizona Law Schools has recognized the significance of Greylord to legal ethics nationally. Hank has arranged for me speak at a number of law schools throughout the country. Terry Kinney and Steve Kessler of the U.S. Department of Justice recognized Greylord's international investigative and ethical importance and invited me to speak in Indonesia in 2014. I especially want to thank my attorney and agent Jay B. Ross for placing this book with Ankerwycke Publishing. Toby Roberts and Nancy Stuenkel of the Chicago Sun Times went out of their way in finding some of the photographs for this book. Finally, I am also grateful to the team at Ankerwycke, especially editors Jonathan Malysiak and Erin Nevius, who greatly improved the book.